MODERN SOCIOLOGY

MODERN SOCIOLOGY

(In 2 Volumes)

Volume 1
(Globalization and Urban Sociology)

Editor

G.S. Mohanty

ISHA

ISHA BOOKS

Delhi-110033

Modern Sociology

(Globalization and Urban Sociology)

Rs. 1800 (Set)
Rs. 900 (Each Volume)

ISBN : 81-8205-207-6 (Set)
ISBN : 81-8205-279-3 (Vol. 1)

Published in 2005 in India by
Isha Books
D-43, Prithviraj Road,
Adarsh Nagar, Delhi - 110033
e-mail : ishabooks@hotmail.com

Laser Typesetting at : Global Printers, New Delhi
Printed at : Chawla Offset Press, Delhi

Contents

Preface

For centuries, cities and towns have been engines of growth and incubators of civilisation and have facilitated the evolution of knowledge, culture and tradition, as well as of industry and commerce. Today they emerge as one of the strategic sites where these macro social trends materialise. Among these trends are globalisation and the rise of the new information technologies, the intensifying of transnational and translocal dynamics, and the strengthening presence and voice of specific types of socio-cultural diversity. Cities are also sites where each of these trends interacts with the others in distinct, often complex manners, in a way they do not in just about any other setting.

From the mid-1980s onwards 'globalisation' become increasingly the buzzword. With the increased pace of globalisation, the world is becoming increasingly a single market place. Communications, including the internet and the mobile phone, rapid air transport, mean that goods and services can move rapidly around the world. The global economic growth is uneven. No country is insulated from competition from some other part of the globe. Globalisation brings opportunities as well as problems, and its impacts are increasingly being observed worldwide, most clearly in the cities.

Rapid urbanisation, the concentration of the urban population in large cities, the sprawl of cities into wider geographical areas and the rapid growth of mega-cities are among the most significant transformations of human settlements. Urban areas strongly influence the world of the twenty-first century, and urban and rural populations are increasingly become interdependent for their economic, environmental and social well being.

The transition into an urbanised world has enormous implications for the world economy, for social conditions, as well as for the state of the world environment. An increasing number of cities have taken on significant roles in the globalisation of the economy, particularly with regard to financial services, commerce, transport and telecommunication. Urban settlements, properly managed, hold the promise for human development and the protection of the world's natural resources through their ability to support large numbers of people while limiting their impact on the natural environment.

This book illustrates the impacts of globalisation in urban life. It covers a range of topics including: cities in the age of globalisation, urban population growth, impacts of globalisation on urban areas, formation of global cities, social transformation in cities, urban streets and complexity, global trends in labour markets and urban criminology. The book will be of great value for sociologists, planners, politicians, researchers, students and social workers.

Editor

1

Cities in the Age of Globalisation

Today, the trend of urbanisation continues, although intertwined with globalisation. Like urbanisation, globalisation brings opportunities as well as problems, and its impacts are increasingly being observed worldwide, most clearly in the cities. The challenge is to develop solutions to problems associated with globalisation, while at the same time strengthening its positive aspects. Human settlements can play a significant role in this process by fostering good governance and effective partnerships.

Globalisation gives shape to the "global village" predicted by the Canadian Marshall McLuhan. The "information era" that it ushers in compresses time and we are now living in a world speeded up as never before. World-wide urbanisation is proceeding at a similar rate and its pace in the poor countries of the South seems terrifying. By 2025, two-thirds of humanity will be living in cities and towns, where the best opportunities in life tend to be.

Globalisation also accentuates a "new urban geography" in both North and South. Islands of rich consumers are springing up in cities amid an ocean of deprived people. More and more unemployed people, immigrants, minorities and the homeless, are pushed into cities by pressure from "market economies". As a result, all urban areas–not just those in the poor countries of the South–will have to deal with growing internal tensions. In New York, for example, the poorest 20 per cent of the population earns 15 times less than the richest 20 per cent.

Cities have always had their smart neighbourhoods and their dangerous areas–the old cities of Europe even more so than those of the Americas, where there is more geographical and social mobility. But such social and geographical segregation has changed in pace and scale because of the growth in the urban population, the increase in "illegal" migrants and rising uncertainty.

In fact, we have entered a period of historical transition, where discontinuities prevail over adjustment. Radical changes in the nature of production and jobs and the incredible concentration of capital in the hands of the financial sector and speculators weigh much heavier in our lives these days than the state's efforts to adjust and improve the market economy. Segregation in cities has been given a new lease of life whose consequences we do not know. It has reached unprecedented dimensions because of the explosive growth of urban areas.

According to one scenario, things will go badly. The growing pace of globalisation will increase uncertainty about the future. Fear and defence mechanisms will grow among people and institutions, fuelling intolerance, xenophobia and mistrust of everything new or foreign. Urban tensions will manifest themselves with increasing violence, and segregation will sharpen. Public areas will be abandoned and become dangerous no-man's-lands, the wretched abode of society's rejects. Cities will lose their original function of being a crossroads for meeting and exchange.

If globalisation also continues to go hand in hand with deregulation of financial markets and an unchanged level of indebtedness of poor countries, the latter will not be able to maintain their urban infrastructures. And if on top of this there is corruption and lack of political will, challenges to the system will increase and violence will grow. Cash-strapped authorities will respond with undemocratic measures and will even ally themselves with financial mafias which provide them with funds.

According to a second scenario, everything will be all right. In line with the principle that "everything the state does is public, but the state doesn't control everything that is public," a new social contract will be drawn up between the state, the market, the working population and civil society, including NGOs. Cities will develop a new quality of life by providing citizens with a forum for exchange. Jobs will be created in the social sector, in the fields of the environment, education, research, culture and leisure, opening up possibilities for young people.

In the countries of the South, long-term development strategies will be drafted and urban planning practised, taking advantage of the opportunities provided by globalisation but without falling into its traps. Town planning will become part of the political process, and the state will work with the private sector, monitored by institutions of civil society. Adequate housing will be built with the help of micro-credit and controls on the price of building materials. Improved infrastructures will enable marginal areas to become part of the civilised part of the city. Democracy will come up with new ways of governing with the help of networks of involved citizens.

In a transitional scenario, action strategies should fall somewhere between these two extremes. They should include social goals so that in big urban areas a society emerges which is founded on participatory democracy and on "capitalism with a human face" or "market socialism".

But the outlook is less clear than ever. Let us hope the present transition will lead rapidly to a new revival of humanism, whose first signs we are already seeing. This would open up the road to a development which is fair, humane and peaceful.

Globalisation and Urban Trends

At the beginning of the twentieth century, 150 million people lived in urban settlements, representing less than ten per cent of the world's population. As the century draws to a close, the world's urban population has increased twentyfold to nearly 3,000 million, i.e. almost half the world's population. Asia accounted for the lion's share (47.5 per cent) of the world's population in 'million' cities and had 143 of such 'million' cities. Asia also has 13 of the world's 23 mega-cities of at least 8 million inhabitants.

Three major urban trends have been observed at the close of the present century. First, contrary to most predictions, population growth rates have slowed down for many cities in developing countries. The largest cities in these countries grew far more slowly in the 1980s than during the previous two decades. Second, the world is less dominated by very large cities than had been forecast. Less than five per cent of the world's population lived in megacities in 1990. The prediction that cities such as Calcutta and Mexico City would grow to gigantic conurbations of 30 to 40 million inhabitants has not come true.

Third, the links between urban change and economic, social, political and cultural change are not clear. Some large and rapidly growing cities have been well-managed and serviced, while some of the worst physical conditions have beset small towns.

Several tendencies in shaping the urban future of the third millennium can be discerned. First, the progressive urbanisation of the globe is certain. It has been estimated that in the first decade of the twenty-first century more than half the world's population will be living in urban settlements.

Second, there will be growing interaction between urbanisation and globalisation. Globalisation is a multifaceted process of drawing countries, cities and people ever closer together through increasing flows of goods, services, capital, technology and ideas. The world cities have come to the fore because they perform special functions in the new global economy.

The third characteristic of the urban future is the likely continuing devolution of powers and responsibilities to local authorities and civil society. This process began in the 1990s when traditional modes of urban governance were found wanting and existing institutions could not adequately deal with the old and new urban problems.

In a globalising world, countries and cities are increasingly linked in interdependent and interlocking relationships. While world cities are important in their own right in a world order in which national boundaries fail to stop cross-border flows of capital, people and ideas, subregional economic entities have emerged.

Called growth triangles, some neighbouring territories involving several countries have sought creative economic co-operative development. Examples of successful growth triangles in Asia are those known as Southern China, with the participation of Hong Kong, Guandong, Fujian and Taiwan, and SIJORI, including Singapore, Johor (Malaysia) and Riau Island (Indonesia). These two growth triangles are centred, respectively, on the world cities of Hong Kong and Singapore. A variant of this theme of subregional development is what some scholars call region-states.They produce sound economic development in some regions that may be parts of a country or may involve several countries.

Another spatial expression of rapid economic development in the global economy is urban corridors which have been observed in East Asia, Europe and elsewhere.

Globalisation has not been a boon to all cities. While it has brought new opportunities and wealth to some cities, it has marginalised others. The marginalised city can be found anywhere in the world, but especially in Africa. It is outside the cyberways, lacks the requisite information infrastructure and is generally not able to plug into the global economy.

Four common features characterise cities in all parts of the world.

First, urban unemployment remains high. This explains the phenomena of 'area boys' — unemployed, able-bodied men, sometimes drug-dependent, in Lagos and 'parking boys' in Nairobi.

Second, urban infrastructure is often inadequately maintained even in developed countries. Water and sewer systems fail in Chicago and Washington, and electricity on the Eastern seaboard. In developing countries the problems are often much worse. Poor infrastructure has led to problems in water supply, urban sanitation and transport. The urban poor suffer most.

Third, environmental problems, especially air, water and noise pollution have grown in many cities of the developing world.

Fourth, growing social conflicts, such as homelessness and crime, plague many cities. These are the result partly of growing competition for jobs and partly of the freer movement of people.

In the next century, the relevant unit of economic production, social organisation and knowledge generation will be the city. World cities will be especially influential in shaping the development of the global economy. Technological advances and easy access to information will enable cities to evolve more efficient ways of production, capitalising on the cheapest sources of materials.

In the information age that has just begun, cities act as generators, processors and depositories of knowledge. Knowledge is generated by research, discovery and innovation. As knowledge is a highly valued resource, cities will be in competition to generate knowledge. The knowledge industry, science parks, technological development zones, technopolies and others will be further developed in the cities of the future.

Cities of the future will have more freedom. Greater freedom will be enjoyed by individuals and institutions because they will be networked electronically. Wired interactions will supplement face-to-face contacts. This will affect urban lifestyles as people can work at home, shop by computers and travel with credit cards. The clamour for greater participation and democracy will see more attention and resources devoted to non-governmental, community-based organisations.

Cities of the future will have the opportunity of reorganising themselves socially and institutionally. With the knowledge and wisdom that humankind has inherited from our ancestors and with new technologies and resources, there is no reason to believe that we are not prepared to face our urban future which is both a daunting challenge and a window of opportunity.

World of Cities

With just under half of its population living in cities, the world is already urbanised. When measured in knowledge, attitude, aspiration, commercial sense, technology, travel and access to information, even the most rural societies on earth are, to one extent or another, woven into a global network of cities.

Thus, the Songye people of the Congo produce masks and statues for purchase in Nairobi by the owner of a Milanese Africana shop. A Canadian rancher flies his own plane to Vancouver to meet a friend from San Francisco. A Brazilian placer miner uses his cell phone to monitor gold prices in London through a broker in São Paolo. A Kazakh folk singer places her music on the Internet in Alma Ata for downloading by a scholar in Shanghai. And a Peruvian expatriate in Perth responds with help to a call, again over the Internet, from the priest in a flooded village in Peru.

The industrial revolution of the late 18th century began the current phase of globalisation. In less than one hundred years, the steam engine, telegraph, telephone and elevator were conveying people, goods and ideas both horizontally and vertically at an unprecedented volume and velocity. Now, in less than another century, low-cost international air transport, digital telecommunication and liberalised trade have the global economy moving at "warp speed."

The focal point of global economic activity has invariably been the city, a place of deals and decisions, take-offs and landings - a place less concerned with the rhythms of nature, where everything can be bought and sold, especially one's ideas and labour.

During the past two hundred years of global economic expansion, the collective population of the world's cities grew from less than 30 million to 3 billion - from one in thirty of the earth's inhabitants to every other person on earth. Now at the beginning of the new century and millennium, the planet hosts 19 cities with 10 million or more people; 22 cities with 5 to10 million people; 370 cities with 1 to 5 million people; and 433 cities with 0.5 to 1 million.

Another 1.5 billion people live in urban areas of less than half a million people. The process of urbanisation will continue well into the 21st century and, by 2030, over 60 percent of all people (4.9 billion out of 8.1 billion) will live in cities.

As isolated seats of power from which to govern rural holdings, cities were, throughout most of recorded history, exceedingly small islands in a vast ocean of rural culture and tradition. With the advent of the industrial age, humanity rapidly evolved into a citydwelling species that is intensely competitive but at the same time cooperative, specialised yet adaptable. Homo urbanus is identified by dense living patterns, a tolerant acceptance of strangers, predictable behaviour based on agreed rules (but with lifestyle variations within the rules), access to great amounts of information and an almost total disconnection from the natural world.

Urbanisation in the twentieth century established a world network of competitive centres that set the physical reference points for today's globalisation. During the great rural-to-urban population shifts over the past half-century, cities became supermarkets for employment, incubators of technology, suppliers of social services and shelter, portals to the rest of the world, processors of agricultural produce, adders of manufactured value, centres of learning, and, above all, places to make money through trade, industry, finance, real estate and, of course, attendant crime and corruption.

In today's globalised world, cities no longer stand apart as islands. They are the nexus of commerce, gateways to the world in one direction and focus of their own hinterlands in the other. Tied together in a vast three-dimensional web of communication and transport, cities are concentrations of energy in a global force field, appearing fixed as concrete and steel. World cities in this urban millennium may be governed more by Quantum theory and Einsteinian relativity than by Newtonian physics and Euclidian geometry. As in quantum physics, simply observing the city can change it, as the political economy responds to public awareness and investor confidence. Almost meta-physically, with minimal regard to space, every place becomes every other place, because distance is measured in nano- and pico-seconds not just kilometres. Innovations and information arrive in waves washing over the whole planet at once, and cities scramble to gain the latest advantage - for as long as it lasts. In a real sense, the world is completely urbanised, as this force field has the power to connect all places and all people into a productive, constantly adapting unity.

In almost every country, the city's share of national output is much higher than its share of the population. Lima, for example, has less than 30 percent of Peru's population but produces over 40 percent of its national output. Bangkok, in an even more dramatic example produces nearly 40 percent of Thailand's output with just over 12 percent of its population, nearly the same ratio of production to population as São Paolo, Brazil. Cities are the generators of national development, which invariably starts with migration. Opportunity is the attractor. The rural poor, the attracted. In an urbanising world, cities, with all their demand and promise, harvest the countryside of people who can no longer tolerate the limitations of rural life or who simply see urban life as presenting more options for livelihood. Rural to urban migration is naturally greater where the benefits of development (that is, decent wages, adequate shelter, longer life) have not been well-distributed over the national landscape. Fifteen years ago, the urban growth rate of developing countries (3.8%) was over four times that of developed countries (0.9%), which had already urbanised. In the coming years, the rate of urbanisation for developing countries will have slowed dramatically compared to the earlier rates. This is natural as excess rural population becomes fully absorbed and because fertility rates tend to decline with urbanisation.

Taking a closer look at the nighttime satellite image, one sees black holes in the fabric of light covering the continents. Swaths of darkness, most remarkably stretching across much of populated Africa, imply exclusion from the modern productive world. The darkness signals a parallel universe where individuals, families, communities, cities and whole countries may be disconnected, not part of the global economic grid.

Has the global economy bypassed these areas? Or, has urbanisation generated insufficient energy to reach a visible threshold? Could one, if sufficiently sensitive, detect low intensity energy emanating from cities and communities within the dark patches? And, if so, would that potential force be on the verge of extinction or would it be just powering up? Compare, also, the brightest metropolitan clusters of eastern North America with the relatively low levels of light emitted by five times as many people in India. Which is more sustainable? Which more amenable? Are the energy-rich cities of highly industrialised countries now what others could become?

Or, do they form an exclusive global club, where the privileged and wealthy members are unwilling, or unable, to open the doors to others?

To answer these questions, one must examine many cities, over time, from all angles and all levels - from the global satellite overview to the gritty footpath of the shanty town. Starting with this 2001 edition, the State of the World's Cities series will take the reader through Africa, the Arab States, Asia and the Pacific, the highly industrialised countries, Latin America and the Caribbean and the countries with economies in transition - to understand better how shelter, society, environment, economy and, above all, systems of governance can contribute to urban vibrancy and viability in a globalising world. From periodic enquiry and regular assessment of urban conditions and trends, practical notions will emerge about how homo urbanus can realise a more sustainable and liveable habitat.

Civilisational Transition in Cities

We are entering a new era, the era of cities, a major civilisational transition. By the year 2000, half of humanity - 3.2 billion people - will be living in cities. Seventy per cent of this urban population will be in developing countries. Eighteen cities in the developing world will have a population of more than ten million.

Given the unprecedented urban explosion in the South, the magnitude of the task ahead is illustrated by the following figures. According to the United Nations estimates, the number of urban dwellers in the South will have doubled from 1980 to the year 2000: from one to two billion. A second doubling is likely to occur in the following twenty-five years, from two to four billion. In less than half a century, three billion people will be added to the urban population of the South. At the beginning of the 21st century, low-income people in Third World cities, many of them crowded in mega-cities, will become the new majority among the world's population.

Each of the continents is affected in a somewhat different way. In several Latin American countries, the degree of urbanisation has reached the levels of Europe and North America. In Africa, the rates of urban growth are excessively high. In Asia, the share size of the population involved is staggering. Nonetheless, this diversity of configurations provides an opportunity for internationally comparative research to gain insight into the contrasting patterns of accelerated social transformations going on in cities throughout the world.

"By 1990, an estimated 1.4 billion people lived in urban centers in the Third World. Of these, at least 600 million are estimated to live in 'life and health threatening' homes and neighborhoods because of the inadequacies in the quality of the housing and in the provision of infrastructure and services associated with housing and residential areas (such as piped water supplies, provision for sanitation, garbage collection and site drainage, paved roads and pavements, schools and health clinics)".

Cities, mirrors of society, reflect maldevelopment and the price of modernity. The predominant picture is one of fragmented or dual cities, characterised by phenomena of social exclusion, spatial segregation and mounting urban violence. The form that economic growth and social change have taken has been critical to the emergence of new problems in cities.

This dismal picture is by no means exclusive to developing countries, even though scales are different between the South and the North, East and West. The focus of a recent OECD report is on the severe concentrations of disadvantage, unemployment, poverty and alienation in many cities throughout OECD Member countries and on the scope for policies to encourage urban regeneration, social integration and the development of more livable environments.

A report of the Commission of the European Communities on the functions of cities in the European Community states that "during the next decade, as Europe moves towards greater economic and political integration, cities will be even more crucial players... They will also be the focus of many acute problems in the 1990s... The future of Europe will substantially reflect that of its cities. Their enormous economic, social and cultural energy must be harnessed to promote social and economic cohesion throughout the European Community. Cities demand a prominent place on its future agenda" . Cities are a major political challenge for both the North and the South.

The urban explosion compounded with severe environmental degradation - the urban poor are the main victims of environmental disruption - will have to be dealt with in a world economy characterised by low rates of growth, mounting unemployment, the pains of structural adjustment and debt servicing, as well as the need in many countries to implement institutional reforms.

The prospect for the cities will, to a great extent, depend on local solutions found for these global problems. It is clear, however, that the urban problem, as well as the environmental concerns, cannot be singled out from the broader context of social and economic styles of development. This puts the issue of political economy of development at the top of the urban agenda.

Even in cities that play a pre-eminent role in the processes of globalisation of the economy, economic progress often goes hand in hand with the persistence of pockets of destitution and ghettos. Hence the danger of paying too much attention to the economic role of cities, while underestimating the social, environmental, political, cultural, psychological and spatial dimensions of the ongoing transformations.

The experience of several industrialised countries shows that provision of reasonable infrastructure and shelter is not sufficient to humanise the cities and to overcome the social tensions. Employment, social integration and effective grass-roots democracy are necessary to create a sense of belonging and co-responsibility - two ingredients of meaningful citizenship. Designing and implementing systemic public policies should not only aim at improving people's quality of life, but also bring social and political stability to our cities, and thereby to our societies.

Nor is it reasonable to expect that complex and, in many cases, unique challenges will be met by merely copying ready-made models, even though these models may have shown their efficiency under other latitudes and in different contexts. "Cities are like people. They belong to the urban species but they have their unique personality.

The response to the urban challenge must take into account the singular configurations of natural, cultural, and socio-political factors, as well as of the historical past and tradition of each city. Instead of proposing across-the-board, homogenising solutions, the diversity of cities should be considered as a cultural value of paramount importance".

The sheer magnitude of the urban explosion compounded by the backlog of unattended employment, housing, environmental, public health and educational needs - "the social debt" - means that the replication in the South of the solutions now existing in the North would only increase the prevailing inequality, benefiting a minority and marginalising a majority of the urban dwellers.

Given the scale and nature of urban change and its likely extent in the future, the conventional model for the development of urban residential areas within market or mixed economies, developed in the North, does not work in the vast majority of urban centers in the Third World, and proved its limits in the North. Hence the need to seek innovative approaches.

The speed with which urban populations have grown in Third World nations has far outpaced the institutional capacity to manage it. The central characteristic of the urban problem is not the scale of population growth but the scale of the mismatch between demographic change and institutional change

Today, cities have emerged as strategic territories for a broad array of social, economic and political processes central to the current era: economic globalisation, international migration, the emergence of the producer services and finance as the leading growth sector in advanced economies, the new poverty, among others, and as strategic sites for their theorisation. This return of the city to the fore of the social sciences agenda can be seen as the representation of the social question in urban terms, the projection of the cleavage between marginalisation and integration.

However, cities are not just territories where social transformations take place, they are actors of this process. Hence it is necessary to determine how cities can play the role of economic, social and cultural driving forces - becoming incubators of innovation - and adapt to our rapidly changing, interdependent and uncertain world, as an alternative to the crisis of the nation-states.

Cities are undergoing a profound metamorphosis, the full consequences of which are still to be completely fathomed. As Francis Godard puts it, "we may then ask ourselves the following question: does the crisis of previous urban development models simply reflect the inability of cities to cope with the new world situation, or are we now instead witnessing the dawn of a new urban civilisation, based on new relationships between cities and labor, and between cities and regions?"

In this turbulent sea of change, the urban challenge constitutes perhaps the most difficult, yet crucial, component of the sustainable human development agenda, and calls for finding concrete ways of harmonising the criteria of social equity, ecological sustainability, economic efficiency, cultural pluralism and integration, and balanced spatial distribution of human activities and settlements, otherwise countries doomed to become one after another urban archipelagos in rural deserts. Meeting these criteria means translating them into a plurality of local ecosystem-specific, culture-specific and even site-specific solutions, devising new resource-use patterns and management procedures, requiring new mindsets, attitudes and values.

In this newly emerging urban civilisation, cities are the locus or crucibles, where major social problems are played out daily and magnified, but also locus of most creative change. The city is a territory that brings into focus and crystallises the major conflicts and contradictions of a society undergoing a deep mutation, and its role is to increasingly manage these accelerated social transformations.

Globalisation, exclusion, multiculturalism and ethnicity, governance, ecology, science and technology, are driving social transformations at work in cities (in various forms and degrees of intensity), presenting a series of continuing challenges to people and to decision-makers.

This is not to underestimate other crucial transformations with profound effect on cities such as demographic and migratory trends - gender struggles, family formation and dissolution patterns, fertility behaviour and sexuality, population structures and growth of the economically active population, international migration; changes in the structure of employment accompanied by growing unemployment and underemployment; fiscal restraint; changing equilibria between population and territory, among others.

The Global City

The last decade has seen a growing literature on the phenomenon known as 'globalisation' and the impact on cities of the major structural trends of our epoch, that is, the formation of a global economy and of the new techno-economic paradigm. For Saskia Sassen "we are seeing the emergence of a new type of urban system at the global and transnational regional levels: these are systems wherein cities are crucial nodes for international co-ordination and servicing of economies that are increasingly international". Economic globalisation promotes both integration and exclusion, decreases national sovereignty and increases autonomy of the market.

"The combination of geographic dispersal of economic activities and integration which lies at the heart of the current economic era has contributed to a strategic role for major cities in the current phase of the world economy... These cities now function as command points in the organisation of the world economy; as key locations and market-places for the leading industries of this period - finance and specialised services for firms - and as sites for the production of innovations in those industries. A limited number of cities emerge as transnational locations for investment, for firms, for the production of services and financial instruments, and for various international markets".

World cities perform a dual role at the intersection of the global economy and the nation-state.

This process leads to competitive struggle between cities to get and to retain world city status. However, this world city status bears considerable social costs: the economic restructuring is accompanied by a growing social polarisation or dualisation in the occupational and income structure, which is paralleled by high levels of spatial and ethnic segregation. Sao Paulo is but one illustration of the contradiction between the "success" of being the world city and the human price that most of its inhabitants must endure to survive. The struggles of people, caught in the trap of relative territorial immobility and the mobility of international capital, are a part of the dynamic which will shape both the world cities and the capitalist world economic system.

The process of globalisation not only changes the economic and social fabric, and the environment, of large urban areas, but remodel their spatial structure as well. The outcomes of this process will differ between particular countries and cities - the links are contingent, and depend to a significant extent on the scale and structure of the welfare state intervention, income distribution, planning policy and the mode of social regulation.

The discrepancy between the rate of company expansion and the rate of urban development is a problem cities, and in particular world cities, have to face. In some cases, urban life is in danger of being stifled by the very high rate of economic growth; the opposite trend can be observed in cities deserted by companies. How can cities and firms reconcile their respective needs?

How do major transformations taking place in the patterns of world economic interdependence manifest themselves in cities functioning as regional and global nodes? How are these processes of internationalisation articulated with other components in the economic and social structure of a large city? What are the consequences of these developments for the general socio-economic conditions of city residents? Recent research shows sharp increases in socio-economic and spatial inequalities within major cities of the developed world: how do global processes affect the daily life in the cites in terms of values, consumption patterns, life styles and political behaviour?

The Fragmented City

Throughout the ages cities have been the crucibles for the advance of civilisation, the melting-pots integrating people of different cultures, languages and creeds, the *loci* of tolerance and conviviality. Synonymous of democratic sociability, today they are too often synonymous of exclusion, racism, xenophobia and violence; a reversal in values. Across Europe, there is a profound unity of processes and logics that lead to hate, fear and growing incapacity to recognise and accept otherness.

Urban exclusion means that a shift has occurred between the paradigm of inequality within a cohesive social entity to the paradigm of fragmentation, isolation, poverty pockets, radical otherness. If nothing is done to stop this shift from integration to segregation, cities will break up into separate sectors: on the one hand, overprotected areas and on the other, dangerous, ghettos and "outlaw zones".

This growing social and spatial polarisation of cities goes hand in hand with mounting urban violence. Many forms of violence in the city are not only political, but are related to social, economic and cultural exclusion. Teresa Caldeira shows how violent crime has increased in Sao Paulo in the last decade, so has the fear of crime and the talk of crime, materially embodied in the city's walls. She argues that "if the fear of crime and the spread of violence are real in Sao Paulo, and if crime is supplying a language to talk about and think of many other de-stabilising processes, it is also the case that with the help of the talk of crime and crisis what is being forged is a much more segregated city and unequal society, and a polity in which the notions of justice and citizenship rights are fading away - for the sake of security and of the proper".

The degree of social inequality, cultural conflict and political fragmentation in cities has sharpened over the last decade. The ghost of social, political and psychological fragmentation haunts our society. Social divisions tear apart the very fabric of urban life and are testimony to the fact that cities and urban life styles lead to conflict and suffering that may weaken society as a whole.

Cities, as political entities, are faced with the following trade-off: will they develop into exclusion-generating systems or will they become promoters of citizenship and well-being, supported by local social contracts? The quest for citizenship seems to be universal. To enable and to guarantee the full exercise of citizenship could be seen as the guiding force of the forthcoming urban civilization.

The Multi-cultural and Multi-ethnic City

Cities are by definition, and tradition, "cosmopolitan". Perhaps the most dramatic change which urbanisation brings is the throwing together, in small, geographical areas, of people from different cultures and backgrounds. As underlined by Mario Polèse, this represents both the chief strength of the city, as a center for social innovation (urban culture), and its Achilles' heel. The collision of cultures can be both a source of creation and of conflict.

The city is a powerful tool for promoting positive social change. However, by bringing strangers together, urbanisation provokes tensions. Values and perceptions collide. How society deals with these tensions is perhaps the most difficult challenge of all. Few societies are immune to the specter of violence and ethnic strife.

To counteract nationalist tendencies, consolidating social integration with respect to ethnic and cultural diversity, and yet inciting them to blossom, is a major public policy challenge facing cities today and tomorrow. What are the principles for an equitable quality of life in cities? What have we learnt from experience about the principles of multi-ethnic coexistence in urban areas and what are the strategies to be implemented to enhance cosmopolitanism of city dwellers?

The Governed City

Cities as magnifiers of general social problems have become crucibles of crises more or less amenable to governance. Changes in thestructure of contemporary urbanisation raise the problem of social, economic and political governability, and in particular, of the emerging large metropolitan complexes.

How did governance - involving the relationship between civil society and government institutions at different levels -

become restructured, on one hand, as a consequence of globalisation and, on the other, the search for greater local democracy, accountability and transparency? What empowerment policies are needed to seek new forms of partnership for development between the State, the city, civil society and the private sector to guarantee the right to the city and the full exercise of citizenship in terms of political, civil, economic, social, psychological and cultural rights which are indissoluble? What new imaginative systems of governance can be found to foster civic engagement and integration of ethnic minorities?

States or markets? Processes of decentralisation, municipalisation and privatisation of functions (urban services) previously carried out by central government, are part of the more general and structural transformations of the State, and the need to rethink local government.

In which ways will urban management issues such as social policy, infrastructure investment, public transportation, land policy, municipal finance and administration, and responses to urban social crises, determine the future of cities, and their capacity to cope with social transformations and guide social change, including the management of desired transitions?

According to Guido Martinotti, particularly in regions with millenary urban history such as Europe, changes in the structure of contemporary urbanisation - strained by the new patterns of social relations emerging in time and space - raise the problem of social, economic and political governance of the large metropolitan complexes.

Local governments are elected by residents, but the economic interests of the metropolis are increasingly dependent on agents, such as big financial and industrial corporations which are not politically accountable from the point of view of the city itself. Traditional municipal policies and institutions seem inadequate to achieve the aim of governing these new entities.

Indeed, the new form of urban morphology is largely the product of the progressive differentiation of several populations gravitating around metropolitan centers. With increased mobility of the population, the very relations between population and territory become highly dynamic. Many of the social problems of contemporary metropolitan societies depend on the coexistence, competition and superimposition of these "urban layers" - inhabitants, commuters, users, metropolitan businessmen - and lead to *de facto disenfranchising* of the urban dweller. Martinotti argues that a great deal of governance problems of the new metropolis can be approached more aptly by acknowledging this intertwinement of morphologies.

The administrative borders of the traditional centers have often become obsolete in the course of the current urban dynamics. So far local democracy was largely understood in terms of some variation of the original idea of political community, but now the validity of this concept is increasingly submitted to erosion by the emerging social and physical morphology of the city.

The Ecological City

A city is a complex natural and social ecosystem, and should be managed accordingly. In terms of quality of life for the populations concerned, the disruption of the urban environment is one of the most difficult problems faced in the mega-cities of the South. A fundamental aspect of the urban environmental problem, emphasised by WHO. is the prevalence of poor health and the premature death of millions of people (mostly infants and children) due to inadequate nutrition and pollution of water, air and soil. Even though the situation in the cities of the North is less dramatic, environmental degradation has long-term effects and prejudices the movement towards sustainable cities.

How cities can play a crucial role in moving our societies toward a more environmentally sustainable future and environmentally sensitive local politics? Designing socially responsive and environmentally sustainable urban strategies that respond to the diversity of ecosystems and their resource potentials, as well as of needs as perceived by local communities, calls to move away from *ex-post* remedial environmental management to *ex-ante* pro-active environmental policies. For this, to promote a more rational resource management so as to increase the efficiency of the urban economy by:

(i) identifying and eliminating the wasteful uses of resources (financial, physical and human) and in this way releasing resources for development;

(ii) extending the useful life of existing infrastructure, buildings, and equipment by better maintenance; and

(iii) mobilising latent, underused, misused or wasted resources, both in the 'legal' and in the 'illegal' city: vacant land, unoccupied public and private buildings, the potential for non-financial investment in self-help housing, waste recycling, energy and water saving.

The Technological City

Science and technology are an essential component of the future of cities. In a highly interconnected world, in which competitiveness will depend largely on the capacity to generate and utilise knowledge, scientific and technological capabilities will strongly influence the pattern of urban development and amenities, and cities' sustainable management. Advances in science and technology have created unprecedented opportunities for improvements in standards of living. However, that progress in material well-being for a growing fraction of the world's population coexists with stagnation and even deterioration in standards of living for the majority of poor people. The clash between rising aspirations and the reality of widespread poverty has become a source of social tension.

Cities of the future call for exploring and assessing the opportunities and threats of science and technology for their management under the new techno-economic paradigm, and in particular advances in new technologies (information technology, biotechnology, new and advanced materials). They call for urban innovations adapted to ecological, cultural and socio-economic contexts, and for designing resource-conserving cities, blending the most advanced and the traditional techniques (skillful management of technological pluralism), both affordable and accessible to developing countries.

How to improve the overall cost-effectiveness of fixed capital investment in urban infrastructure, in services and in shelter by means of developing and demonstrating new cost-effective, resource-efficient, environmentally sustainable technological solutions? How can the trend towards flexible specialisation and the concomitant communication revolution characteristic of the "second industrial divide" alter rural-urban configurations, by "diffuse industrialisation" *à l'italienne*?

Acknowledging the growing importance of science and technology should not lead to celebrate the marvels of what they offer to mankind and cities' future. Science and technology are a social process among others, hence the need to refute urban management anchored on the mystification of the "technological fate".

"Development is an uncertain quest in which the seekers are doomed to rely more and more on science and technology. The quest is uncertain not only because there is no prior guarantee of success (nor that it will be lasting), but above all because it raises questions about the price of modernity: the benefits that a country can expect to derive from it, in political, economic, social, and cultural terms, as well as the sacrifices that it is prepared to make on its behalf...In short, despite what was promised by the rationalism of the Enlightenment and even more by positivism of the nineteenth century, scientific and technological progress does not necessarily coincide with social and moral progress... In the upheavals marking the end of the twentieth century... the whole world is in quest of new paths and alternatives leading to a better social order... Science and technology can contribute a great deal to development, but they cannot do everything, and above all they do not offer a ready-made solution to the problem of values that is raised by the clash between tradition and modernity... Development requires... a mastery of the consequences of scientific and technical change".

Challenges of Cities

Cities, a multi-faceted problem, are confronting daunting challenges continuously altered by the constellation of political, economic, social, cultural, environmental, scientific, and technological changes. The choices and challenges are many.

In Africa, only one-third of all urban households is connected to potable water. In Latin America, urban poverty stands at 30 per cent. In Asia Pacific, a mere 38 per cent of urban households are connected to a sewerage system. In Europe, processes of social exclusion marginalise many low-income and minority households, while urban crime and the decline of peripheral housing estates undermine the social cohesion of many communities. In North America, problems of residential segregation, discrimination in housing markets and affordability persist, particularly in the larger cities, despite recent economic growth. Worldwide, hundreds of millions of people live under conditions of abject poverty or experience highly unequal access to resources.

While some population groups have improved their housing conditions, a disproportionate share of the world population has seen its situation deteriorate further. In many countries, real incomes have fallen, the costs of living have gone up and the number of poor households has grown, particularly in urban areas. Sixty countries have become steadily poorer since 1980. Many studies portray increasing economic disparities between nations, cities, neighbourhoods and households, revealing strong increases in polarisation and growing global inequality.

The growing demand for public services in many countries is increasingly being met by local authorities and, in some cases, by the private sector, as these entities take on responsibility for functions previously ascribed to national governments. Furthermore, as civil society becomes more organised, effective and politically active, municipal institutions are becoming more democratic and adopting more participatory local structures.

Local political coalitions, together with representative groups from civil society, are attempting to shape their cities and towns in ways that help to maximise the opportunities as well as to minimise the social and economic disadvantages associated with globalisation. Whether this involves campaigns against crime or plans to improve the local environment in order to attract tourists, or whether it involves strategies to reduce local taxes or develop more comprehensive educational or health systems, municipal officials and their partners are increasingly responsive to the potential benefits of competitive strategies.

As a result, many cities have experienced a shift in the policies of urban government from managerialism to entrepreneurialism. This entrepreneurial attitude views the city as a product that needs to be marketed. The emphasis on marketing underpins the restructuring of cities so that they appeal to global investors. By the same token, cities that do not always have the resources to attract outside interest and investment may find themselves even more bereft and impoverished. Local capacity building is essential to reducing the risk of global polarisation.

In this connection, it is encouraging that international cooperation in the form of city-to-city exchanges is rapidly growing in popularity. Public–private partnerships are also increasingly being broadened to include civil society groups and there is increasing evidence of the potential of community-based networks based on direct people-to-people interactions. The challenge at national and international levels is to create an enabling legal framework in which the various forms of community-to-community cooperation can be intensified and strengthened.

Megacities, comprising urban cores and associated hinterlands, are theoretically able to address all kinds of technical problems, including urban service provision and environmental management. However, they are facing difficult governance challenges, owing to obsolete municipal political structures and inhabitants who are more and more concerned with only their immediate individual and local neighbourhood interests than with their common future as citizens of the same city.

Urban planners are inescapably caught up in this dynamic of the new urban political economy. Urban planning today is less codified and technical, and more innovative and entrepreneurial. It is also more participatory and concerned with projects rather than whole urban systems. Planning expertise is increasingly sought not only by states, but also by the corporate sector and civil society which seek to forge agreements through negotiation and mediation among contesting parties. Urban planning is no longer the prerogative of national and local governments, who previously claimed to possess privileged knowledge about the 'public interest'. What is controversial is not urban planning per se, but how to reconcile its multiple goals of efficiency, equity and liveability.

Globalisation not only increases competition but also fragmentation, with contradictory effects on cities. To compete effectively, cities must act as a collective unit. However, their growing social, political, economic and physical polarisation hampers their capacity to build coalitions, mobilise resources and develop good governance structures. Given that metropolitan areas are the chief arenas for global competition, it is necessary to strengthen them by giving them greater authority and autonomy. However, the enabling and regulatory role of governments must be broader than just facilitating the functioning of markets. It must also include responsibility for social cohesion, equity and conflict resolution.

Managing the Challenges

To face these formidable challenges cities are faced with a dilemma: either to reaffirm blind faith in the power of economic growth, synonymous of modernisation and progress, and the hidden assumption that the gains of economic growth will "trickle down" to the poor and make cities fit to live in; or cities strive for explicit societal development subordinated to values of social equity, ecological sustainability, economic efficiency, political participation , and cultural pluralism and integration. The specter of social, political and psychological fragmentation haunts our society; to halt it constitutes the real challenge as we approach the twenty-first century. To fight exclusion and discrimination, and to promote human rights and peace, are the motto.

The ongoing process of globalisation can be seen as "a narrative of eviction" of the symbolic meaning of places and people's quality of life, as if the place where we live no longer matters. On the contrary, the process of social (re)construction of spaces - public spaces - by enabling citizenship, as opposed to this loss of the place-boundedness, is not only complementary, but crucial, to the globalisation of capital if we do not want to move towards a world of "non-lieux".

To resume with the art of the city and its symbolic meaning is crucial. Augustin Berque offers a beautiful journey across Japanese cities illustrating the intertwining of social link and places, that is, in fact, to nature. Manuel Castells pleads in favor of "a series of political, economic and technological strategies that could contribute to the reconstruction of the social meaning in the new historical reality characterised by the formation of the space of flows as the space of power and functional organisations... The new techno-economic paradigm imposes the space of flows as the irreversible spatial logic of economic and functional organisations. The issue then becomes how to articulate the meaning of places to this new functional space. The reconstruction of place-based social meaning requires the simultaneous articulation of alternative social and spatial projects at three levels: cultural, economic, and political..."

The ethics of the city is to serve people and not the economy, hence the need to depart from an economicist vision of the city, the urban economy and macroeconomic performance framework, and explicitly assert the coronation of the citizen and, as a corollary, the process of expansion of citizenship rights - civil, political, and social. This principle must be upheld if cities are to become safe and democratic places to live.

The search for socially and environmentally sustainable urban development strategies should be guided by the principles outlined in the Rio Declaration on Environment and Development, and in particular Principle 1: "Human beings are at the center of concerns for sustainable development. They are entitled to a healthy and productive life in harmony with nature."

Hence, managing social transformations in cities should become a process of expanding people's capabilities and entitlements, of enlarging the range of people's choices. This shift in development thinking towards the concept of human development, that is development *of* people, *for* people, including the creation of economic opportunities for all, and *by* people, requiring participatory approaches, should become the driving force of urban management, and, thus, elevate "city governance and democracy" to the forefront of urban futures.

The challenge ahead is to promote alternative urban futures towards:

— cities, managers of social transformations and guides of deliberate social change;
— cities of solidarity and multiculturalism, capable to nurture an environment of tolerance and social sustainability;
— cities, promoters of citizenship and well-being;
— resourceful cities, designed to use natural resources sustainably.

In this imagined future of modernism, the right to the city, vector of social integration and humanism, can be fostered through:

— Fighting the fragmented city and struggle against social exclusion before its territorial crystallisation - the French urban policy illustrates the limits of the territorial management of exclusion - by policies to alleviate urban poverty, promote social integration and generate employment. Unemployment is often the trigger of exclusion, however exclusion is not only economic and social, but political, cultural, and symbolic - the question then becomes how to satisfy the claim for dignity of the marginalised population.
— Building partnerships for change between the civil society, the State and the market in the context of 'mixed economies' with special emphasis on participatory management and increased citizen involvement.
— Empowering of local communities through enablement strategies for urban self-reliance by making available the resources and techniques that cannot be mobilised locally, in particular funding community initiatives; even if not easy, community involvement is indispensable for social cohesion.

— Strengthening of local capabilities to cope with the rapidly changing environment, and therefore changing priorities.

— Implementing a holistic and multi-sectoral approach to urban regeneration, targeted at neighborhoods, as the essential building block of urban change.

Beyond the conceptual challenge of envisioning cities as the enhancement of human capabilities, and hence endorsing an ethical stand - the right to the city, vector of social integration and humanism, by enabling the exercise of citizenship, there is an urgent need for a very profound reconceptualisation of the intellectual and empirical tools for the study of urban social facts and processes because many of the established intellectual tools used to depict the urban phenomenon were built on a radically different urban morphology, and are strained by the new patterns of social relations emerging in time and space.

Scholars of urban phenomena, and social scientists in general, are faced with the challenging task of radically redefining the object of our field, and its conceptual representation. To appreciate fully the challenges and options available it is necessary to develop new conceptual frameworks, habits of thought and willingness to move to highly disaggregated modes of thinking, as well as to reinterpret past experience in a rapidly changing context.

According to Guido Martinotti, if we want to understand the current urban dynamics and related social problems, we must adopt a new visual angle based on the idea that the study of cities is systemic in character and that at present the system we have to consider tends to have planetary extension. One of the aspects of our conceptual apparatus that needs radical reconsideration has to do with the implicit or explicit intellectual heritage of social ecology where the residential function is largely prominent.

Another one has to do with the challenge of change and policy relevance, that is to cope with uncertainty and change;

to enhance "organisational learning"; to bridge the gap between theory and practice by fostering reflection-in-action; to implement the socially desirable futures through the strategic planning process viewed "as a loose co-operative learning process that involves a multiplicity of actors throughout the whole fabric of society, that seeks to attain increasing levels of shared perceptions on objectives and goals, and that aims at agreeing on specific anticipatory and actual decision on the basis of temporary consensus", and to foster innovation. Furthermore, a methodological reflection on empirical categories is called for: the history of concepts - distinction between universal tendencies versus local phenomena - and their specific meanings in given cultural contexts, through a multicultural viewpoint examining how spaces and urban territories are categorised in various linguistic areas and different countries.

2

Urban Population Growth

The world population reached 6 billion in 1999. Remarkably to note, it took a century to grow from 1 billion to 2 billion people; 30 years (1930-1960) to reach 3 billion; 15 years (1960-1975) for the next billion; and 12 years to grow from 4 billion to 5 billion. At the current rate the world will have 7 billion people soon after the year 2010. The overwhelming share of world population growth is taking place in developing countries (89.9 % in 1970-80; 92.2 % in 1980-90, 95.2% in 1990-2000; 97.6% in 2000-10; and 98.4% in 2010-20). The population of developing countries has more than doubled in 35 years, growing from 1.89 billion in 1955 to 4.13 billion in 1990.

Significant proportions of population increases in the developing countries have been and will be absorbed by urban areas (45.6% in 1970-80; 58.7% in 1980-90; 71.8% in 1990-2000; 83.4% in 2000-10; and 93.4 in 2010-20). Urban settlements in the developing countries are, at present, growing five times as fast as those in the developed countries. Cities in the developing countries are already faced by enormous backlogs in shelter, infrastructure and services and confronted with increasingly overcrowded transportation systems, insufficient water supply, deteriorating sanitation and environmental pollution.

Rapid urbanisation, the concentration of the urban population in large cities, the sprawl of cities into wider geographical areas and the rapid growth of mega-cities are among the most significant transformations of human settlements.Urban areas will strongly influence the world of the twenty-first century, and urban and rural populations will be increasingly interdependent for their economic, environmental and social well being. Among the economic and social factors influencing this process are population growth and voluntary and involuntary migration, real and perceived employment opportunities, cultural expectations, changing consumption and production patterns and disparities among regions"

By the year 2006, every second human being is expected to live in urban settlements, while in 1975 only 37.8% of humanity lived in towns and cities, this rate has risen to 45.3% in 1995 and projected to grow further. Recent estimations show urbanisation level of 61.1% for the year 2030.

A well managed urbanisation has the potential to lead to improvements in the living standards of the world's population. The transition into an urbanised world has enormous implications for the world economy, for social conditions, as well as for the state of the world environment. An increasing number of cities have taken on significant roles in the globalisation of the economy, particularly with regard to financial services, commerce, transport and telecommunication.

During the course of history, urbanisation has been associated with economic and social progress, the promotion of literacy and education, the improvement of the general state of health, greater access to social services, and cultural, political and religious participation. Democratisation has enhanced such access and meaningful participation and involvement for civil society actors, for public-private partnerships, and for decentralised, participatory planning and management, which are important features of a successful urban future.

Cities and towns have been engines of growth and incubators of civilisation and have facilitated the evolution of knowledge, culture and tradition, as well as of industry and commerce. Urban settlements, properly managed, hold the promise for human development and the protection of the world's natural resources through their ability to support large numbers of people while limiting their impact on the natural environment.

Larger and larger proportions of the population live in 1,000,000+ cities. In the developed countries 26% of the total population lived in such cities in 1990, compared with 19% thirty years ago. This increase is more startling in the developing countries, where this proportion more than doubled from 5% in 1960 to 12% in 1990. The concentration of urban populations 1,000,000+ cities is becoming particularly characteristic for developing countries. In 1990, for example, 36 percent of the urban population of the developing countries lived in such cities, compared to 22% in 1950. In the developed countries these proportions changed from 29% in 1950 to 35% in 1990.

Globally, there were 245 1,000,000+ cities in 1985, while twenty-five years earlier there were only 112 and a century ago there were only five. By the turn of the century, worldwide there will be 372 metropolitan cities and it is anticipated that this number may rise to 527 in 2015. In 1950, the industrialised countries had only 49 1,000,000+ cities. By 1975 that number had nearly doubled, and it is expected to have tripled by the year 2000, when the number will reach 117. In 1970, the developing countries had about the same number of metropolitan cities as the industrialised countries. However, it is forecast that, by the turn of the century, they will have twice as many as the industrialised countries. By the year 2015, it is expected that 22% of the world's total population and 41% of the world urban population will live in 1,000,000+ cities.

Increasingly, cities have a network of linkages that extends far beyond their boundaries. Sustainable urban development requires consideration of the carrying capacity of the entire ecosystem supporting such development, including the prevention and mitigation of adverse environmental impacts occurring outside urban areas. The unsafe disposal of waste leads to the degradation of the natural environment: aquifers, coastal zones, ocean resources, wetlands, natural habitats, forests and other fragile ecosystems are affected, as are the homelands of indigenous people.

Most countries of the developing world with high rates of urbanisation in the last decade also experienced higher economic growth. The world has witnessed economic and social progress during the last decades. This is shown in, among others, higher life expectancy, lower infant mortality, higher literacy, and increased participation of disadvantaged groups. But economic and social gains are, however, unequally distributed. Back in 1960, the 20 per cent of the world's population living in countries with the highest per capita income had incomes 30 times greater than the world's poorest 20 per cent; by 1990, the richest 20 per cent were getting 60 times more.

Poorly managed cities and towns contribute to unsustainable production and consumption patterns. They also generate unmanageable wastes, which negatively impact on land and water resources as well as on the atmosphere. Sustaining healthy environments in the urbanised world of the 21st century represents a major challenge for human settlements, development and management. Social gains have lagged behind economic gains. A large proportion of the world's population remains deprived of basic services such as water supply and sanitation. The marginalised population is particularly large in those countries of the South where economic progress was slow.

Every day in a course of this decade, the developing countries have to accommodate 150,000 additional urban dwellers. For the next decade this figure will grow up to 180,000 inhabitants daily or more than one million people weekly. While large cities in some developing countries have been growing at rates of up to 5 per cent per annum, slums and squatter settlements in some of them have been growing as twice as quickly.

Slums and squatter settlements dwellers present a significant part of population in many cities of the developing countries (for example, from 30 to 40% in Caracas, Dakar, Dhaka, Lima, Nairobi, Madras, Manila, Rio de Janeiro, Sao Paolo; 40-50% - Calcutta, Mexico City, Tunis; 50-60% - Bogota, Bombay, Delhi, Buenos Aires, Lagos, Lusaka; 60-70% - Dar es Salaam, Kinshasa; more than 70% in Addis Ababa, Cairo, Casablanca, Luanda).

It has been estimated that, 17 per cent of the world's stock of housing consists of one-room shelter, of which some three quarters are to be found in the developing countries. Some 42 per cent of rural and 35 per cent of urban dwellings in Africa are single-roomed. The overwhelming shelter problem in the developing countries is the shortage of affordable housing for the low-income majority of households in urban areas. This has resulted in the proliferation of slums and squatter settlements.

An assessment in 1991 suggested that around half the urban population in the developing countries had water piped into their houses while around a quarter were supplied through less convenient means - public standpipes, yard taps, protected dug wells and bore-holes/hand-pumps. The remaining 350 million urban dwellers did not have a safe, protected water supply. The latest estimates indicate that the number of urban dwellers without suitable water services had increased.

At least one third of the South's urban population lacked provision for sanitation in 1991. Of those that had provision for sanitation, most had a simple latrine; only some 550 million had a house connected to a public sewer with around 220 million having a septic tank system. Estimates for 1994 suggest that the number of people lacking adequate sanitation in urban areas in the South had increased considerably during the early 1990s, to 588 million up from 452 million in 1990. Projections to the year 2000 show that if the present rates of provision of sanitation services are maintained, the number of people without adequate sanitation will total 3.31 billion, that is more than half the world's population. This will include 846 million urban dwellers.

Most cities in both developed and developing regions experience a polarisation of their populations into affluent and poor neighbourhoods. Trends are often towards further segregation rather than social integration of the poor and marginalised urban population groups. Poverty is a growing problem worldwide both in the rural and urban areas and impacts negatively on human settlements. At least 600 million urban dwellers in Africa, Asia and Latin America live in "life-and-health threatening homes" and neighbourhoods because of the very poor housing and living conditions and the lack of adequate provision for sanitation, drainage, removal of garbage and health care. An increasing number of the urban poor are also homeless in both developed and developing countries, with current estimates of the homeless population being over 100 million.

In many countries, the rates of urbanisation exceed the capacity of national and local governments to plan and organise this transformation. As a result, new forms of urban poverty have emerged, manifested through poor housing conditions, insecure land tenure, urban crime and homelessness. Moreover, poorly managed cities have negative impacts on environmental conditions. In most countries in Africa, Asia and Latin America, the absolute level of resources available to local governments is seldom adequate to provide even the most minimal level of services.

New Urban Habitats

Rapid growth of population and its concentration in cities around the world are affecting the long-term outlook for humanity. Despite four millennia as centres of civilisation and economic activity, cities never attracted more than a few percent of the global population until the last century. Now, at the beginning of the 21st century, systems of cities have become a dominant factor in the world's social, economic, cultural and political matrix.

Burdened with all the problems of growth, cities are increasingly subject to dramatic crises, especially in developing countries. Unemployment, environmental degradation, lack of urban services, deterioration of existing infrastructure and lack of access to land, finance and adequate shelter are among the main areas of concern.

Table 1. World urban population and growth rate in percentage

	Urban Population as a % of total population			Urban Population annual growth rate (%)	
	1970	1995	2015	1970-1995	1995-2015
Least Developed	12.7	22.9	34.9	4.6	5.1
All Developing	24.7	37.4	49.3	2.9	3.8
Industrialised	67.1	73.7	78.7	0.6	1.1
Low HDI	18.2	27.4	38.6	3.7	4.1
Medium HDI	23.0	37.7	52.7	2.8	3.3
High HDI	52.8	70.9	78.5	1.7	3.9

For better or for worse, the development of contemporary societies will depend largely on understanding and managing the growth of cities. The city will increasingly become the test bed for the adequacy of political institutions, for the performance of government agencies, and for the effectiveness of programmes to combat social exclusion, to protect and repair the environment and to promote human development.

Urbanisation and human development There is a strong, positive link between national urbanisation and national levels of human development. Urban population, as a share of total national population in both highly industrialised countries (HIC) and those countries with a high Human Development

Index (HDI1), is above 70 percent. Urbanisation falls to less than 30 percent in countries that are classified as Least Developed Countries (LDC) or have a low HDI. All HICs score high in their provision of urban services and infrastructure to all citizens and low in incidence of absolute poverty. Development and urbanisation, thus, proceed handin-glove. Without substantial investment in the infrastructure and services that support both, neither can occur.

Moving toward urban-rural equilibrium The current worldwide rate of urbanisation is about 0.8 percent, varying between about 1.6 percent for all African countries to about 0.3 percent for all HICs. Worldwide, nearly all cities continue to grow in absolute terms. The rates at which they are capturing a portion of a country's total population, however, vary. In Asia and North America, cities are still taking in national population at an increasing rate, although the rate in North America is very low at 0.26 percent.

In Africa, Europe and Latin America, urbanisation rates are slowing. In Latin America, urbanisation rates - now at about 0.5 percent - have been slowing since 1950 when the average for all countries in the region was 1.8 percent per year. With the exception of the small island states of Oceania, that actually had negative urbanisation rates since 1975 and are now moving into positive territory, rates of urbanisation are projected to drop in all regions after 2015. Slowing urbanisation rates mean that the combined rate of

(1) domestic rural-tourban migration,

(2) immigration of foreigners directly to cities and

(3) the natural rate of population growth in cities is dropping off.

Population in Mega Cities

The rise of the mega-city (cities of at least 10 million people) in developing countries over the past twenty years is of concern because of incapacity to increase the provision of housing and basic services at the same pace. There is currently an extremely rapid displacement of developed country cities on the list of the world's 30 largest cities by those in developing countries. Between 1980 and 2000 Lagos, Nigeria, Dhaka, Bangladesh, Cairo, Egypt, Tianjin, China, Hyderabad and Lahore, India, along with several others in developing countries, were added to the list. By 2010 Lagos is projected to become the third largest city in the world.

At the same time Milan, Italy, Essen, Germany, and London, United Kingdom have all disappeared from among the top 30 cities, and New York, USA, Osaka, Japan and Paris, France will have slipped farther down the list by 2010. Among developed countries, only Tokyo will have held its place - as the largest urban agglomeration in the world - for 30 years.It should be noted that none of these great cities, with the possible exception of London, will have lost population over the 30 year span.

Mega-cities are still growing, but in the developed world they are part of the general slowdown of urban growth rates to a global rate of about one-third of one percent per year. The overall urbanisation rate in Asia, in contrast, is four times that and is reflected in the growth of its mega cities. The urban population in the countries with economies in transition (ET) will approach 420 million, or 78 percent of its projected total population of 541 million, by 2020.

Economies in Transition

Today, urban areas account for 70 percent, or 382 million of the total population of 543 million. The urban share of total population ranges from 40 percent in most of the central Asian republics to nearly 75 percent in Russia, about the same as the HIC and Latin American countries. Of the central Asian republics that were part of the former Soviet Union, four - Kyrgyzstan, Kazakhstan, Tajikistan and Turkmenistan - recorded negative urban growth rates between 1990 and 1995.

Table. 2. Trading Places on the Top 30 List
(population in millions)

	980		1990		2000		2010	
1	21.9	Tokyo	25.1	Tokyo	26.4	Tokyo	26.4	Tokyo
2	15.6	New ork	16.1	New York	18.1	Mexico city	23.6	Bombay
3	13.9	Mexico City	15.1	Mexico city	18.1	Bombay	20.2	Lagos
4	12.5	São Paulo	15.1	São Paulo	17.8	São Paulo	19.7	São Paulo
5	11.7	Shanghai	13.3	Shanghai	16.6	New York	18.7	Mexico city
6	10.0	Osaka	12.2	Bombay	13.4	Lagos	18.4	Dhaka
7	9.9	Buenos Aires	11.5	Los Angeles	13.1	Los Angeles	17.2	New York
8	9.5	Los Angeles	11.2	Buenos Aires	12.9	Calcutta	16.6	Karachi
9	9.0	Calcutta	11.0	Osaka	12.9	Shanghai	15.6	Calcutta
10	9.0	Beijing	10.9	Calcutta	12.6	Buenos Aires	15.3	Jakarta
11	8.9	Paris	10.8	Beijing	12.3	Dhaka	15.1	Delhi
12	8.7	Rio de Janeiro	10.5	Seoul	11.8	Karachi	13.9	Los Angeles
13	8.3	Seoul	9.7	Rio de Janeiro	11.7	Delhi	13.9	MetroManila
14	8.1	Moscow	9.3	Paris	11.0	Jakarta	13.7	Buenos Aires
15	8.1	Bombay	9.0	Moscow	11.0	Osaka	13.7	Shanghai
16	7.7	London	8.8	Tianjin	10.9	Metro Manila	12.7	Cairo
17	7.3	Tianjin	8.6	Cairo	10.8	Beijing	11.8	Istanbul
18	6.9	Cairo	8.2	Delhi	10.6	Rio de Janeiro	11.5	Beijing
19	6.8	Chicago	8.0	Metro Manila	10.6	Cairo	11.5	Rio de Janeiro

20	6.3	Essen	7.9	Karachi	9.9	Seoul	11.0	Osaka
21	6.0	Jakarta	7.7	Lagos	9.6	Paris	10.0	Tianjin
22	6.0	Metro Manila	7.7	London	9.5	Istanbul	9.9	Seoul
23	5.6	Delhi	7.7	Jakarta	9.3	Moscow	9.7	Paris
24	5.3	Milan	6.8	Chicago	9.2	Tianjin	9.4	Hyderabad
25	5.1	Teheran	6.6	Dhaka	7.6	London	9.4	Moscow
26	5.0	Karachi	6.5	Istanbul	7.4	Lima	9.0	Bangkok
27	4.7	Bangkok	6.4	Teheran	7.3	Bangkok	8.8	Lima
28	4.6	Saint Petersburg	6.4	Essen	7.2	Teheran	8.6	Lahore
29	4.6	Hong Kong	5.9	Bangkok	7.0	Chicago	8.2	Madras
30	4.4	Lima	5.8	Lima	6.9	Hong Kong	8.1	Teheran

The aggregate urban populations in the first and last of these countries is still decreasing. On average, municipalities of the ET countries capture about US$275 per capita in revenue per year.

It is primarily the former centrally planned economies of Eastern and Central Europe, plus the CIS countries, that have become known as economies in transition. Some of these were among the first industrialised urban societies in the world but in recent decades have failed to modernise their cities. The enormity of the task of their transforming to market economies and upgrading their cities is now manifesting itself to a full extent. At present, there are very few ETs whose transition is complete.

Although the transition from centralised to free market economies has delivered considerable social benefits, it has also proven a costly process. Transition started with general impoverishment – in 1996, real wage levels in many ETs had fallen to half or less compared to 1989. Next came rises in unemployment, followed by sharp increases in poverty and inequality, a striking deterioration of public services and a fall in the provision of educational services. The elderly – often sentenced to poverty - became major losers in the transition process, as well as many middle-aged people, since retirement was widely used to reduce unemployment. Half the region's poor citizens live in cities.

There are, indeed, sharp differences among the various countries with economies in transition, notably in criminality, corruption and democracy. Some, particularly in Central Europe, have clearly started to adjust to the market economy promoted by the West. But, although the laissez-faire model was assumed by many experts to be the solution, experience during the past decade indicates that this does not necessarily hold true for all. The informal sector in a number of countries will play an increasing role, as a consequence of growth in the labour force without a matching response in the level of formal employment opportunities.

In several of the region's countries, newly enfranchised city governments often have neither the experience nor the capacity to deal with the huge deficiencies built up over the years. In spite of quantitative transfer of tasks to local authorities, demands frequently overshadow administrative and financial capacities. It is, therefore, important to strengthen both the institutional and financial bases of local authorities to enable them to participate effectively in the development process.

Local government income figures suggest that decentralisation has not been achieved since the national government transfers are still very high. There are, however, capacity building programmes ongoing in such countries as Poland and Romania, and, in the Balkans, cities are undergoing not only reconstruction but "re-invention."

Sustainable urban development in ET countries will depend upon the creation and maintenance of efficient land and property markets; the development of housing finance; a greater emphasis on municipal finance and institution building; the strengthening of urban utility systems; a growing interest in the preservation of cultural assets and heritage; and the responsiveness to such emergencies as earthquakes and flooding.

Vulnerability of the Urban Poor

The growth of large cities in the developing world is accompanied by an upsurge in urban poverty.From a number of perspectives, national and local authorities are not prepared to manage urban development in favour of the poor, who usually take up illegal residence on the periphery of the city. Without basic services, secure tenure and formal employment opportunities, these settlements become slums of the most appalling nature, offering their inhabitants little hope of improving their lives.

It is estimated that between ¼ and 1/3 of all urban households in the world live in absolute poverty. Vulnerable to a number of hazards, the urban poor are always at risk. They live densely packed, subject to heavy rains or sudden fires that can wipe out their homes. They have precarious employment, in the formal or informal sector. They are exposed to higher incidence of disease, arbitrary arrest and forced eviction. Neglected by formal institutions, they are often left unprotected against violence, drug dealers, corrupt officials, unscrupulous slumlords and organised crime.

Lack of resources and, therefore, lack of political power, is one of the main causes of their vulnerability. Low levels of assets make poor people especially vulnerable to negative economic shocks, setting in motion a downward spiral that worsens deprivation in the long term. Pulling children out of school to earn extra income; making quick land sales at desperately low prices; slowing nutritional intake below the levels necessary to sustain health all contribute to greater vulnerability in the future.

Urban indicators, based on local definitions of poverty, reveal that the cities of Africa have the highest rates of poverty of all regions: over 40 percent and rising. Latin America has significantly higher percentage of woman-headed households living in poverty than the percentage of all households in poverty (36 against 25 percent). Thirty-four Latin American cities report more woman-headed households in poverty against 23 with less. Cities of North Africa show a different pattern than the other Arab States, with more woman- headed households in poverty. In most Asian cities, poverty incidence is higher in woman-headed households than in all households.

Social and political forces, as well as markets, have their effects on poverty. Public expenditure patterns, gender discrimination, accountability, corruption, having a voice in public affairs, as well as global factors such as environmental degradation, health advances, and agricultural productivity each play a role in increasing or reducing poverty. Statistics on health, education and income, however, do not capture the micro-level realities of living poor, such as the impact of domestic violence on women's lives. Patterns of poverty evolution are so enormously varied that one should not expect simple causal explanations, much less a uniform set of policy prescriptions.

Increasingly, identifying and overcoming conditions of local poverty is seen as a local authority responsibility - for higher level institutions to support and facilitate.

In terms of income poverty it appears that relative equality in assets and relative stability of the economic growth path can have significant effects on poverty reduction. In this regard a fair and predictable legal system and the ability to dampen short term shocks with targeted assistance programmes will have positive long-term consequences. Strengthening institutions, norms and values, and building the social capital generated by reciprocity - or the give and take within networks - is also important in reducing levels of poverty.

Just as it is becoming clear that poverty reduction demands more effective local response and more supportive enabling policies at the national level, the urban poor face additional risk. In the 1970's, the world embarked on a phase of globalisation aimed at deregulating labour markets, privatising government functions and liberalising finance.

Financial liberalisation was supposed to move savings from developed to developing countries, lower the costs of borrowing, reduce risk through new financial instruments, and increase economic growth. Much the opposite materialised: savings have flowed from poor to richer countries, interest rates have generally increased, risk has risen and economic growth throughout the world has slowed for the vast majority of countries, rich and poor.With global liberalisation, job and income security worsened in both rich and poor countries.

Competition for foreign investment and the greater ability of employers to shift production to other locations have undermined job security and collective bargaining. Mergers and acquisitions, now the most prevalent form of foreign domestic investment (FDI) in developing countries, have commonly produced corporate restructuring and massive layoffs. Then, in 1997-1998, the economic crisis in Asia struck a blow against economies in the developing world that had been held up as models of liberalised success.

The crisis was caused in part by poorly regulated financial systems that allowed an excessive flow of credit to weak borrowers and to high risk projects.Banks were weakened by growing levels of unreported non-performing debt. In mid-1997, market confidence collapsed. In one country after another, starting in Thailand and spreading to Malaysia, Indonesia, the Philippines and the Republic of Korea, the Asian crises exposed the risks inherent to close integration of national economies with the global financial markets. Human impacts were severe and will persist long after economic recovery.

In the two decades prior to the crises, East and Southeast Asian countries made spectacular welfare gains, primarily because growth was largely inclusive - the poor shared the benefits. The number of poor people had fallen and the severity of poverty had declined. Life expectancy at birth, infant mortality, and literacy all improved. The economic crisis in Asia caused the biggest setback for poverty reduction in several decades. It caused lay-offs, real wage declines, weak demand for new labor market entrants, and falling margins in the informal sector.

In Thailand, unemployment increased by 50 percent. In the Republic of Korea, unemployment reached two million people during 1998, up from one-half million the year before. In the Philippines, one million additional people joined the ranks of the jobless.

Job losses hit women, youth and unskilled workers hardest. Families under stress were taking children out of school. Increasing domestic violence, street crime and suicides were reported in most of the countries as a result of increased social stress and family fragmentation. More people live in poverty today in Asia than in the mid-1990's.

Good Governance

In Asia, cities became the locus of bad debt generated in large part by a vast oversupply of middle and upper-class housing estates, condominiums, hotels and office towers. The Asia crisis revealed the destructive side of globalisation. The prospect of global markets fueled the desire of many entrepreneurs and some government officials to cash in quickly. It increased the opportunities for crony capitalism and corruption.

Expecting a rising tide to float all ships, it diverted attention from the basic needs of those who are normally excluded or could not participate.

As the Asian crisis and those that occurred in Mexico, Brazil and Russia have demonstrated, all urban communities, not only the poor - who are always at greatest risk - are vulnerable to malfunctions of global economic system. It is only a matter of time before another systemic shock shakes investor confidence and capital abandons even stronger economies.

At this moment, rising oil prices, falling stock prices and a series of global food supply problems are causing politicians and investors no small concern. Local authorities, who know the micro-realities of poverty and are on the front line in responding to all social, economic and environmental crises, urgently require different and more effective tools for securing the lives of their citizens and ensuring that the urban poor have some protection against global market hazards.

The silver lining is that the increased pace of urbanisation and its linkages to economic globalisation have reinvigorated interest in good urban governance and its links to economic growth. The combined effect of economic foibles and failures is helping to define the fundamentals of good governance, made conspicuous by their absence: fiscal discipline, fair and transparent resource allocation, effective and predictable regulatory systems, fiduciary responsibility, strategic planning, independent and just mechanisms for conflict resolution, participatory decision-making, safety and security for all, open information flows and ethical behaviour.

In the name of a global economy, international institutions are taking steps to liberate markets from the regulatory authority of nations and their autonomous subdivisions - the provinces and cities. That authority can be pre-empted by such instruments as the proposed Multilateral Agreement on Investment (MAI), which was read by many local authorities as restricting their abilities to:

1. condition new major investments within their jurisdictions on performance requirements in support of local economic development;
2. prohibit contracts with entities that violate international human rights, labour and environmental laws; and
3. prohibit public entities from conditioning the receipt of public funds on compliance with human rights laws or other criteria reflecting community values.

Local Canadian and United States officials noticed that the MAI put in question the ability of municipalities, acting in the public interest, to limit the use of property through zoning, among other instruments. An international coalition, using Internet to organise opposition, scuttled the MAI.

3

Impacts of Globalisation on Urban Areas

Globalisation increases competition between different areas throughout the world. This can be seen easily when looking in a grocery store. Not all of the produce in a grocery store is produced in one area or region; rather the products are obtained from numerous places and regions throughout the world. Ideally, the most efficient producers will be able to control the market. This however is only the case when government subsidies are not implemented in the given industry. The agricultural market in some countries is subsidised and in others are not, creating an unfair advantage for those farmers who live in the subsidised regions. For instance, the United States has subsidised the American farmers but the Canadian market does not subsidise its farmers as much, therefore creating an unfair playing field.

In addition a simple change or decline in transportation costs can allow a product to travel from areas further away at lower or at the same costs. This causes an increase in supply and if the supply is not demanded then prices are reduced. Thus, reducing the amount of revenue that goes to the farmer. With increased corporate farms, and the above problems, it is virtually impossible for the family farm to survive in this increasingly competitive world.

On top of these problems, globalisation creates a strengthening of the urban realm. New and better transportation means increases the distance that people can live from their urban job or career. This creates a greater need for suburban land for residential and other related uses. "Due to Niagara's close proximity to Toronto and other expanding cities there is a great demand for housing, infrastructure and industry which is detrimental for agriculture".

Moreover, clusters of urban development can now take place free from the city center. Soja, in the book Variation on a Theme Park: The New American City and the End of Public Space, describes this process as an exopolis, a city without a city center. These clusters of development often take over places that were once agricultural lands. Urban pressures for development infringe on rural land not only on the urban fringe but also deep within rural and agriculturally rich areas.

Globalisation thus, causes a decrease in rural and agricultural land and an increase in commodity rich land uses, such as those economic processes that are located within a city. "In the past decades [urban] development has sprawled over much of the specialty land in the Niagara Region". Some types of specialised agricultural land have been able to survive the increased urban pressures and globalisation, because of their commodity rich nature and economical determination. One example of this is the wineries in the Niagara Region. For further information on a wineries ability to survive urban and global pressure see the link Agri-tourism on the previous page.

Lands in the Niagara Region are owned by the Crown therefore, planning departments, local governments, the region and provincial policies control land-uses of a given city, town or hamlet. Crown land is land that belongs to the Queen hence land owners do not have the final say over the landuse of the property that they bought, rather the province, region and local government have the final say in the way the land is used. The areas of government are then influenced by; private sector developers, consultants, non-profit organisations, concerned residents of the area, the media and the rest of the public.

There are many policies and regulations that are implemented at these different levels that try to ensure that agricultural land is protected. Unfortunately, these portions of government are also pressured by the economic success of an area and the need to make voters happy. It is extremely challenging to have all of the above governments resist the temptation to accept forms of urban development in agriculturally rich areas.

Even if the local planning department feels that a given building or residential area should not be built on a specific piece of agricultural land, the issue still has to be presented and approved or not approved by the local government, and then possibly but not always the regional government). The result of this is highly fragmented decision making, with little or no coordination to consider regional needs or regional consequences of local action or inaction. In addition, the people that are often asking for approval for such development may have given financial contributions to the city, which makes it hard for the City to say no to the developer. Moreover, the provincial policy statement permits expansion into areas that are agriculturally rich. The Provincial Policy states that development can occur, only where;

1. There are no reasonable alternatives, which avoid prime agricultural areas, and
2. There are no reasonable alternatives with lower priority agricultural lands in the prime agricultural area.

As can be seen in the Font hill Kame example this legislation can have drastic affects on the land if the land is proven to be unsuitable for large scale tender fruit growth. In addition the language of the policy allows for urban expansion to take place on prime agricultural land if there are no alternative places to put such a landuse. This unfortunately allows for an increase in the number of consents in areas of prime agricultural land which reduces agricultural crop sizes.

Spaciality/Temporality of Economic Globalisation

The global has specificity in its conditionalities and contents. Two key pieces in this formulation are the locational and institutional embeddedness of economic globalisation at least partly in the national, and secondly, the specificity and social thickness of the global. The global economy needs to be implemented, reproduced, serviced, financed. It cannot be taken simply as a given, or a set of markets, or merely as a function of the power of multinational corporations and financial markets.

There is a vast array of highly specialised functions that need to be executed, infrastructures that need to be secured, and legislative environments that need to be rendered hospitable. This holds even in the case of what we might think of as the mere cross-border spread of certain "national" forms, whether Anglo-American accounting standards or US styles of food and entertainment. Not all would agree. Much of the scholarship on economic globalisation has either rejected its specificity, and even reality, or it has confined its conceptualisation to cross-border trade and capital flows thereby denuding the global of much of its social thickness.

Among those who grant it specificity and presence, the tendency has been to understand the spatiality of economic globalisation in terms of the hypermobility and neutralisation of distance made possible by the new technologies. With this comes inevitably a notion about the compression of time: instantaneous integration and so-called real time simultaneity. What both of these mainstream accounts tend to leave out of the analysis is the fact that hypermobility and time-space compression need to be produced, and that this requires vast concentrations of very material and not so mobile facilities and infrastructures.

Thus the spatiality/temporality of economic globalisation itself contains dynamics of mobility and of fixity. While these may easily be classified as two distinct types of dynamics from the perspective of mainstream categories, they are in fact not distinct. One presupposes the other and this raises a whole series of empirical, theoretical and political questions about the spatiality/temporality of economic globalisation that go beyond a unitary conception of hypermobility and time-space compression.

The global city is emblematic here, with its vast capacities for controlling hypermobile dematerialised financial instruments and the enormous concentrations of material and human, mostly place-bound resources that it takes to have the former circulating around the globe in a second. This is one way in which economic globalisation can be said to be characterised by locational and institutional embeddedness. If the global is indeed rich in contents and conditionalities, then its insertion in an institutional world which has been historically constructed as overwhelmingly national, is eventful. It is the combination of this embeddedness of the global along with its specificity which gives meaning to the notion of overlap and interaction among the multiple spatialities and temporalities of the national and the global. Much of the enactment of these overlaps and interactions is in formation as the global is still in the process of producing the particular forms of its specificity as well as its social thickness. It is already different today from what it was only 15 years ago.

To what extent the global today resembles earlier eras which scholars have identified as having strong parallels is a subject of much debate. Of interest here is Braudel's examination of the times and spaces of Europe. His treatment of the distinctiveness of the major cities—his "supervilles"—of the 14th and 15th centuries compared with their surroundings, shows us the co-existence of several spatialities and temporalities. But a significant difference is that these were largely mutually exclusive zones, cores and peripheries articulated at best through relations of hierarchy.

What we positing is different from Braudel's mutually exclusive zones. For instance, in the case of the global economy, the capital fixity necessary to produce hypermobility can be seen as instantiating a spatiality and temporality that is distinct from that of the circulation of hypermobile dematerialised financial outputs. This means that the spatiality of the global economic cannot be fully contained in either one, but overlaps both. Yet both are contained within the specificity of the global.

On the other hand, what Appadurai identifies as disjunctural in global cultural flows might find a parallel when it comes to the global economy in the efforts to deregulate financial markets across the world and the efforts and resources allocated to compensate investors for losses due to the financial crises which are a regular outcome of that same financial deregulation.

The strategic spaces where many global processes are embedded are often national; the mechanisms through which new legal forms, necessary for globalisation, are implemented are often part of state institutions; the infrastructure that makes possible the hypermobility of financial capital at the global scale is embedded in various national territories. This insertion of global projects, coming not only from the outside but also from inside the national, produces a partial unbundling of national space.

It is partial because the geography of economic globalisation is strategic, it is not diffuse nor is it an all encompassing condition. Further, this unbundling is partial in the sense that national space was probably never a unitary condition, even though institutionally constructed as such. The doctrine of extraterritoriality was precisely developed to accomodate the fact that it was not a unitary condition and to secure the extension of state authority beyond the geographic boundaries of national territory.

One way of conceptualising this insertion of the global in the national is as a partial and incipient "de-nationalisation" of what has been constructed as the national, or rather, particular elements of the national. These developments signal a transformation in the particular form of the articulation of sovereignty and territory that has marked the recent history of the modern state and inter-state system, beginning with WWI and culminating in the Pax Americana period.

Analytic Borderlands

Specifying these borderlands has its own particular challenges: how to produce the contents and the activities that mark such borderlands, and the needed theoretical tools to resist its collapse or folding into a line that simply separates two differences. Far more work on this issue has been done in fields other than those dealing with the global economy. For instance, Homi Bhabha's explorations and theorisations of spaces of intersection and the in-between forms of difference, can be seen as contributing to the specifying of such as analytic borderlands. We also read such an effort in the extraordinary new book by Palumbo-Liu where he posits that his construction "Asian/American", at once implying both exclusion and inclusion, "marks both the distinction installed between "Asian" and "American" and a dynamic, unsettled, and inclusive movement".

Interactions and Overlaps

A second issue concerns the level of complexity that these interactions and overlaps can assume given the specificity and social thickness of both the national and the global. An important contribution is Appadurai's conceptualisation of global cultural disjunctures and his insistence that there is a dynamic and uncertain interaction among the various disjunctures he has famously identified in the language of scapes. Thus, for instance, he argues that the relationship between cultural and economic levels is not simply a one-way process "set wholly by, or confined wholly within, the vicissitudes of international flows of technology, labor, and finance" which would only call for a "modest modification of existing neo-Marxist models of uneven development and state formation;" on the contrary, these dynamics are producing distinct formations that need to be empirically specified and theorised on their own terms. Secondly, he posits that more than perhaps was the case in earlier periods, today an actor is likely to live, and an entity to operate, in overlapping domains of the national and the global.

Researches report that what we think of as a new economic dynamic, i.e. the global dominated by finance, emerges out of the juxtaposition of the national and the global. This is particularly so, perhaps, when it comes to the temporalities embedded in institutional and organisational settings associated with respectively the national as constructed in developed countries in the post WWII era and the global as constructed over the last decade.

Juxtaposed Temporalities and New Economies

The question of duration and temporality in the economy brings up the familiar notion of how technology has altered the duration of a whole variety of economic practices. But it is not only acceleration. It is indeed, the sharply different rates of acceleration in different economic activities that are decisive. It is not a homogeneous or homogenising process of overall acceleration. The differences engender the possibility of differing temporalities. It is this that matters.

The ascendance of finance and the dematerialisation of many economic activities assume their full meaning in the juxtaposition of different temporalities and are an enactment in the economy of this sharpened differentiation—between their temporality as dematerialised/digitalised activities and other sectors of the economy which still deal with the material and hence are going to be slower.

This strategic difference can be illustrated through the differences in the form of capital mobilised in, respectively the manufacturing of a car and the financial services: the temporality of the first is about 9 months, that of the second, significantly shorter, i.e. it could be a day or less. These are produced temporal orders, each embedded in a complex institutional world, belonging to different spatio-temporal configurations. In the exchange, in the trade-off between these two lies a world of business opportunities. This is not necessarily a new event.

But the organisation of respectively manufacturing capital and financial capital represents one of the specific contents and conditionalities that the national and the global can assume today. The sharper the differentiation between these two temporalities has grown (with dematerialisation/digitalisation) the more intense this world of new business opportunities will be. This is one way in which economic globalisation today is constituted: the particular features of finance enable it to subject other sectors of the economy to its rhythms.

The emergence of this new world of business activities at the interface of the distinct temporalities of different economic sectors in advanced economies brings with it new questions and agendas for theory and research. Insofar as many of these new activities tend to locate in cities and create new sources of growth and new hierarchies of profitability, it concentrates much of this new analytic effort on the city.

Analytically this new world of business activities is a sort of borderzone, it does not belong to either of the two or more sectors among which it negotiates its own existence and sources for profit. These are business opportunities which negotiate different temporalities and extract new types of profits from their co-existence and their sharpened difference.

There are particular sites where these intersecting temporalities and spatialities assume especially thick and consequential forms. Among such sites are global cities, the new architectures for governing the global economy, and the cross-border migration of people. Each one of these is only partly constituted in terms of the global and is in fact embedded in the spatialities and temporalities of both the national and the global.

Temporality of the national

The temporality of the national has to some extent remained submerged, an unnamed condition, partly because it is the given condition, the assumed built-in time of much social science, compared to the new accelerated time that has become a master image for globalisation and that has been constructed as a distinct object of study. Further, insofar as some of the institutional orders within which the time of the national is embedded are becoming destabilised by economic globalisation, the national may well contain a deteriorating temporality.

The time of the national is slippery and requires excavation. It is constructed through a look to the past of the founding myths of a nation and through a look at the future given the construction of the nation as a necessary condition for the state, which reveals this future to be actually an inherited project and hence also located partly in the past. The way in which John and Jean Comaroff locate their work against a broader set of conceptual and historiographic practices can help us understand something about the temporality of the national even though their focus is not on this issue. "While, at least in one obvious sense, the making of the modern world has run its course, its grand narrative has been rendered all the more enigmatic by the sheer unexpectedness of its closing scenes... the jury is still very much out on some of the enduring issues of social theory."

The privatisation of resources and regulatory functions which is one of the marking features of the current global economic era contains within it an instantiation of a shift in temporalities that has not been named as part of the dynamic by scholars on the subject. When a firm goes from the public sector to the private sector much more happens than a mere shift in ownership regime. Insofar as the shift is through foreign investment—which has been the norm in much of the world—it is likely to entail entry into global economic circuits, that is to say, an institutional world that operates according to different constraints in terms of speed and profitability.

There is also a shift of regulatory functions, from being embedded in public bureaucracies to their reconfiguring as private specialised corporate activities. Also here there is a shift out of the temporal order of public bureaucracies, in principle subject to often slow moving governmental processes of adherence to rules and subject to public accountability via legislatures and judiciaries. Becoming part of private "regulatory" mechanisms entails entering what is likely to be a far more accelerated dynamic.

Finally, the growth of privatised self-regulation can also be read as a shift from an institutional order characterised by certain temporal features to one that is quite different. Much scholarship on national public bureaucracies and public settlement mechanisms, notably courts, has given us good insights into how these institutional orders function, including their time cycles and duration of procedures. This is a scholarship guided by very different questions from those we are after; and it does not speak of temporalities. Yet they are unwittingly describing, without naming it, the temporal order within which these institutions operate. By giving content to the temporality of some of the institutional orders of the national, this scholarship can help specify how these shifts to the private and increasingly globalised sphere of leading sectors, incorporates these privatised firms into a different type of temporal order. One illustration of this is private international commercial arbitration.

Cross-border Spatialities

There is a specific kind of materiality underlying the world of new business activities even if they take place partly in electronic space. Even the most digitalised, globalised and dematerialised sector, notably global finance, inhabits both physical and digital spaces. These firms' activities are simultaneously partly deterritorialised and partly deeply territorialised, they span the globe yet they are highly concentrated in very specific places.

This produces a strategic geography that cuts across borders and across spaces yet installs itself also in specific cities. The spatiality thus produced can be thought of as a crossborder network of specific sites embedded partly in the national but constituted through spatial and temporal practices that distinguishes these from others, notably those of the national as historically constructed. It is a geography that explodes the boundaries of contextuality and the traditional hierarchies of scale.

In so doing it contributes to a partial unbundling of national territory. We can then think of the global economy as materialising in a worldwide grid of strategic places, uppermost among which are major international business and financial centers. We can think of this global grid as constituting a new economic geography of centrality, one that cuts across national boundaries and across the old North-South divide.

The most powerful of these new geographies of centrality at the inter-urban level binds the major international financial and business centers: New York, London, Tokyo, Paris, Frankfurt, Zurich, Amsterdam, Los Angeles, Sydney, Hong Kong, among others. But this geography now also includes cities such as Sao Paulo, Buenos Aires, Bombay, Bangkok, Taipei and Mexico City. The intensity of transactions among these cities —particularly through the financial markets, transactions in services, and investment—has increased sharply, and so have the orders of magnitude involved.

At the same time, there has been a sharpening inequality in the concentration of strategic resources and activities between each of these cities and others in the same country. The growth of global markets for finance and specialised services, the need for transnational servicing networks due to sharp increases in international investment, the reduced role of the government in the regulation of international economic activity and the corresponding ascendance of other institutional arenas, notably global markets and corporate headquarters, for the governance of the global economy—all these point to the existence of transnational economic processes with multiple locations in more than one country. We can see here the formation, at least incipient, of a transnational urban system.These cities are not simply in a relation of competition to each other. There are elements of a division of labor among them as well.

By the late 1990s it has become evident that there is a cross-border system at work in the relations among these cities. In some cases this is becoming formalised, notably the strategic alliance between London and Frankfurt's financial markets and the current effort to create an alliance among 8 of the leading stock markets in continental Europe. There is also a significant degree of hierarchy in this cross-border network. New York and London are, doubtless, the leading international business and finance centers, while Tokyo remains the main exporter of capital though it has lost strategic servicing capacities to other centers. These features also underline the need to rethink the distinction between the global and the local, notably the assumption about the necessity of territorial proximity in the constitution of the "local."

One of the tasks here has to do with rethinking spatial hierarchies that are usually taken as a given: local/national/global. For example, both the new international professionals and immigrant workers operate in contexts which are at the same time local and global, thereby overriding these conventional hierarchies of scale. The new professionals of finance are members of a cross-border culture that is in many ways embedded in a global network of "local" places—a set of particular international financial centers, with much circulation of people, information, capital among them.

Further, as financial centers, London, New York, Zurich, Amsterdam, Frankfurt, are all part of an international yet very localised work sub-culture. We see here "proximity" but not embedded in territorial space; rather, a deterritorialised form of proximity. And many immigrants will tend to be part of a cross-border network that connects specific localities —their new communities and their localities of origin in home countries. Though in a manner different from the financiers, they nonetheless also have the experience of deterritorialised local cultures, not predicated on locational proximity. These workers operate in labor markets that are local even though not characterised by territorial proximity as standard models of such markets hold.

This type of analysis points to a space economy for major new transnational economic processes that diverges in significant ways from the duality global/national presupposed in much analysis of the global economy. Economic globalisation does indeed extend the economy beyond the boundaries of the nation-state and hence reduces the state's sovereignty over its economy. But these boundaries are not simply geographic; they are also institutional and located inside the national rather than at its geographic borders.

These cities and the globally oriented markets and firms they contain mediate in the relation of the global economy to nation-states and in the relations among nation-states. In that regard they contribute to destabilise the hierarchy we have tended to accept as a given, going from the sub-national to the national and on to the inter-national. This cross-border grid of strategic sub-national sites connected via intense transactions and flows of professionals is one instantiation of a de-nationalised spatiality and temporality.

Unbundling of the National

Another instantiation of the emergece of overlapping spatialities and temporalities is that of national state sovereignty in today's context of globalisation. The kinds of questions and research foci in this case are quite different from those explored in the preceding section. National state authority has long been represented as territorially exclusive and absolute.

The encounter of a global actor—firm or market—with one or another instantiation of the national state can be thought of as a new frontier zone. It is not merely a dividing line between the national and the global. It is a zone of politico-economic interactions that produce new institutional forms and alter some of the old ones. Nor is it just a matter of reducing regulations or the role of government generally.

For instance, in many countries, the necessity for autonomous central banks in the current global economic system has required a thickening of regulations in order to de-link central banks from the influence of the executive branch of government. This zone of interaction is highly charged and potentially the outcomes of this interaction can make for epochal change.

It is not simply the push by global firms and markets that is shaping the dynamics of interaction as is implied in much of the literature on the declining significance of the national state under globalisation. States are also shaping the dynamics of interaction and are doing so not merely in the form of resistance. In doing so, however, they are reconfigured. This reconfiguring is shaped both by trends towards standardisation, as is the growing convergence in the role of central banks, and by national particularities, e.g. the different responses of Argentina, Indonesia and Malaysia to the financial crisis of 1997-78.

Beyond the inadequacy of simply accepting the general proposition of a declining significance of the state, there is also the problematic acceptance of a simple quantitative measure of globalisation. Simply to focus on the fact of the often minimal share of foreign inputs in national economies overlooks, again, some of the marking features of the current phase of the global economy. It is indeed the case that in most developed countries the share of foreign in total investment, the share of international in total trade, the share of foreign in total stock market value, are all very small.

However, to infer from this that economic globalisation is not really a significant issue, misses at least three crucial features. One is that economic globalisation is strategic rather than all-encompassing: it does not require "majorities" to succeed. The second is the fact that most global processes materialise in national territories and do so to a considerable extent through national institutional arrangements, from legislative acts to firms, and are thereby not necessarily counted as "foreign." Third, in theoretical terms, it denies the possibility that the global economic may be enacted through a specific spatiality, which while imbricated with the national has its own sociological reality.

Economic globalisation entails a set of practices which destabilise another set of practices, i.e. some of the practices that came to constitute national state sovereignty. In their enactment these practices produce distinctive and complex spatialities which cannot simply be subsumend under the national. Thinking about the global in terms of specific spatialities which while partly embedded in the territory of the national have their own specificity helps us extricate analytically the fact that a global dynamic or process may partly operate through a national institution. Thus we cannot simply assume that because a transaction takes place in national territory and in a national institutional setting it is ipso facto national.

The imbrication of global actors and national institutions is far more ambiguous. The case of the central banks today also illustrates another key aspect in the process whereby national economies accommodate a global economic system: a country's central bank can be a key institution for implementing—in its national economy—some of the new rules of the global game, notably some of the standards in IMF conditionality. This signals that "national" institutions can become home to some of the operational rules of the global economic system.

One of the distinctive features of the current phase is the combination, on the one hand, of an enormously elaborate body of law which secures the exclusive territoriality of national states to an extent not seen in the 19th century and on the other, the considerable institutionalising of the "rights" of non-national firms, the "legalising" of a growing array of cross-border transactions, and the growing, and increasingly institutionalised, participation by supranational organisations in national matters. This sets up the conditions for a necessary engagement of national states in the process of globalisation: certain components of the national state operate as necessary instrumentalities for the implementation of a global economic system.

We can see here overlapping and intersecting dimensions between the global and the national. Our argument is that the tension between: a) the necessary, though partial, location of globalisation in national territories and institutions, and b) an elaborate system of law and administration that has constructed the exclusive national territorial authority of sovereign states, has c) been partly negotiated through i) processes of institutional de-nationalisation inside the national state and national economy, and ii) the formation of privatised intermediary institutional arrangements that are only partly encompassed by the inter-state system, and are, in fact, evolving into a parallel institutional world for the handling of cross-border operations. In terms of research this means, among other tasks, decoding what is national today in what has historically been constructed as national, and establishing what are the new territorial and institutional conditionalities of national states.

Globalised Localities

If we want to take the concept of globalisation both serious and critically, not least to address and think about cultural transformations in the world, the term needs to be given some precision. What we need to know, as Crang suggests is how globalisation takes place through 'conceived, perceived and lived spaces', in changing patterns of spatial consumption, for example.

But we also need to know how a very clearly structured system of global political economy (not least related to the imperial and colonial past) has produced, and continues to produce, on one hand, cultural difference and so-called "ethnic minorities" and the differential spaces they inhabit, as well as, on the other hand, economic and social spaces of privilege and exclusion. We need, Crang suggests, to see globalisation as a discontinuous rather than a homogenous space, a notion of discontinuity that we could also extend to historical time.

Globalisation is not a single set of activities or a single 'one world' movement but a number of partially interlocking global networks which have been historically, geographically, politically, and culturally constructed. Here, we want to turn to another way of "re-worlding the world", a different theoretical representation which fundamentally critiques this idea of a "singular", globular view, and gives due recognition to these historical developments: postcolonial theory and criticism.

Postcolonial Criticism

One of the phenomena we've been trying to understand recently are the conditions accounting for the quite spectacular growth in the anglophonic academy - particularly American, British, Canadian, Australian, maybe elsewhere - and particularly in the humanities such as English, comparative literature, art history, and more recently geography, architecture - of the new knowledge paradigm of postcolonial theory and criticism. And while the theorists of the critique are not invariably independent of those developing theories of globalisation, the reverse is generally true.

Postcolonial criticism, according to Robert Young 'itself forms the point of questioning Western knowledge's categories and assumptions'; it 'demands a rethinking of the very terms by which knowledge has been constructed. Such statements take for granted that, in the early part of the twentieth century, Europe held roughly 85 per cent of the earth as colonies, protectorates, dependencies, dominions and colonies which, roughly between 1947 and the early 1960s, technically at least, became independent states. Technically, because to cite Gayatri Spivak , postcoloniality is 'the failure of decolonisation' .

Postcolonial consciousness, however, is not necessarily one thing. The editors of *Postcolonial Space(s)* state: 'postcolonial space is a space of intervention into those architectural constructions that parade under a universalist guise and either exclude or repress differential spatialities of often disadvantaged ethnicities, communities or peoples'. Australian geographer, Jane Jacobs, writes 'Spectacles of postmodernity are entwined in a politics of race and nation which cannot be constructively thought of without recourse to the imperial inheritances and postcolonial imperatives which inhabit the present.

The rise of postcolonial studies is not just, as has been suggested, because of the presence of Third World intellectuals in the West, but, much more importantly, results from the considerable growth of the proportion of academics as well as students from ethnic minority backgrounds between the late 1980s and early 1990s. In addition, the very substantial growth of international students in all anglophone countries has, in the relevant subject areas, given a huge boost to the growth of, and support for, postcolonial studies.

We can, of course, ask how far the academic 'postcolonial' agenda is being driven by the interest of postcolonial and ethnic minority audiences in the West (as a critique of Eurocentricism and cultural racism in the academy) or by the "situation on the ground" in postcolonial countries themselves - but this does not undermine its relevance as a particular frame for addressing equally particular questions, whether these relate to the system of knowledge production, education and, not least, the production of space.

But we also have to ask what analogies, or comparisons, can be made between the histories and outcomes of different European imperialisms in Asia, Africa and the Americas, and more recent, different forms of imperialism in Europe. Can the centralised state rule of the Soviet Union be seen from a similar perspective? Clearly, there are many forms of colonialism and their outcomes are not alike.

That there is no single 'colonial/postcolonial narrative', let alone a common set of principles to account for all cases of postcolonial urban development is most clearly evident in Abidin Kusno's recent book on postcolonial Indonesia, and the fifty year history of the development of urban planning in Jakarta, first, under Sukarno, and then, the 32 year rule of Suharto. The problem of postcolonial studies, according to Kusno, has been a tendency to examine colonial discourse as part of an undifferentiated critique of 'the West' - without acknowledging that colonialism can come in many different forms.

What Kusno argues is that, until the demise of Suharto's 'New Order' regime in 1998, Indonesia maintained a colonial regime in all but name. Moreover, Kusno departs from a key theme in postcolonial criticism, arguing that colonialism did not bring about a displacement of indigenous culture. Indeed, as the Dutch promoted the Indonesian language throughout the archipelago and also developed indigenous forms and styles of design, they helped construct a sense of nationalism in the new state. The spatially divisive system of planning, however, has been exacerbated after independence. Therefore, broad- anging theoretical discourses, whether of globalisation, or postcolonialism, need to pay very careful attention to particular political, cultural and historical conditions.

Hybrid Modernities

Typically, we assume that the spatial, built form manifestations of what we crudely refer to as 'globalisation' are in the CBD, the downtown, evidenced by the appearance of multinational corporation headquarters, international banks or the pervasive sign of franchised global corporations - the golden M, perhaps, in some sort of vernacular disguise. What has been neglected is 'globalisation' and postcolonialism in the suburb, both as a cultural process and especially, as a spatial, built form - phenomena conceived in regard to Crang's "conceived, perceived and lived spaces".

Both Roger Silverstone, in his Visions of Suburbia and Peter Taylor, in Modernities, while both focusing on the anglophone world of the USA, Australia and the UK, see the contemporary suburb as the paradigmatic embodiment of modernity, the classic modern suburb of single family houses in large gardens in tree lined roads. "This landscape of consumer modernity", Taylor writes, "represents the culmination of four centuries of ordinary modernity". Probably conceiving of the suburb in terms of the immense proportion of society's resources invested in it, Taylor states that it is "the modern equivalent of the great Gothic cathedrals of the high middle ages in feudal Europe". With some license, he writes that, with the era of American hegemony, "the middle class suburb has spread to cities across the world".

Similarly, for Silverstone,

> "Suburban culture is a consuming culture. Fueled by the increasing commoditisation of everyday life, suburbia has become the crucible of a shopping economy. It is a culture of, and for, display. The shopping mall, all glass and glitter, all climate and quality control, is the latest manifestation of the dialectic of suburban consumption. The hybridity displayed in the shopping mall is a representation, a reflection and a revelation of the hybridity of suburbia. Suburbs are places for transforming class identities. The differences grounded in the differences of position in the system of production have gradually, as Bourdieu states, been overlaid and replaced by the differences grounded in the system of consumption"

While we agree largely with Taylor and Silverstone here, there is, however, a major omission in their accounts. Neither pays sufficient attention to the dependence of suburbanisation, both as an economic as well as a physical, spatial , ideological, and architectural phenomenon, on the internationalisation of the economy, not least, through the processes of imperialism, colonialism and the workings of the world economy and international division of labor.

In the nineteenth century in the West, as the industrial bourgeoisie got larger, the suburb represented a move to an imaginary, more exotic, even foreign universe, one represented by new names, new spaces, new forms, new plants and shrubs, imported from all over the colonial world. Quite early in the development of the spatialised social differentiation that became the suburb, three spatial forms were appropriated from other cultures to give new meanings to suburban life: the villa, the verandah and the bungalow.

Villa, both as term and architectural idea, came into the English language from the Italian as a response to a renewed interests in the classics in the l7th century. However, it entered into the fashion conscious vocabulary of England only from the late l8th century during the first spurt of the expansion of the bourgeois classes It also entered Germany about the same time. Its transplantation to the USA early in the nineteenth century was an outcome of similar conditions.

'A villa' wrote A J Downing, the architectural writer, 'is the country house of a person of competence or wealth sufficient to build it with taste and elegance'. Where a cottage could be looked after by a family, ' a villa requires the care of at least three or more servants'. The verandah, another exogenous space and term, imported originally from Spain and Portugal via colonial routes from India, was an additional spatial device devoted to conspicuous consumption. The bungalow - the classic single-storey suburban dwelling - in the country but not of the country - was equally a product of imperialism, by the first decades of the 20th century, becoming the suburban house of choice, first in California, then throughout the USA, Canada, before being transplanted to Australia, New Zealand, Britain, South Africa and elsewhere in the mid twentieth centur.

Neoligisms

Suburb, as we know, is a term and phenomenon that has been around at least since the fourteenth century, even though massive suburban expansion in Western cities was a nineteenth, early and then mid- twentieth century phenomenon. The idea of the suburb as a lifestyle however is especially associated with the late nineteenth century when the term suburbia first entered the OED.

We don't have to be Latin scholars to recognise that sub-urb originally implied that the suburban settlement was 'sub' the city - a generic growth out of the city. What we want to suggest here is that, today, in many cities round the world, we no longer just have sub-urbs - we also have supraurbs whose origins - economic, social, spatial, architectural - are not only no longer generated from the city, or even the country, but develop from outside the nation - state itself. They fly in, touch down at the airport and are nourished by umbilical cords that are not only infinitely extendable but no-one knows where they end - taking in imagery from films, TV and transnational travel. But rather than attempting to account for these developments simply in terms of the contemporary gloss of "globalisation"

The suburbs of today continue to be generated by forces of imperialism, colonialism, nationalism, as well as the diasporic migratory cultures and capital flows of global capitalism. Examples come from the USA, China, and India. They illustrate the very different transnational, postcolonial or neo-imperial flows of capital and culture, migration and urban and architectural design, as well as the particular dynamics of locality that help account for them.

Supraburbs and Globurbs

The new migrations which have largely helped to form supraurbs/ globurbs - mostly, but not all, Asian (and later, Asian-American) were, and are, in different degrees, tied to American foreign policy as well as patterns of colonialism and nationalism. Asian Americans, as well as Latinos/as have arrived in the United States as a result of colonialism in the region and the ensuing colonial wars. Immigrants of Asian and Central American descent - with their local suburban economies as also their distinctive mall architectures - carry the traces of wars.

For government, military, and intelligence reasons, "Pentagon connections are today highly significant for first wave refugees from a number of countries to North Virginia". Near Seven Corners in Fairfax County, the Eden Center/Plaza replicates a small Vietnamese marketing town", with its Saigon East store, typical (gold) jewelry shops and cultural entertainments. It is the center of attraction for some 50,000 Vietnamese Americans in the metropolitan area. In the mid 1990s, however, Vietnamese were 'second only to the Salvadoreans in the number of immigrants entering the Washington metropolitan area', largely represented in restaurants, food stores and in the (inherently suburban) landscaping business.

Koreans, another war-related community, are largely centered on Annandale, where they support a large suburban mall, grocery and distribution center for Korean goods and several restaurants. Other war-refugee groups from East Africa - Somalis, Eritraians, Ethiopians - refugees of some status, often educated in the US, are also to be found in this area.

Unrelated to America's overseas wars are the significant numbers of highly-educated Indians in other Washington suburbs, linked mainly to high tech industries in the region, with their commercial and cultural centers, and Bollywood movie house at Loehman's Plaza on Arlington Boulevard. Iin the long duree, this Indian presence must also be accounted for by the long-term colonial anglophonic connection, with Indians taking up almost 50 per cent of the 200,000 highly sought-after H1-B visas for professionals issued in 1999. Though language is not the only factor taking postcolonial anglophonic Hindi speakers to a postcolonial America where indigenous, native American languages have been virtually wiped out, it is one, among others, that makes Germany, for example far less attractive.

Villa Phenomenon in Beijing

In examining the cultural and spatial transformations taking place in Beijing, the first thing to note are the 55 million overseas Chinese who bring some $30 billion investment into the country every year- 60 per cent of it from, and through, Hong Kong, 15 per cent from Taiwan.

In the early 1950s, Chairman Mao, with the help of Soviet planners, erased swathes of the ancient fabric round the Forbidden City to make way for a socialist "people's space" of Tianenman Square. Today, Mao (as well as previous emperors) would no doubt turn in his grave to see central Beijing transformed into an "International Metropolis" , and major global financial center.

The developments described below, therefore, need to be seen in the context of a Beijing (population 12.5 million) where the urban fabric, consisting of the ancient Forbidden City at the center, a rapidly diminishing area to its north of traditional, single-storey 'hutong' settlements, masses of 6-8 storey walk-up apartment complexes from the socialist era, and a very rapidly-growing array of huge and expensive private apartment buildings often over thirty stories.

'Traditional' housing is being replaced by 'modern' housing with a vengeance (but only in the 'collective', apartment house form). In the 1990s, however, the shape of housing has taken a completely new (capitalist) direction. In 1998, Beijing had a stock of 21,000 units of residential property especially "designed for overseas buyers" either "quality apartments" or "single family houses". The major clients for these are foreign multinational firms, overseas investors but also local Chinese, suddenly grown rich with the shift to free market capitalism.

In the mid 1990s, villas were a major sell to overseas Chinese. At Regent on the River, 17 KM west of the city center is a 19 acre estate of luxury suburban homes "surrounded by lovely woodland, rivers and streams". The nomenclature and designs of these "European and US style houses" are chosen to reach a more residentially discriminating Euro-American-Chinese clientele - "The American, the Nordic, the Baroque, Mediterranean, Classic European, The Georgian". "River Garden Villas or Phoenix Garden Villas are located near "the only world class 18 hole golf course, managed by Japan Golf Promotions".

Alternatively, there are Garden Villas, King's Garden Villas, the Beijing Eurovillage - for the managers of global capital flows. Images of Beijing Dragon Villas, "beautiful American-Canadian residences," provide more precise evidence of the transcontinental connectivity of places, linking this transmigratory, diasporic overseas Chinese business class around the world.

The villas are compared to other houses in Beverly Hills in California, Long Island in New York, and Richmond in Vancouver, Canada.5 This latter is especially interesting as, with the influx of (especially) Hong Kong migrants into Vancouver in the decade from the late 1980s, residents of Chinese descent in this upmarket suburb of Richmond increased from 7 to 37 per cent of all residents. By summer 2000, there were something over one hundred of these 'luxury residential' complexes clustered in seven locations, predominantly round the outskirts of the built up area of the city, accessible from the 4th Ring Road, and with the main concentration around the Airport Expressway. Those closest to town (in Sanlitum and the 'second Diplomatic Area'), some thirty in all, are largely tall apartment complexes.

The villa developments are (expectedly), further out, closer to the airport, or to the north, beyond the Asian Games Village. For their (mainly) transnational residents - employed, for example, by IKEA, Hoechst, BASF, BP, Siemens, Audi, NOKIA, Coopers and Lybrand, Hewlett Packard and others - they are within reach of (non-indigenous) facilities such as the German School, Beijing International School, Montessori KG, Family Hospital, in this case, in the 'third Diplomatic Area'. In these outlying areas, carefully located by the Beijing planning system in the middle of open country, far from the noise, pollution, and not least, intense crowding of the Chinese capital, are the Purple Jade Villas, King's Garden Villas, Fragrance Garden, Beijing Riviera Villas, Capital Paradise Villas, Silver Lake Villas, Legend Garden Villas, Regent on the River, Dynasty Gardens - all powerfully promoted on huge hoardings as one drives along the otherwise building-free, excellently surfaced, tree-lined highways towards the airport.

All developments have appeared in the last eight years. Seen for the first time, the Beijing 'villa phenomenon' brings to mind two phrases: Robert Hughes 'Shock of the New', being suddenly confronted by a 'built environment experience' produced by the juxtaposition of one completely new cultural product within the cultural space of another and Homi Bhabha's 'white, but not quite' in that, on a closer look, the 'local' becomes apparent through the 'global', or better, the 'Chinese' obtrudes through the 'American'.

The extent of the 'luxury' is perhaps best conveyed by the price. In a city where average wages are in the region of 2000 RMB villa prices in the Beijing Riviera complex are from some $765,000 to $1.3 million (total floor area for the lower range about 250 square metres to 464 square meters for the more expensive). Rentals (for a 400 sq m villa and above) range from $9,000 to $13,000 p.m., plus a management fee (for owners and renters) of between $492-$677 p.m. and a membership fee for the Club (providing a wide range of recreational/sporting facilities) of $120 p.m.

In its promotional literature, Beijing Riviera markets itself as 'North American style in the Beijing suburbs. Beijing Riviera has succeeded in replicating North American Life and Architecture'. The Capital Paradise Villas are 'a leading expatriate society in Beijing with 500 European style villas'. Over the last twenty years, according to the Beijing Riviera literature, 'Beijing has exerted itself as one of the world's greatest international capitals.

With over 100,000 expatriates from over fifty countries, Beijing offers an opportunity for interaction unrivaled in most other Asian cities'. The complex, a walled and gated compound with 'electric sliding gates', houses 700 residents, 'ambassadors, embassy staff, executives of the world's leading companies', representing twentyeight countries. Thirty per cent of whom are from the US, and from four to seven per cent from each of France, Australia, Germany, UK, Taiwan, Singapore, as well as China.

For these prices, the villas come with the most up-to-date American fittings - bathrooms, kitchens, home theater, gym, bar - and a full complement of top class, leading edge interior furnishing and furniture. A regular shuttle bus runs between each of these developments for the 20 minute journey to the city. The architects, developers, mortgage banks, as far as can be ascertained, are Chinese firms in Hong Kong and Singapore.

The major feature marketed by these developments is security. Dragon Villas, the most expensive of these luxury villas, 231 'residences fit for royalty' with fourteen different designs (from 341 to 886 sq meters) and 'utilising North American style architecture' are 'behind carefully guarded stone gates'. Dragon Villas 'puts residents' safety first. An infra-red alarm system seals the community's outer walls; at each villa, closed circuit TV and coded alarm systems ensure residents' safety and security'. The presence of (at least some of) the two hundred security guards - paid at the rate of 800 RMB p.m. ($80) - is pervasive.

The facts of uneven development are as glaring as the reproduction, in the grossest of senses, of the spaces and sociopolitical conditions of colonial cities - not least, Shanghai in the 1930s. What is particularly striking, however, is the massive and rapid shift over a period of less than one decade from collective to individual forms of housing - represented by the individualised Western villa, as the epitome of the individualised, consumption-oriented suburb8.

Though superficially 'similar' to some North American suburban developments, these Beijing globurbs are no more perfectly mimetic of their generative models in 'the West' than were the colonial houses before them. Local conditions are paramount. With some singular exceptions, plot sizes are minuscule compared to what might normally be assumed, in the West, to be appropriate for such huge villas. High land costs may be an explanation; but Chinese house-owners, whether in China or Vancouver, unlike Anglo-Saxons, put higher values on inside than outside territory. Wide open spaces are American, not Asian longings. High, solid, and impenetrable walls - the historically enduring feature of Chinese domestic architecture - divide the handkerchief sized plots from each other. Glazed roof tiles lend an Italian housing idea a Sinicized finish.

Above all, the regimental system of management control exercised on these developments totally contradicts the individualised treatment and serendipitous semi-neglect often characteristic of private suburban property in 'the West' Delhi and Bangalore The overall conditions producing new forms of transnational (and especially, supraburban) space in India are, in some ways, comparable to China but the results are also very different, not least because the large diasporic Indian population have very different political histories, cultures, and diasporic geographies.

The Indian diasporic population can be grouped, historically and geographically, into five main clusters, the largest, and probably the wealthiest, of the five groups being the four million in the USA (1.3 million), the UK, Canada, Australia and other western countries . This latter group, well-educated, often in professional occupations, have been called the "priviligentsia". In total, all overseas (or non-resident) Indians contribute some $10 billion in annual remittances and deposits in Indian banks of Non-Resident Indians (NRI's) amount to about $23 million.

The social, spatial and cultural transformations taking place around particular cities - Delhi, Hyderabad, Bangalore - has to be seen (if we can believe the advertisements) in the context of two or three phenomena. One of these is the transnational process of transmigration, in which migrants move regularly between "home" and the "destination country, shifting capital between them.

More especially, however, it has to be understood through the particular stance of the Indian state which, first, has legislated two distinctive categories - the Non Resident Indian, giving particular privileges and gaurantees regarding the investment of property capital in India, and the PIO, Person of Indian Origin (with similar financial and legal privileges) . Both of these categories carefully cultivate an Indian identity: one of belongingness to the state, but another, transnational identity, that can operate in the market.

The third factor to note, however, is the distinctive postcolonial identity in which property advertisements represent the new suburban developments with which developers tempt NRI's worldwide to invest. Much of the advertising is directed to flattering the cosmopolitan nature of the potential investor, people "who have known the very best the world has to offer", who recognise that apartments are "world class", and for those who move between the business worlds of the US, the UK and France. Here, if we can believe the ads, a transnational, if still anglophonic, domestic suburban villa architecture is in process - with villas emanating or labeled from the US, England, Scotland, postcolonial Britain though also Morocco.

Globalisation: Negative Impacts on Urban Areas

In the industrialised world, we enjoy good standards of living, but often we fail to appreciate the damage that our economies and lifestyles do to others. Very often, our prosperity is based on exploitation of others, usually poorer people in developing countries. For example we go into supermarkets, looking for the cheapest bargains, unaware that the reason those goods are cheap is the appalling working conditions that people in developing countries were forced to work in to make them. In some cases the goods may have been produced using - literally - slave labour. Or we drive our car to work or fly abroad for our holidays, forgetting that the pollution from the gasoline we burned to get us there will very likely help to kill some people in some developing country, for example by contributing to a drought because of its effects on the world's climate. There are really three separate issues to do with this exploitation: Unfair trading, pollution, and human rights abuses. The first two issues, along with some related human rights abuses, have come to be known by the term globalisation.

Unfair Trading

Most Western countries have vigorously pursued policies of opening up the world to free market competition. The trouble is that what might work inside industrialised democracies doesn't always work so well in other places. In many industries, multinational companies can exert monopoly or oligopoly powers in small poorer countries. In the UK or Germany or America, if you don't like your salary or working conditions, you just find another job. But if you're for example a banana or coffee or cocoa worker in many countries you can't because there are no other jobs. The companies will demand what they want. They may expect you to work with toxic chemicals without any protective precautions. They will pay you a wage that gives you scarcely enough to buy food for your family. Complain and the company may circulate a blacklist to prevent you from ever finding work again. You may even find yourself getting tortured as an incentive to 'behave'. All this happens as part of the so-called free trade system, in order for us to be able to buy cheap goods at our supermarkets.

Pollution

global warming is the most serious problem facing humanity at the present time. And despite the attempts of certain internationally well known politicians and certain oil companies to pretend otherwise, the overwhelming scientific consensus is that the problem is real and is caused by our carbon dioxide emissions from burning oil, coal and gasoline etc. And the overwhelming scientific consensus is that we must start reducing those emissions urgently.

As for how serious the problem is, we can do no better than quote Paul Brown:

> Among the predictions is that sea levels will rise so fast in the next 50 years that some low lying island nations may disappear altogether. In the unprotected river deltas of Bangladesh, Egypt and Vietnam there are a total of 30 million people living within 1m (3ft) of the high water mark. They have no safeguard. Equally horrifying is the fate of others who will go hungry as crops fail. There are 10 million people in ten sub-Saharan African states who are already living on the edge of starvation because of prolonged droughts in 1991092. These droughts are believed to be one of the first signs of climate change.

This was written in 1996 but the science hasn't substantially changed since then - except that the evidence has become stronger.

Human rights Issues

Many governments torture their civilians, deny basic human rights, deny freedom of speech, or systematically oppress ethnic or religious minorities. To some extent of course you could argue that that's not our doing so why should it be our responsibility. The problem is that often our own Governments tolerate this repression for our own economic or political benefit. For example we rightly condemn Robert Mugabe when he sends his thugs out to terrorise the people of Zimbabwe so that he can hold on to power, yet we largely remain silent when China does the same thing in Tibet (a country which by any moral standards doesn't even belong to China anyway - China invaded Tibet in 1950 and has occupied it ever since).

Urban Poverty and Anti-social Issues

When people live as close together as they do in urban settlements, some social problems will eventually occur. Differences between social classes and pressure from the environment may cause social disorder. People often get problems when they feel that they are socially incompetent or that they have failed to realise their dreams, when they feel isolated or just happen to know the wrong people. For instance, social problems occur when people are drawn into the swamp of drugs. Moreover poverty is a significant cause of crime, hopelessness and feelings of hatred towards the wealthy people in the city.

Cultural diversity and differences within the social classes in urban societies may cause disorder among people. Poverty for instance, feeds hostility towards political authority and those better off and is one of the reasons why young people commit crimes and why many poor people are addicted to drugs. As a result of, for instance, the pressure to have a career among the rich, or gang fights among the poor, individuals may experience personal disorder and social deviation. In the lower classes rates of schizophrenia are high while in the middle and upper classes rates of manic depression are high.

The social deviation is also reflected in the crimes committed in the different social classes. Among the lower classes crimes such as burglary and other violent crimes are usual, while among the middle classes adult crimes involve fraud and embezzlement. Sexual crimes such as rape, child molesting and incest are more usual in the lower classes than in the middle and upper classes. As for the cultural differences, people from different cultures may have trouble understanding each other and because of that conflicts rise between them. An intercultural marriage for instance may end in trouble in one way or another; a divorce or maybe even a child kidnapped and taken to another country.

As we have seen drug addiction can lead to prostitution and prostitution in turn can lead to a drug addiction. Many prostitutes are involved in crime syndicates and have problems with their private social life and intimate relationships. In G. B. Shaw's play, *Mrs Warren's Profession,* Mrs Warren becomes a prostitute because she is poor and furthermore the play reflects the attitude towards her profession. As for addiction, the addict is demoralised by the drugs and may turn to prostitution and theft to finance the habit. As a final conclusion to this we would say that poverty among people is a problem that has to be solved. If the poverty in urban society could be fought and all citizens could live a decent life, fewer people would turn to crime, drugs and prostitution. But it is not only the poverty that is the problem. Technology has taken us so far that man can walk the surface of the moon before people can walk safely in some slums of our large cities but the technology of today has not helped to make the streets safer. The root of social problems lies in mankind and the people in a society are the ones who have to take care of the problems.

Drug Addiction

As said before poverty is one of the reasons why people become addicted to drugs, but poor people are not the only ones who get addicted. The use of drugs is found in all social classes but the ones that people notice, as drug addicts, are the less fortunate ones found in the streets who are so into drugs that they do not care about their appearance or their behavior. Statistics show that men and singles are more likely to take drugs than women and married, city-dwellers and younger people are more likely to take drugs than rural residents and older people. Furthermore there is a high incidence of drug abuse among prisoners and street children.

In 1989 the Drug Use Forecasting Program of the United States National Institute of Justice examined the use of drugs among recently arrested persons. The study took place in selected cities and included only male persons charged with serious non-drug-related offences. The study showed that 76 percent of the persons tested in New York were drug positive for cocaine. The percentage of positive result was higher in large cities and lower in smaller cities. In comparison with New York the tests in San Antonio showed that 24 percent of the persons tested were positive for cocaine. Considering the results of the test one draw the conclusion that indeed the drug problem is an urban problem.

In the upper middle class people have the money to maintain both their wealth and their use of drugs. It is also easier for wealthy people to undergo expensive treatment and see professional people to keep their craving for drugs in check and to go back to the clinics if they have a relapse. Poor people do not have the same opportunities as rich people to deal with their addiction partly because they are poor. With the addiction comes a need of money and therefore poor people often turn to crime in order to finance their addiction. As a result of this they are put in jail instead of being given the opportunity to undergo professional treatment. Since the craving for the drug is so intense in the drug addict, it is difficult for him or her to get off the drugs and stay clean. The number of rehabilitated addicts who go back to drugs is therefore high. An addict who tries to stay away from drugs experiences several physical aches. The addict shivers, sweats, has muscular cramps and feels nausea. The physical aches and the psychological pain make the addict want drugs even more to relieve the pain. Hence the addict connects the drugs with, maybe not health, but a state similar to that, a state of having no troubles and no pain in body or mind.

Prostitution

Drug addiction is one of the reasons why people turn to prostitution since prostitution is a way of making good money fast. Some prostitutes are involved in crime syndicates though, who in exchange for protection take part of their profit. As a prostitute a woman is exposed to venereal diseases and the risk of getting beaten or even molested. After a few months as a prostitute the women get physical as well as psychological problems. The prostitute's fear of physiological injuries is often accompanied by low self-esteem and feelings of degradation. A study by Harold Greenwald showed that 15 out of 20 prostituted women attempted suicide.

Many prostitutes use drugs to ease the anxiety they feel partly because of the risk of getting caught and the personal problems connected with prostitution. As a consequence of their impersonal sexual relations with their clients, prostitutes may encounter problems in their own private sexual life. The prostitutes' habit to restrain their feelings in their work may effect their ability to feel positive feelings in their private sexual life. It may also be difficult for a prostitute to maintain a normal social relation with relatives and friends since prostitution in many cultures is viewed with disgust. Despite this common attitude towards the occupation, even women may appreciate the prostitutes. An example of this is a Western town where many migratory workers lived. The women who lived there were in favor of prostitution in their town, in segregated areas though, but still they did not mind prostitutes because they felt safer with prostitutes around. Considering this one may say that prostitutes may well offer ordinary women a sort of protection from sexual assault in areas where there are a great number of single men.

4

Formation of Global Cities

The population explosion and massive rural to urban migration in the developing countries during pre post-World War II period are among the key determinants of the rapid growth of the megacities in the developing world. In addition, policies and measures to promote economic development and industrialisation in the developing countries have been transforming predominantly agricultural and rural societies to more industrialised and urbanised societies in a relatively short period.

The growth and structural transformation of the third world cities are integral parts of national development. Furthermore, global economic integration, increased international trade, capital flows, telecommunication, new waves of technologies, and shifts in the comparative advantage of production continue to play a central role in integrating major urban centers and shaping the spatial organisation of national economies at the world level. At the center of this global economic integration and structural adjustments is the interlinkage of mega-cities and other major metropolises, which form a world city system.

The rise and slow-down of OPEC cities; the debt burden of Latin American metropolises; the collapse of commodity prices and stagnation of import-substitution industries in African urban centers; and the rising role of Asian cities as new, dominant trade and financial centers in East Asia and the world economy clearly demonstrate how the major metropolitan centers in the world have been affected by the current globalisation process occurring in the recent past.

The new wave of techno-economic paradigm is in the process of replacing the old production paradigm and reshaping the major metropolitan centers in both developed and developing countries, a process that will continue in the decades to come. Lewis Mumford wrote in 1961 that the "megalopolis is fast becoming a universal form, and the dominant economy is a metropolitan economy, in which no effective enterprise is possible without a close tie to a big city." Whether they should be called megalopolises, mega-cities, or world cities, their role at the world or national levels is increasingly associated with their economic capacity and external linkages as the world economy has increased its interdependency in the recent years.

During the1980s and 1990s, the world economy underwent a series of economic upheavals, in addition trends of globalisation and new wave of technologies that have changed the configuration of mega-cities and defined new conditions for their transformation in the early twenty-first century.

These powerful and omnipresent changes have, as well, sent the ascendancy of large cities, particularly mega-cities and world cities, in the global political economy. Mega-cities are simply very large cities by virtue of their population size and world cities can be distinguished by the functions they perform in the new global economy. The present global economy is underpinned by a functional world city system.

Since the 1980s the world economy has changed, rapidly and fundamentally, in its nature, operating modes, and relationships among countries and cities. These changes have been driven by several emerging mega-trends that have led to global structural adjustments.

First, a debt crisis emerged among the resource-exporting developing countries owing to the precipitous drop in the prices of primary commodities and fuel in the early 1980s and the corresponding advances in material sciences leading to a sharp reduction in the use of raw materials in manufacturing production. This created unprecedented difficulties for the developing countries, which have traditionally depended on the export of these products to finance their national development.

Countries in Africa, whose export earnings are dependent upon up to 90 per cent of these primary goods exports, have been severely affected. They were, moreover, increasingly burdened by fast-growing national debts. Similarly, South-East Asian countries that had hitherto depended heavily on the export of primary products for their export income were adversely affected. They were able to free themselves from the impasse because the period fortuitously coincided with a phase of rapid manufacturing development, propelled by East Asian economies' readiness to search for foreign locales to decentralise its industrial plants and secure its competitive edge in world markets in the wake of the Plaza Accord in 1985. That event caused the Japanese yen to double in value against the US dollar almost overnight. This led to a massive flow of foreign direct investment to the large cities and new industrial locations in South-East Asia, but not to Africa and Latin America.

Secondly, the relative decline in traditional raw materials in manufacturing has been accompanied by a commensurate increase in the importance of capital, especially transnational capital, as a determinant in economic development. Nations and cities are in the race for foreign direct investment (FDI). Transnational corporations, on the other hand, are basing their decisions on the selection of locations for investment largely on the comparative advantage of factors of production, namely, land, labor, and capital.

In the 1990s, the inflow of FDI from mostly America and Europe, accompanied by new technologies, increased its momentum in the Asia Pacific region. This has further intensified the structural interdependency of the world economy, linking cities in Europe, North America, and Asia. The movement of FDI has also strengthened the structural interdependency of production and marketing in cross-country linkages of city networks.

Thirdly, a key factor that has permitted breathtaking changes since the early 1980s has been technological innovations. Rapid advances in micro-electronics, telecommunications, robotics, biotechnology, and new materials have come in rapid succession in developed countries and selected newly industrialising economies. All these are, by nature, resource saving and reinforce the relative decline in material inputs in manufactured products mentioned above. Increasingly, the world economy is facilitated by the new information technologies, in which ideas, capital, and people move rapidly and in large numbers.

The impact of these mega-trends has varied within the different regions of the world. The traditional factors affecting the location decisions of industry have been greatly weakened and they have been superseded by new considerations of access to information through the latest technologies, the availability of capital, and changing comparative advantage. The location of industry is now based on a flexible mode of production at convenient points on information highways, challenging the Fordist techno-economic paradigm that dominated manufacturing before the 1980s. The rise of the information economy has the effect of lessening the importance of boundaries, including national boundaries - so much so that a borderless global economy has emerged.

In other world, telematics and globalisation have neutralised place and distance. The geography of globalisation is characterised by a dynamic of dispersal and centralisation. There is a new geography of rapid development and of marginality, highly conditioned by new information technologies, service intensity, and new kinds of spatial correlates. New forms of centrality are constituted by electronically generated spaces. Cities have emerged as elevated economic entities by virtue of their heightened centrality. Consequently, at the national and international levels there is keener competition among cities and, at the city level, intrametropolitan decentralisation, first of residences, then jobs, occurs. Specifically in North America, economic trends experienced globally affect intrametropolitan distribution of activities, including the shift towards services, the pull of an increasingly suburbanised labor force, the diffusion of agglomeration economies, and the effect of changes in the level of congestion. All this has resulted in firms being more footloose than ever. Increased economic and cultural polarisation within world cities has also been observed.

The new dynamics of global production and changing comparative advantage have been conducive to the formation of regional trading blocs. Essentially, the present world economy is dominated by three trading blocs, namely the North American Free Trade Area, the European Union, and the loosely structured Pacific Asia entity. Together, they accounted in 1995 for 84.5 per cent of the world's GDP. It is clear that they form, by and large, more integrated regions of sustained development, although country and city economies within Western Europe and North America have been undergoing basic restructuring. Blue-collar jobs have been lost rapidly in such cities as Detroit, Pittsburgh, Manchester, Liverpool, Belfast, and Naples.

OECD countries have adjusted their economies, such that between 60 and 70 per cent of their GDP is derived from the service sector. By contrast, the Western Pacific Rim has emerged as the fasting-growing region, supported by expansion of the manufacturing sector. The countries within it are at different stages of economic development and are able to capitalise on their varied factor endowments for effective complementarity and cooperative development for industrialisation.

A so-called "flying geese" pattern of industrialisation has been noted for light manufactured goods, involving the staged development of Japan, the Asian newly industrialising economies (NIEs) of Hong Kong, South Korea, Singapore, and Taiwan (otherwise known as the Four Little Dragons), the countries of the Association of South-East Asian Nations (ASEAN), and China. One expression of rapid economic development has been the formation of urban corridors and growth triangles in the Pacific Asia.

Uneven development has been an inevitable outcome of the new global economy. Regions, countries, and cities that are not heavily crossed by cyber-routes and digital highways are not active participants in the evolving patterns of development. In fact, for most of the period since 1980, countries in Africa and Latin America have been undergoing a painful process of structural adjustment under the twin burden of falling commodity prices and accumulating national debts. Alan Gilbert has portrayed the situation in Latin America. He maintains that the debt crisis that has befallen most countries in the region would not have occurred without financial globalisation.

The Mexican financial crisis in December 1994 turned a paragon of economic success into a basket case overnight. The Mexican crisis poignantly reveals the economic and social volatility of economic globalisation. It has also deepened economic inequality and social polarisation. However the upshot of a period of economic stagnation and social protest has prompted several countries in the region to seek a new path of rapid economic development. They have pursued export-oriented industrialisation very much along the lines of the Asian NIEs. This provides a more positive prospect for the future.

Of all the regions, Africa appears to have been most adversely affected by processes of globalisation. Notwithstanding the euphoric expectations of rapid development following the wave of independence movements in the 1950s and the 1960s, the disenchantment began to be felt in the 1970s. By the 1980s, most African countries were badly hit economically by the sharp fall in commodity prices. Historically, they have evolved a relationship with the world economy by depending on export earnings from primary products for more than 90 per cent of their GDP.

By 1990, national debts in African countries became the heaviest among developing countries, as measured in relation to exports of goods and GDP. The structural adjustment programmes administered by the International Monetary Fund and the World Bank in fact created more immediate difficulties, despite their good intentions. The sub-Saharan countries have been most seriously affected by widespread poverty and economic stagnation. Globalisation has thus failed to generate positive impulses in Africa; rather, it tends to marginalise the competitive edge of African countries, leading Carole Rakodi to conclude that no world cities as yet exist on that continent.

Mega-Cities and World Cities

Although great cities emerged as a global phenomenon in the nineteenth century, attracting scholarly attention, the world of large cities grew ever more strongly as the twentieth century proceeded. In the 1960s, some scholars portrayed the future metropolis of man-made environments. At the beginning of the twentieth century, there were only 11 cities with over a million inhabitants. By the early 21st century, it has been projected that the world will have 400 "million" cities.

In the twentieth century, one of the most striking phenomena is not just the rapid growth of population and of cities in developing countries since 1945, but the rise of very large cities, or mega-cities, in these countries since 1975. Mega-cities are defined as those with populations exceeding 8 million, following the Untied Nations definition. By 1990, 14 mega-cities were located in developing countries, as opposed to 6 in more developed countries (counting Moscow in Russia). Within the developing world, the level of urbanisation and the size of urban population vary sharply among the major regions. In 1994, there were 1,653 million urban dwellers in developing countries, at a level of urbanisation of 37.0 per cent. Africa was the least urbanised at 32.4 per cent, with a total urban population of 240 million. Latin America reached an exceedingly high level of urbanisation at 73.7 per cent, with 349 million urban dwellers. Asia was slightly above Africa at 33.4 per cent urbanised, but its urban population was huge at 1,064 million. In Asia, age-old agricultural practices oriented to food production have been holding population in the rural areas, but the situation is apparently changing fast.

Take the extreme example of China. Temporary migration of population towards the coastal cities, largely since 1984 when population migration controls relaxed as a feature of economic reforms, had already reached an estimated total of 70 million in 1988 . The potential is even more staggering when one notes the estimated rural labor force of 450 million, with 300 million likely to leave the rural areas for lack of jobs by 2000. Looked at from this perspective, it is vitally important to improve population-holding capacities in the rural areas in Asia, and hence the importance of such concepts as extended metropolitan regions.

Indeed, rural-urban relations have undergone visible and substantive change as a result of globalisation. Space-time collapse has resulted from transactional space change. Globalisation processes at first affect the cities, then economic interactions, population mobility, and remittances radiate influences to as far as 150 km in the rural areas in Asia. The "new" rural-urban dynamics have blurred the traditional rural-urban divide, whereby people, commodities, and capital move ever more freely and imperceptibly than before. What is unquestioned is that Asia is still, cn the whole, in the early stages of the urban transition. However, in parallel with rapid economic development in this region, a massive rural-to-urban migration is emerging as a mighty trend. Asia's present mega-cities are not simply big; they mirror a telescoped process of urbanisation.

Because of the growing number of mega-cities that have mushroomed in development countries, city governments have to contend with a host of problems, which have attracted scholars and policy makers. Because most of these cities are also hamstrung by limited financial and other resources, issues such as urban poverty, lack of jobs, governance, crime, and the environment have overwhelmed many of their administrators. At least increasing international resources and attention have been focused on them in recent years. Although mega-cities have become a global phenomenon and have acquired national importance in the countries in which they are located, there is another class of cities that are critical to the new global economy. These are called world cities or global cities, because they perform certain functions that differentiate them form others and that help drive the global economy.

In a recent book, Lo and Yeung have developed the concept of the functional world city system, which began to grow and network countries in the world through trade and commerce in the thirteenth century. However, it is primarily since the 1980s, when globalisation processes gathered momentum in a new international division of labor, that world cities have come to the fore.

One key element of the functional world city system is that new networks and linkages are created in the system and world cities are at the points of convergence of these networks and thus acquire growing centrality and importance. Network functions are engendered through financial flows, headquarter-branch relations, high-tech service intensity, and telecommunications networks. The new wave of technologies since the late 1980s in electronics, robotics, telecommunications, new materials, and biotechnology has given rise to a new technology paradigm that accentuates the role of world cities.

Innovation and continuous technological change are used to create new growth markets as demand for outdated products declines. The commercialisation of many more innovations based on this new techno-economic paradigm awaits the economic incentives to create new mega-demands. According to UN sources, it is estimated that the potential from information technology will increase 10 times more in the 1990s than in recent decades. It should be noted that the Asian NIEs have been investing heavily in high-technology industries in recent years and are beginning to take a growing share of world trade.

World cities are extremely complex but constitute, historically, points of international articulation. Consequently, in the present era of large-scale and rapid exchange of goods, people, and ideas, the importance of ports, airports, and teleports (indeed infrastructure as a whole) cannot be overemphasised. In order to prepare a world city to perform the functions it is supposed to discharge, there is a need for cities to plan, invest, and carry out a process that may be briefly described as world city formation.

Many of the world cities in Pacific Asia have spared no effort and expense to do precisely this, so that they are better prepared for the continued rapid economic growth that has been forecast for this region in the twenty-first century. Tokyo, for instance, has emerged as a dominant world city since the 1980s. It has been actively reaching out to Asia and beyond through joint ventures and direct foreign investment through scanning of global markets and technologies by its transnational corporations.

As linkages of cities assume greater importance, there is increasing tension and competition between them within countries and regions. Certainly, in many European cities there is concern about the trade-off between efficiency and equity. Two metaphors are commonly used to depict the relations of cities in Europe. On the one hand they are likened to grapes, which captures the essence of multicentrality, but leaves out the sense of spatial polarisation or the center of power. Alternatively, European cities have been compared to a bunch of bananas, whereby the sense of centrality is vividly conveyed.

One of the effects of globalisation on world cities is rapidly growing social and economic polarisation. This impact, as alluded to before, is most pronounced in mega-cities in Latin America. Rio de Janeiro is a world city that has suffered through economic recession and a wave of social unrest. However, it still has some specialised financial services with which the city has maintained its comparative advantage. Given that the revenue base of the city is constrained and circumscribed, social infrastructure investment appears to be an avenue by which the urban poor can be materially assisted.

Role of Globalisation in Formation of New Cities

Place is central to the multiple circuits through which economic globalisation is constituted. One strategic type of place for these developments, and the one focused on here, is the city. Including cities in the analysis of economic globalisation is not without conceptual consequences. Economic globalisation has mostly been conceptualised in terms of the duality national-global where the latter gains at the expense of the former. And it has largely been conceptualised in terms of the internationalisation of capital and then only the upper circuits of capital.

Introducing cities in an analysis of economic globalisation allows us to reconceptualise processes of economic globalisation as concrete economic complexes situated in specific places. A focus on cities decomposes the nation state into a variety of sub-national components, some profoundly articulated with the global economy and others not. It also signals the declining significance of the national economy as a unitary category in the global economy. And even if to a large extent this was a unitary category constructed in political discourse and policy, it has become even less of a fact in the last fifteen years.

Why does it matter to recover place in analyses of the global economy, particularly place as constituted in major cities? Because it allows us to see the multiplicity of economies and work cultures in which the global information economy is embedded. It also allows us to recover the concrete, localised processes through which globalisation exists and to argue that much of the multiculturalism in large cities is as much a part of globalisation as is international finance. Finally, focusing on cities allows us to specify a geography of strategic places on the global scale, places bound to each other by the dynamics of economic globalisation. We refer to this as a new geography of centrality, and one of the questions it engenders is whether this new transnational geography is also the space for a new transnational politics.

Insofar as our economic analysis of the global city recovers the broad array of jobs and work cultures that are part of the global economy though typically not marked as such, it allows us to examine the possibility of a new politics of traditionally disadvantaged actors operating in this new transnational economic geography. This is a politics that lies at the intersection of economic participation in the global economy and the politics of the disadvantaged, and in that sense would add an economic dimension, specifically through those who hold the other jobs in the global economy — from factory workers in export processing zones to cleaners on Wall Street.

The centrality of place in a context of global processes engenders a transnational economic and political opening in the formation of new claims and, hence, in the constitution of entitlements, notably rights to place, and, at the limit, in the constitution of "citizenship." The city has indeed emerged as a site for new claims: by global capital which uses the city as an "organisational commodity", but also by disadvantaged sectors of the urban population, frequently as internationalised a presence in large cities as capital.

Global capital and the new immigrant workforce are two major instances of transnationalised categories that have unifying properties internally and find themselves in contestation with each other inside global cities. Global cities are the sites for the over-valorisation of corporate capital and the de-valorisation of disadvantaged workers. The leading sectors of corporate capital are now global, in their organisation and operations. And many of the disadvantaged workers in global cities are women, immigrants, people of colour. Both find in the global city a strategic site for their economic and political operations

The analysis presented here grounds its interpretation of the new politics made possible by globalisation in a detailed understanding of the economics of globalisation, and specifically in the centrality of place in a context where place is seen as neutralised by the available capacity for global communications and control. It is important to dissect the economics of globalisation in order to understand whether a new transnational politics can be centred in the new transnational economic geography. Secondly, we think that dissecting the economics of place in the global economy allows us to recover non-corporate components of economic globalisation and to inquire about the possibility of a new type of transnational politics. Is there a transnational politics embedded in the centrality of place and in the new geography of strategic places, such as is for instance the new world-wide grid of global cities? This is a geography that cuts across national borders and the old North-South divide.

Immigration, for instance, is one major process through which a new transnational political economy is being constituted, one which is largely embedded in major cities insofar as most immigrants, whether in the US, Japan or Western Europe are concentrated in major cities. It is one of the constitutive processes of globalisation today, even though not recognised or represented as such in mainstream accounts of the global economy.

Place and Production in the Global Economy

We think of the mainstream account of economic globalisation as a narrative of eviction. Key concepts in that account — globalisation, information economy, and telematics — all suggest that place no longer matters and that the only type of worker that matters is the highly educated professional. It is an account that privileges the capability for global transmission over the material infrastructure that makes such transmission possible; information outputs over the workers producing those outputs, from specialists to secretaries; and the new transnational corporate culture over the multiplicity of work cultures, including immigrant cultures, within which many of the "other" jobs of the global information economy take place. In brief, the dominant narrative concerns itself with the upper circuits of capital; and particularly with the hyper-mobility of capital rather than with that which is place-bound.

Massive trends towards the spatial dispersal of economic activities at the metropolitan, national and global level are indeed all taking place, but they represent only half of what is happening. Alongside the well-documented spatial dispersal of economic activities, new forms of territorial centralisation of top-level management and control operations have appeared. National and global markets as well as globally integrated operations require central places where the work of globalisation gets done. Further, information industries require a vast physical infrastructure containing strategic nodes with hyper-concentrations of facilities. Finally, even the most advanced information industries have a work process — that is, a complex of workers, machines and buildings that are more place-bound than the imagery of information outputs suggests.

Centralised control and management over a geographically dispersed array of economic operations does not come about inevitably as part of a "world system." It requires the production of a vast range of highly specialised services, telecommunications infrastructure, and industrial services. These are crucial for the valorisation of what are today leading components of capital.

A focus on place and production displaces the focus from the power of large corporations over governments and economies to the range of activities and organisational arrangements necessary for the implementation and maintenance of a global network of factories, service operations and markets; these are all processes only partly encompassed by the activities of transnational corporations and banks.

Global cities are centres for the servicing and financing of international trade, investment, and headquarter operations. That is to say, the multiplicity of specialised activities present in global cities are crucial in the valorisation, indeed over-valorisation of leading sectors of capital today. And in this sense they are strategic production sites for today's leading economic sectors. This function is reflected in the ascendance of these activities in their economies. What is specific about the shift to services is not merely the growth in service jobs but, most importantly, the growing service intensity in the organisation of advanced economies: firms in all industries, from mining to wholesale buy more accounting, legal, advertising, financial, economic forecasting services today than they did twenty years ago. Whether at the global or regional level, cities are adequate and often the best production sites for such specialised services. The rapid growth and disproportionate concentration of such services in cities signals that the latter have re-emerged as significant production sites after losing this role in the period when mass manufacturing was the dominant sector of the economy.

The extremely high densities evident in the downtown districts of these cities are the spatial expression of this logic. The widely accepted notion that agglomeration has become obsolete when global telecommunication advances should allow for maximum dispersal, is only partly correct. It is, we argue, precisely because of the territorial dispersal facilitated by telecommunication advances that the agglomeration of centralising activities has expanded immensely.

This is not a mere continuation of old patterns of agglomeration but, one could posit, a new logic for agglomeration. Information technologies are yet another factor contributing to the new logic for agglomeration. These technologies make possible the geographic dispersal and simultaneous integration of many activities. But the distinct conditions under which such facilities are available have promoted the centralisation of the most advanced users in the most advanced telecommunications centres .

A focus on the work behind command functions, on the actual production process in the finance and services complex, and on global marketplaces has the effect of incorporating the material facilities underlying globalisation and the whole infrastructure of jobs typically not marked as belonging to the corporate sector of the economy. An economic configuration very different from that suggested by the concept information economy emerges. We recover the material conditions, production sites, and place-boundedness that are also part of globalisation and the information economy.

And we recover the broad range of types of firms, types of workers, types of work cultures, types of residential milieu, that are also part of globalisation processes though never marked, recognised, or represented as such. Nor are they valorised as such. In this regard, the new urban economy is highly problematic. This is perhaps particularly evident in global cities and their regional counterparts. It sets in motion a whole series of new dynamics of inequality.

The new growth sectors — specialised services and finance — contain capabilities for profit-making vastly superior to those of more traditional economic sectors. The latter are essential to the operation of the urban economy and the daily needs of residents, but their survival is threatened in a situation where finance and specialised services can earn super-profits.

This sharp polarisation in the profit-making capabilities of different sectors of the economy has always existed. But what we see happening today takes place on another order of magnitude and is engendering massive distortions in the operations of various markets, from housing to labour. We can see this effect, for example, in the unusually sharp increase in the beginning salaries of MBAs and lawyers entering the top firms and in the precipitous fall in the wages of low-skilled manual workers and clerical workers. We can see the same effect in the retreat of many real estate developers from the low- and medium-income housing market in the wake of the rapidly expanding housing demand by the new highly paid professionals and the possibility for vast overpricing of this housing supply.

What we are seeing is a dynamic of valorisation which has sharply increased the distance between the valorised, indeed over-valorised, sectors of the economy and de-valorised sectors even when the latter are part of leading global industries. This de-valorisation of growing sectors of the economy has been embedded in a massive demographic transition towards a growing presence of women, African-Americans and third world immigrants in the urban workforce, a subject we return to later.

We see here an interesting correspondence between great concentrations of corporate power and large concentrations of "others." Large cities in the highly developed world are the terrain where a multiplicity of globalisation processes assume concrete, localised forms. A focus on cities allows us to capture, further, not only the upper but also the lower circuits of globalisation. These localised forms are, in good part, what globalisation is about. We can then think of cities also as one of the sites for the contradictions of the internationalisation of capital. If we consider, further, that large cities also concentrate a growing share of disadvantaged populations —immigrants in Europe and the United States, African-Americans and Latinos in the United States— then we can see that cities have become a strategic terrain for a whole series of conflicts and contradictions.

Centrality and Marginality

The global economy materialises in a world-wide grid of strategic places, uppermost among which are major international business and financial centres. We can think of this global grid as constituting a new economic geography of centrality, one that cuts across national boundaries and across the old North-South divide. It signals the emergence of a parallel political geography, a transnational space for the formation of new claims by global capital; we return to this in the next section.

Global grid of cities: the possibility that it creates a new geography, transnational for politics, the formation of identity and formation of claims. Return to this in last part when we address the matter of the formation of new claims, new transnational space.This new economic geography of centrality partly reproduces existing inequalities but also is the outcome of a dynamic specific to the current forms of economic growth. It assumes many forms and operates in many terrains, from the distribution of telecommunications facilities to the structure of the economy and of employment. Global cities are sites for immense concentrations of economic power and command centres in a global economy, while cities that were once major manufacturing centres have suffered inordinate declines. The most powerful of these new geographies of centrality at the inter-urban level binds the major international financial and business centres: New York, London, Tokyo, Paris, Frankfurt, Zurich, Amsterdam, Los Angeles, Sydney, Hong Kong, among others. But this geography now also includes cities, such as Sao Paulo, Buenos Aires, Bangkok, Taipei and Mexico City.

The intensity of transactions among these cities, particularly through the financial markets, transactions in services, and investment has increased sharply, and so have the orders of magnitude involved. At the same time, there has been a sharpening inequality in the concentration of strategic resources and activities between each of these cities and others in the same country.

One might have expected that the growing number of financial centres now integrated into the global markets would have reduced the extent of concentration of financial activity in the top centres. One would further expect this given the immense increases in the global volume of transactions. Yet the levels of concentration remain unchanged in the face of massive transformations in the financial industry and in the technological infrastructure this industry depends on. For example, international bank lending grew from US$1.89 trillion in 1980 to US$6.24 trillion in 1991 — a fivefold increase in a mere ten years. Three cities accounted for 42 percent of all such international lending in 1980 and for 41 percent in 1991 according to data from the Bank of International Settlements, the leading institution world-wide in charge of overseeing banking activity. There were compositional changes: Japan's share rose from 6.2 percent to 15.1 percent and the UK's fell from 26.2 percent to 16.3 percent; the U.S. share remained constant. All increased in absolute terms. Beyond these three, Switzerland, France, Germany, and Luxembourg bring the total share of the top centres to 64 percent in 1991, which is just about the same share these countries had in 1980. One city, Chicago, dominates the world's trading in futures, accounting for 60 percent of world-wide contracts in options and futures in 1991.

The growth of global markets for finance and specialised services, the need for transnational servicing networks due to sharp increases in international investment, the reduced role of the government in the regulation of international economic activity and the corresponding ascendance of other institutional arenas, notably global markets and corporate headquarters — all these point to the existence of transnational economic processes with multiple locations in more than one country. We can see here the formation, at least incipient, of a transnational urban system.

The pronounced orientation to the world markets evident in such cities raises questions about the articulation with their nation-states, their regions, and the larger economic and social structure in such cities. Cities have typically been deeply embedded in the economies of their region, indeed often reflecting the characteristics of the latter; and mostly they still do. But cities that are strategic sites in the global economy tend, in part, to disconnect from their region. This conflicts with a key proposition in traditional scholarship about urban systems, namely, that these systems promote the territorial integration of regional and national economies.

Alongside these new global and regional hierarchies of cities, is a vast territory that has become increasingly peripheral, increasingly excluded from the major economic processes that fuel economic growth in the new global economy. A multiplicity of formerly important manufacturing centres and port cities have lost functions and are in decline, not only in the less developed countries but also in the most advanced economies. This is yet another meaning of economic globalisation. But also inside global cities we see a new geography of centrality and marginality. The downtown of cities and metropolitan business centres receive massive investments in real estate and telecommunications while low-income city areas are starved for resources. Highly educated workers see their incomes rise to unusually high levels while low- or medium-skilled workers see theirs sink. Financial services produce super-profits while industrial services barely survive. These trends are evident, with different levels of intensity, in a growing number of major cities in the developed world and increasingly in some of the developing countries that have been integrated into the global financial markets.

Global Rights for Capital in the New Urban Grid

The analysis presented above points to a space economy for major new transnational economic processes that diverges in significant ways from the duality international/national presupposed in much analysis of the global economy. Economic globalisation does indeed extend the economy beyond the boundaries of the nation-state and, hence, reduces the state's sovereignty over its economy, an observation that by now has become a basic proposition in discussions of the global economy. This is particularly evident in the leading information industries.

Existing systems of governance and accountability for transnational economic activities and entities leave much ungoverned when it comes to these industries. Global markets in finance and advanced services partly operate through a "regulatory" umbrella that is not state-centred but market-centred. Yet a focus on the space economy of information industries elaborates and specifies the meaning of deregulation insofar as important components of these industries are embedded in particular sites within national territories and others are located in electronic spaces that escape all conventional jurisdictions or borders.

A focus on a strategic sub-national unit such as is the global city illuminates these two conditions that are at opposite ends of the governance challenge posed by globalisation and are not captured in the more conventional duality national-global. On the one hand, a focus on leading information industries in global cities introduces into the discussion of governance the possibility of capacities for regulation derived from the concentration of significant resources, including fixed capital, in strategic places, resources that are essential for participation in the global economy.

The considerable place-boundedness of many of these resources contrasts with the hyper-mobility of information outputs. The regulatory capacity of the state stands in a different relation to hyper-mobile outputs than to the infrastructure of facilities, from fibre optic cable served office buildings to specialised workforces, present in global cities. At the other extreme, the fact that many of these industries operate partly in electronic spaces raises questions of control that derive from key properties of the new information technologies, notably the orders of magnitude in trading volumes made possible by speed. Here, it is no longer just a question of the capacity of the state to govern these processes, but also of the capacity of the private sector, that is, of the major actors involved in setting up these markets in electronic space.

Elementary and well-known illustrations of this issue of control are stock market crashes attributed to program trading, and globally implemented decisions to invest or disinvest in a currency or an emerging market which resemble a sort of world-wide stampede facilitated by the fact of global integration and instantaneous execution world-wide.

The specific issues raised by these two variables, i.e., place-boundedness and speed, are quite distinct from those typically raised in the context of the national-global duality. A focus on this duality leads to rather straightforward propositions about the declining significance of the state vis a vis global economic actors. The overarching tendency in economic analyses of globalisation and of information industries has been to emphasise certain aspects: industry outputs rather than the production process involved, the capacity for instantaneous transmission around the world rather than the infrastructure necessary for this capacity, the impossibility of the state to regulate those outputs and that capacity insofar as they extend beyond the nation-state. And this is by itself quite correct; but it is a partial account of the implications of globalisation for governance.

The transformation in the composition of the world economy, especially the rise of finance and advanced services as leading industries, is contributing to a new international economic order, one dominated by financial centres, global markets, and transnational firms. Correspondingly, we may see a growing significance of other political categories both sub- and supra-national.

Cities that function as international business and financial centres are sites for direct transactions with world markets that take place without government inspection, as for instance the Euro-markets or New York City's international financial zone (International Banking Facilities). These cities and the globally oriented markets and firms they contain mediate in the relation of the world economy to nation-states and in the relations among nation-states.

A key component in the transformation over the last fifteen years has been the formation of new claims by global capital: the claim on national states to guarantee the domestic and global rights of capital. Transnational economic processes inevitably interact with systems for the governance of national economies insofar as those processes materialise in concrete places. National legal regimes are becoming more internationalised in some of the major developed economies and we are seeing the formation of transnational legal regimes.

Transnational legal regimes have become more important and have begun to penetrate national fields hitherto closed. The hegemony of neo-liberal concepts of economic relations with its strong emphasis on markets, deregulation, free international trade has influenced policy in the 1980s in the USA and the UK and now, increasingly, also in continental Europe. This has contributed to the formation of transnational legal regimes that are centred in Western economic concepts of contract and property rights.

Through the IMF and IBRD as well as GATT this regime has spread to the developing world. Deregulation and transnationalisation are key characteristics of the space economy of today's leading information industries. Deregulation has been a crucial mechanism to negotiate the juxtaposition of the global and the national. What deregulation in finance makes clear is that it has had the effect of partly denationalising national territory: e.g., the International Banking Facilities in the U.S., almost all located in New York City, can be seen as such an instance. In other words, it is not simply a matter of a space economy extending beyond a national realm. What globalisation does, as illustrated by the space economy of advanced information industries, is de-nationalise national territory.

Transnational Politics

Typically, the analysis about the globalisation of the economy privileges the reconstitution of capital as an internationalised presence; it emphasises the vanguard character of this reconstitution. At the same time, it remains absolutely silent about another crucial element of this transnationalisation, one that some, like myself, see as the counterpart of that of capital: this is the transnationalisation of labour. We are still using the language of immigration to describe this process. Secondly, that analysis overlooks the transnationalisation in the formation of identities and loyalties among various population segments that explicitly reject the imagined community of the nation. With this come new solidarity and notions of membership. Major cities have emerged as a strategic site for both the transnationalisation of labour and the formation of transnational identities. In this regard, they are a site for new types of political operations.

Cities are the terrain where people from many different countries are most likely to meet and a multiplicity of cultures come together. The international character of major cities lies not only in their telecommunication infrastructure and international firms: it lies also in the many different cultural environments in which these workers exist. One can no longer think of centres for international business and finance simply in terms of the corporate towers and corporate culture at its centre. Today's global cities are, in part, the spaces of post-colonialism and, indeed, contain conditions for the formation of a post-colonialist discourse.

The large Western city of today concentrates diversity. Its spaces are inscribed with the dominant corporate culture but also with a multiplicity of other cultures and identities. The slippage is evident: the dominant culture can encompass only part of the city. And while corporate power inscribes these cultures and identities with "otherness" thereby devaluing them, they are present everywhere. For instance, through immigration a proliferation of originally highly localised cultures now have become presences in many large cities, cities whose elites think of themselves as cosmopolitan, that is transcending any locality. An immense array of cultures from around the world, each rooted in a particular country or village, now are reterritorialised in a few single places, places, such as New York, Los Angeles, Paris, London, and most recently Tokyo.

Immigration and ethnicity are too often constituted as "otherness." Understanding them as a set of processes whereby global elements are localised, international labour markets are constituted, and cultures from all over the world are deterriotorialised, puts them right there at the centre of the stage along with the internationalisation of capital as a fundamental aspect of globalisation today.

There has been growing recognition of the formation of an international professional class of workers and of highly internationalised environments due to the presence of foreign firms and personnel, the formation of global markets in the arts, and the international circulation of high culture. What has not been recognised is the possibility that we are seeing an internationalised labour market for low-wage manual and service workers. This process continues to be couched in terms of the "immigration story," a narrative rooted in an earlier historical period.

There are representations of globality which have not been recognised as such or are contested representations. Among these is the question of immigration, as well as the multiplicity of cultural environments it contributes in large cities, often subsumed under the notion of ethnicity. What we still narrate in the language of immigration and ethnicity we would argue is actually a series of processes having to do with the globalisation of economic activity, of cultural activity, of identity formation. Immigration and ethnicity are constituted as otherness.

Understanding them as a set of processes whereby global elements are localised, international labour markets are constituted, and cultures from all over the world are de- and re-territorialised, puts them right there at the centre along with the internationalisation of capital as a fundamental aspect of globalisation. This way of narrating the migration events of the post-war era captures the ongoing weight of colonialism and post-colonial forms of empire on major processes of globalisation today, and specifically those binding emigration and immigration countries. While the specific genesis and contents of their responsibility will vary from case to case and period to period, none of the major immigration countries are innocent bystanders.

Making Claims on the City

These processes signal that there has been a change in the linkages that bind people and places and in the corresponding formation of claims on the city. It is true that throughout history people have moved and through these movements constituted places. But, today the articulation of territory and people is being constituted in a radically different way at least in one regard, and that is the speed with which that articulation can change. One consequence of this speed is the expansion of the space within which actual and possible linkages can happen. The shrinking of distance and of time that characterises the current era finds one of its most extreme forms in electronically based communities of individuals or organisations from all around the globe interacting in real time and simultaneously, as is possible through the internet and kindred electronic networks.

Another radical form assumed today by the linkage of people to territory is the loosening of identities from what have been traditional sources of identity, such as the nation or the village. This unmooring in the process of identity formation engenders new notions of community of membership and of entitlement.

The space constituted by the global grid of global cities, a space with new economic and political potentialities, is perhaps one of the most strategic spaces for the formation of transnational identities and communities. This is a space that is both place-centred in that it is embedded in particular and strategic sites; and it is trans-territorial because it connects sites that are not geographically proximate yet intensely connected to each other.

It is not only the transmigration of capital that takes place in this global grid, but also that of people, both rich, i.e., the new transnational professional workforce, and poor, i.e., most migrant workers; and it is a space for the transmigration of cultural forms, for the re-territorialisation of "local" subcultures. An important question is whether it is also a space for a new politics, one going beyond the politics of culture and identity, though at least partly likely to be embedded in these.

Yet another way of thinking about the political implications of this strategic transnational space is the notion of the formation of new claims on that space. Has economic globalisation at least partly shaped the formation of claims? There are indeed major new actors making claims on these cities, notably foreign firms who have been increasingly entitled to do business through progressive deregulation of national economies, and the large increase over the last decade in international businesspeople. These are among the new city users. They have profoundly marked the urban landscape. Their claim to the city is not contested, even though the costs and benefits to cities have barely been examined.

City users have made an often immense claim on the city and have reconstituted strategic spaces of the city in their image: there is a de facto claim to the city, a claim never made problematic. They contribute to change the social morphology of the city and to constitute what Martinotti calls the metropolis of second generation, the city of late modernism. The new city of city users is a fragile one, whose survival and successes are centred on an economy of high productivity, advanced technologies, intensified exchanges. On the one hand, this raises a question of what the city is for international businesspeople: It is a city whose space consists of airports, top level business districts, top of the line hotels and restaurants, a sort of urban glamour zone. On the other hand, there is the difficult task of establishing whether a city that functions as an international business centre does in fact recover the costs involved in being such a centre: the costs involved in maintaining a state of the art business district, and all it requires, from advanced communications facilities to top level security .

Perhaps at the other extreme of conventional representations are those who use urban political violence to make their claims on the city, claims that lack the de facto legitimacy enjoyed by the new "city users." These are claims made by actors struggling for recognition, entitlement, claiming their rights to the city. There are two aspects in this formation of new claims that have implications for the new transnational politics. One is the sharp and perhaps sharpening differences in the representation of these claims by different sectors, notably international business and the vast population of low income "others"— African-Americans, immigrants, women. The second aspect is the increasingly transnational element in both types of claims and claimants. It signals a politics of contestation embedded in specific places — global cities — but transnational in character. At its most extreme, this divergence assumes the form of

a) an over-valorised corporate centre occupying a smaller terrain and one whose edges are sharper than, for example, in the post-war era characterised by a large middle-class; and

b) a sharp de-valorisation of what is outside the centre, which comes to be read as marginal.

A question here is whether the growing presence of immigrants, of African Americans, of women, in the labour force of large cities is what has facilitated the embedding of this sharp increase in inequality. The new politics of identity and the new cultural politics have brought many of these de-valorised or marginal sectors into representation, into the forefront of urban life. Globalisation is a contradictory space; it is characterised by contestation, internal differentiation, continuous border crossings. The global city is emblematic of this condition.Global cities concentrate a disproportionate share of global corporate power and are one of the key sites for its over-valorisation. But they also concentrate a disproportionate share of the disadvantaged and are one of the key sites for their de-valorisation. This joint presence happens in a context where :

1. the globalisation of the economy has grown sharply and cities have become increasingly strategic for global capital; and
2. marginalised people have found their voice and are making claims on the city as well.

This joint presence is further brought into focus by the sharpening of the distance between the two. The centre now concentrates immense power, a power that rests on the capability for global control and the capability to produce super-profits. And marginality, notwithstanding little economic and political power, has become an increasingly strong presence through the new politics of culture and identity, and an emergent transnational politics embedded in the new geography of economic globalisation.

Current Trends and Future of Global Cities

If you want to see where globalisation is really taking place, look no further than global cities. However, while it is impossible to imagine globalisation occurring without urbanisation, academia still lacks a clear understanding of the social and cultural dynamics that make a city truly "global."

The rise of the world's cities has gone hand-in-hand with global integration, according to Lisa Benton-Short. Today, 3.1 billion of the world's 6.2 billion people live in urban areas. More than 75% of the populations of the United States, Canada, Argentina, Brazil, Australia, New Zealand, Japan, and many countries in western Europe now live in urban areas. We will soon see this trend repeated in Central Asia and sub-Saharan Africa, she added.

Cities with a population greater than 10 million are more accurately called "mega-cities," Benton-Short explained. The largest of these is Tokyo, which now boasts 28 million souls. However, the size of a city does not necessarily indicate its importance, she said. Dhaka, Bangladesh, for example, is home to 13 million people yet barely registers in global financial flows.

Benton-Short reported that most urban geographers agree that the three cities of key importance to the global economic and political system are London, New York, and Tokyo. These metropolises form the core of a network rooted firmly in the northern hemisphere.

However, vast gaps exist in contemporary research into global cities, stated Marie Price. Social and cultural indicators of cosmopolitanism are often overlooked in favor of criteria such as financial flows when giving cities global rankings. As a result, a city like Washington, D.C. is typically not considered "global" – despite welcoming migrants from more than 190 countries since the 1990s, said Price.

Early research findings suggest that, even allowing for new social factors, the most globally impcrtant cities are still likely to be London, New York, and Tokyo, according to Price. However, look a little further down the rankings and we find that among the most global of cities is Abu Dhabi in the United

Arab Emirates, where 75% of the population is foreign-born. "Vancouver is the poster child for complex global cities," added Price, as almost 35% of the Canadian city's residents were born abroad. In contrast, Seoul in South Korea – a prominent contributor to world industry – is startlingly lacking in diversity. Just 0.14% of its population was born abroad.

In the future, Price and Benton-Short predict several directions their research might take. For example, they plan to look at whether migrants are ghettoised or geographically-dispersed in cities that they move to. Dispersion, according to Benton-Short, is a good indicator of the integration of migrant communities. The growth of towns and cities was initially driven by industrialisation – not global integration. However, it is impossible to conceive of globalisation occurring without the benefits produced by urban societies, such as literacy and large, concentrated markets, she said.

Benton-Short adds that one of the practical implications of their research is that it will help to understand remittance flows. Financial remittances from migrants to developing countries have become major income sources, she stated – for example, they account for 22% of Jordan's GDP. As a result, maintaining remittance flows is a major policy priority for many countries.

Urban Future

Cities have always been centers of civilisation and vitality that have through the years led to human progress and material and scientific advances. In the dawn of the twenty-first century, mega-cities and world cities, are no different in their nature and character. The processes they are subjected to, however, are different. Whatever the outcomes of these processes, the urban future of humankind will be much influenced by them.

The single most important factor that will bear heavily on the future of mega-cities in developing countries is overall population growth and the related extent of rural-urban migration. This issue should be viewed against the backdrop of the world population being estimated to be more urban than rural in the early years of the twenty-first century and more heavily concentrated in developing countries.

The inexorable growth of population in these countries is already difficult to deal with because of their often large population base, but the prospect of sizeable rural-urban migration will create problems of gargantuan proportions. As noted earlier, the urban population share for most countries in Asia and Africa is only 30-40 per cent. Any major shift of population from the rural areas will play havoc in the cities in unimaginable ways.

Overall, the world population must be able to stabilise at a certain level such that sustainable development can be achieved. It is expected that the world population will be around 10 billion by the year 2050, allowing modest growth from the 1999 figure of 6 billion.

Given their hypermobility in capital, ideas, and people, large cities of the future will perforce be centers of transport, telecommunications, and increasing connectivities. Peter Rimmer has identified city networks that are connected to freight, telecommunications, and air passengers. By 2010, the 25 largest urban agglomerations will have a population of more than 10 million each and, as such, improved access by transport and telecommunications will be vital. Improved city networks should be a general target and should be premised by three principles: planned inter-city division of labor, strengthening of comparative advantage of individual cities, and greater cooperation and synergy among cities.

Finally, the sustainability and stability of the urban future depend on, among other things, one key factor that figures very prominently in the present global economy - the financial flows around the world and their effect on the regional, national, and subnational economies. In this respect, the importance of world cities as financial centers merits careful analysis.

The rapid expansion of international finance, reflecting the growth in exports and imports of commodities in the last two decades. Financial intermediaries have grown in tandem and have faced up to competition in different ways. Thus, the keenest competition among financial centers is over acquiring the world regional and branch offices of global intermediaries as evidenced in the recent Asian financial crisis. All these new developments will be important trends in world city formation for years to come. There are several reasons for the increase in rural versus urban land disputes, however all of the reasons are related or linked to globalisation.

5

Social Transformation in Cities

According to recent estimates, cities are likely to account for over 47 per cent of total world population by the turn of the century. This large concentration of nearly 3 billion people within rather Limited space has had and will continue to have tremendous impact on the scope, tenor and rate of social transformation. within individual countries and cumulatively in the world as a whole. Some of these impact are already proving to be of some revolutionary significance. However, it is important to stress that considerable regional differences in urban concentrations do exist from one part of the world to the other. The simple division into developed and developing countries fails to capture the nature of the present diversity in the urban circumstances of countries.

For one thing, developing countries now straddle a wide range of transformed situations. They span from the newly industrialising countries of the Pacific rim to the still largely underdeveloped economies of sub-Saharan Africa. For another, some of the developing regions, notably the countries of Latin America, already have over 70 per cent of their populations urbanised, with already deleterious consequences on societal conditions. Others, such as in sub-Saharan Africa, still have a preponderant percentage living in rural areas and constituting a high potential for future migrations to the cities.

Nonetheless, this diversity provides an unprecedented opportunity for internationally comparative research to gain insight into the contrasting pattern of accelerated social transformation going on in cities throughtout the world. For as has been rightly observed, all cities are relatively large, dense, and permanent settlements of socially heterogeneous individuals whose capacity for tremendous social transformation is a function of their having to accommodate, adapt to and capitalise on the diverse potentialities of this heterogeneous population. They have arisen in the history of human development as a result of increased agricultural productivity and the ability of local and regional economies to support an increasingly large proportion of non-agricultural producers committed to enhancing societal productivity by streams of organisational and technological innovations. Over time, they have continued to grow in size and complexity and it no longer appears fruitful to talk about an optimal size of cities. Today, the tremendous transformation taking place in all sectors Or societal life makes it even courageous to argue that the present megacities with their population of over 10 million represent the final possibility in urban concentration.

Any concern with accelerated social transformation must begin with the tremendous changes that have taken place in the character of work and workplaces aces in the cities of the world. In one sense, these changes reflect the extent to which development in a given country has become fully exposed to the forces of a free enterprise economy. Where this has taken place, work and workplaces are having constantly to adjust to streams of technological and organisational innovations. In recent times, there is no doubt that the cascade of electronic inventions going from the computer, the fax machine, the electronic mail to satellite communications has simply revolutionised the way business is conducted throughout the world. This has had a somewhat bi-polar consequences. On the one hand, it has encouraged the rise of more and more big, transnational corporations. On the other, hand, it has promoted the emergence of a more sophisticated informal sector economy even in developed countries.

For the big, transnational corporations, the challenging fact is that investment finance information on a global scale is now available everywhere on an instant basis through satellite communication. Decisions made in one country are now-conveyed instantaneously and immediately influence productive activities in another country however far removed in space. All this is already creating a sense of global interdependence whose social consequences are still far from being fully appreciated. It is, for instance, a major factor in the new and compelling tendency to create large, regional trading blocks such as the European Community (EC) and the North American Free Trade Area (NAFTA). How all these developments will affect the movement of peoples, the pattern of urban development, the nature of business organisations, the working conditions and general personnel relationship are only starting to be gleaned.

On the other hand, a new type of respectable, private informal sector is starting to emerge based on these same series of cascading stream of sophisticated technological developments. This allows individuals to transact considerable amount of business profitably without stepping out of their homes. In some developing countries, these equipment are already being acquired and used by some enterprises in the conventional informal sector with tremendous consequences for their productivity and profitability. This is not to say that the character of informal sector activities which provide no more than subsistent employment for a sizeable proportion of the urban population of most developing countries has changed dramatically. Of course, organisationally there have been some changes, for instance, in the manner in which credit is being mobilised in the sector.

Various countries notably Bangladesh, Peru and Nigeria have recorded some notable achievements in this regard. Moreover, there is growing evidence that within the sector property rights and relations are becoming increasingly appreciated and acknowledged. What all these do, however, is to emphasise that even in this sector changes are going on in the nature of work and workplaces that are accelerating the rate or social transformation. More than this, these changes underscore a point, often ignored in the literature, namely that the capacity of urban centres to raise social productivity and increase the gross domestic product of countries are progressively being enhanced even by the informal sector.

It is when we turn to look at urban homes that the magnitude of acceleration in social transformation is better appreciated. In the first place, the concept of home as the residence of a nuclear family comprising of a man, his wife and children has changed significantly in many cities. Now, society has had to come to terms with many homes being female headed and the women concerned not even having been married. Moreover, such women need not be social delinquents living on welfare doles but a highly trained professional earning quite respectable income. Indeed, cities have increasingly encouraged societies to be willing to accept different concepts of what a home is, the newest in this regard being a home made by homosexual adults.

All of this has been possible because of the tremendous progress in the emancipation of women. This has been achieved because of the rapid expansion in the education of women and their growing capabilities world-wide to control their fertility. As the number of children desired by a woman decreases with her enhanced status, it has been possible to vastly improve the life chances of also the children. However, in many developing countries where rural-urban migrations, especially of illiterate women, are still of enormous proportions and these changes have not become pervasive in the urban areas, the phenomenon of street children is becoming a major social dilemma and menace.

In the average urban homes, nonetheless, tremendous changes in life style are noticeable. Consumerism is becoming increasingly a fact of life everywhere. It is being pushed by advances in advertising techniques and in the concept of savings, time purchase and non-deferred consumption. The result is a physical home with a growing range of gadgets and equipment unprecedented in the history of mankind.

Apart from the tremendous convenience, enlightenment and life quality enrichment which all these make possible, they have also raised the level of domestic environmental hazards and disasters. Within cities, solid and liquid wastes pollutions of increasing toxic severity are becoming the order of the day. Acid rains, unintended radioactive exposure, growing ozone layer depletion are the more serious and pernicious environmental hazards arising from recent urban lifestyles. They do raise the issue of how sustainable are these life-styles especially as it is becoming so easy to transfer them to cities in less developed regions of the world.

The almost incredible changes in urban life-styles throughout the world has been possible because of the fantastic rate of urban productivity increases since the end of the second world war. This, in turn, has occurred because of the virtual erosion of ascriptive privileges and the increasing determination of human worth on the basis of some universalistic standards.

Upward social mobility has thus thrown the individual very much. on his own, bereft of dependence on the circumstances of his birth or other primordial affiliations. His life chances thus become a matter of personal choice and his determination to succeed. Social relations in cities, moreover, have become preeminently dominated by the money-nexus, driving everybody to want to be moderately or inordinately wealthy in a materialistic sense. This trend underscores the deep sense of deprivation which the urban poor feel when they can lay no claims to any assets of their own or seek to earn income on any sustainable basis.

The pre-eminence of the money-nexus has thus had some contradictory consequences on social life in the city. For many, it has given rise to a stressful concern with or a crisis of identity. The strains and stresses of the daily struggle of existence in the city has provoked a wide range of psycho-somatic disorders in individuals. For others, the situation has been challenging, liberating and fulfilling. It has promoted an advanced concept of individual worth and an increasingly enlightened appreciation of human rights. These have had profound implications for the growth of democratic values and practices in urban and national affairs. They are also reflected in the emerging need to understand how the complex interface of political democracy and economic liberalism in society unleashes the creative potential of the human mind and makes for further advances socially, culturally and technologically.

The role of cities in accelerating upward social mobility and promoting individualism, human rights and general democratic values has in turn encouraged a complementary appreciation of the importance of community. This level of social collectivity is increasingly being recognised as critical for ensuring sustained commitment to these values and to broad-based, humane economic development generally.

Whether in cities of the developed or the developing countries, there is growing interest in the role of the community as a vehicle for pulling people up by their bootstraps or for helping them maintain a safe, healthy and congenial environment for all and sundry. Nonetheless, it 112.5 not been possible AS yet to fully determine how to integrate this level of societal organisation into the General management of cities. In mans countries, neighbourhood community organisations operate as the political or administrative equivalent of the informal economic sector.

Changes in the enhanced capacity for geographic mobility in cities have not been without their own accelerating impact on social transformation. Mass transit provision is becoming a vital infrastructure in many emerging metropolitan centres today and is partly responsible for the almost indeterminable expansion of the modern city with all its social consequences.

In countries where such provision is weakly developed or where development has not kept pace with demand, peak-hour traffic congestion has impaired family life in significant respects. Parents are kept away from their children for long hours or their needs force one of them to remain unemployed or underemployed. Where the communities are well organised, this strains may be minimised by the institution of school bussing or the establishment of child-care centres. Nonetheless, the cost of transportation to and from workplace takes a toll in. the family time and cash budget and greatly affects their overall sense of well-being and security.

Cities have also promoted vast changes in the pattern of leisure activities. The rise of television games and entertainment either through national network or global satellite communication has, on the one hand, encouraged more family- or household-based leisure activities. This has meant, as it were, bringing global events right into the household. On the other hand, it has made it possible to increase the excitement for world-wide travels even among lower income families.

Packaged international air travels have exposed more urban dwellers to the pleasures and educational advantages c; seeing far away places and meeting peoples of different cultures and customs. They have also made urban dwellers more sensitive to events and incidents in other parts of the world. This enhanced cosmopolitanism has meant that many cities have had to strive to raise their basic infrastructural facilities to minimally acceptable international standards. In some developing countries, this has resulted in the emergence of two-sector cities, one sector of which can at least cater to the needs of foreign tourists.

The enhanced cosmopolitanism of city dwellers has made them increasingly better disposed to accepting the need for the maintenance of higher standards of environmental quality both nationally and internationally. It has made it easier to canvass amongst them the urgency of preserving fragile environments in distant lands or endangered species in various parts of the world. It has also stimulated a high level of humanitarian concerns for people in somewhat precarious 2nd 1 if e-threatening circumstances world-wide.

This high level of global consciousness in cities fosters the idea of the world becoming increasingly a global village. These developments, however, cannot be regarded as taking place autonomously without some positive direction by the State. Indeed, increasingly, there is a profound recognition of the direct relation between State policies and actions and the rate of social transformation in cities. Consequently, it is of. considerable comparative research interest to examine the role of the State in different countries in accelerating the rate of social transformation in their cities.

Role of the State

There are several ways in which the manner of functioning of the State in different countries affects the scope, depth and character of social transformation in cities. Pour of these are particularly of interest. These are: the management *of the* macro-economy of the country; the policy and programmes for the and promotion and acquisition of technological innovations, the investment in human capital development and the measures taken for reducing levels of income and social inequality.

The management of the macro-economy of particular countries has become very critical for the quality of life and the social circumstances of vast majority of city dwellers. A sound and efficient system of financial and investment transactions serves to keep the economies of the cities robust and strong. This entails a highly controlled rate of inflation and strenuous effort to minimise price distortions. It also requires sectoral policies that promote increased production and productivity and stimulate a relatively high rate of export activities. Where these policies are vigorously pursued, they ensure a high level of gainful employment among the urban population and to guarantee most of them income-levels well above the poverty line. Otherwise, cities become better noted for their high level of unemployment, their high rate of crime and their appearance of pervading poverty.

A growing and robust urban economy encourages a willingness to try out or acquire new technologies, to increase productivity or to introduce new production processes. In many countries, these are matters for serious policy considerations at the level of the State.

Policies on the acquisition of intellectual properties from other countries, on the payment of royalties and licensing fees, on the employment of foreign consultants and the transfer of dividends to foreign partners could greatly affect the rate of growth of big businesses in particular countries. In turn, these exert a not inconsiderable influence on the character of work and workplaces in cities, greatly affect the organisational forms of the urban economy and strongly determine social relations between the classes.

None of these activities of the State, however, has as much direct impact on the accelerating rate of social transformation in cities as its investments or human capital development. Human capital development refers to the enhancement of the capabilities and general well-being of the citizens of the country. It relates to the systems of education and training available to the youths and the range of continuing educational programmes which adults can undertake to make their skills and expertise continually relevant to the changing job opportunities in cities. The more technologically sophisticated these jobs, the more critical is the importance of investment in such outreach educational facilities to ensure that the human capital remains in prime form.

An important emphasis in this respect is the education of girls and women. who make up at least half of the total labour force. The rate of social transformation in cities of countries which have failed to give adequate attention to gender issues in their human development programmes is invariably much lower than expected.

Similar magnitude of investment in health-care facilities and services also makes substantial difference. Here again, where special emphasis is not given to children and mothers as well as to the aged and other vulnerable groups, the quality off social transformation is greatly impaired. Particularly in respect of mothers, elaborate facilities for family planning help to ensure that they do not end up having more children than they desire or can care for. Enhanced educational opportunities for girls have been shown to correlate strongly with their desire for a small family of one, two or three children.

In cities where this is the case, the limited number of children per family makes it possible to invest substantially in providing them. with a warm, enabling environment and giving them maximum advantage to continually improve on the social and economic life of cities.

An aspect of human capital development relates to the magnitude of investment which the State commits to ensuring adequate nutritional status for the majority of the population. This is not simply a matter of investing in appropriate agricultural programmes or ensuring adequate availability- of food through international trade. It entails paying attention to regional variations in the profile of available food and ensuring that any quantitative and qualitative deficits are easily made up through the provision of adequate and appropriate transport and wholesaling facilities.

More than this, there are the problems at the household level of distributional practices as between men and women, adults and children In many countries already, to ensure that the vulnerable groups, particularly the children, do not suffer unduly in this regard, most urban schools provide at least mid-day meals for the children.

Finally, an important role for the State is in minimising the deleterious consequences of a high level of income inequality in a country. This it does through a progressive tax policy. This makes the wealthy pay proportionately much more than the less wealthy, the difference being used in providing services at rates which the latter *can* afford. This has made it possible to provide many cities with infrastructural facilities of roads, water supply, electricity and telecommunications as well as educational and health-care services of above average standards.

The increasing ability of the State to intervene in this manner has been very catalytic in accelerating the rate of social transformation and in reducing the proportion of the total urban population that could have been marginalised in the process. However, where as in many developing countries, the state has proven too weak to intervene in this manner, the majority of city dwellers remain poorly serviced and feel greatly alienated from the scheme of things. Their lack of a proprietary pride in the city is exhibited in their destructive or vandalising attitude to urban infrastructure and facilities.

While it is possible to articulate other roles of the State which directly impact on social transformation in cities, it must be admitted that we do not know enough about the trajectories of these impacts or the nature of the relationships among many of the variables they generate. These trajectories and relationships can be expected to follow varying paths in their evolution.

Not all of these are likely to be benign- or indifferent in their consequences. Nonetheless, a better appreciation of their incidence and magnitude allows for more informed attempts to improve on city life. For these reasons are given the prospects of still further acceleration in the process of social transformation as we move into the 21st century, the-e is an imperative necessity to undertake research into various facets of urban life in different parts of the world.

Culture and Economic Development

Culture can be defined in a broad manner, as a way of life and a way of living together. This includes the values that people hold, tolerance for others (race and gender), outward as opposed to inward orientations and inclinations, and so on. Of course culture can also be defined in a narrower sense as an expression of art, music, literature and so forth.

Western ethnocentrism has customarily been employed as the implicit basis of thinking about development. The paradigm equating development to modernisation and modernisation to Westernisation has long been, and still is, the conventional wisdom, although it has been recognised that there are several alternative strategies of development. One of the many paradoxes that has accompanied internationalisation and globalisation is that local peculiarities are now being stressed more than before. Globalisation stimulates localisation, it would appear. Or rather, globalisation leads to cultural interpretations which, in turn, lead to a multiplication of permutations and the growth of new "local" cultures. Cultural pluralism is increasingly becoming an all-pervasive feature of societies, and ethnic identification is often a normal and healthy response to pressures of globalisation. The impression of growing global uniformity may, therefore, be misleading as people turn more and more to culture as a means of self-definition and mobilisation. Could it be, therefore, that globalisation marks the true beginning of a search for a range of development models based on local differences?

Forcing a uniform model on diverse country and cultural situations may endanger the economic future of these countries as well as that of the world at large. We seem to be at a crossroads now, where alternative approaches have to be pursued and diversity rather than uniformity must be chosen.

The point to be made is that each region would be well-advised to establish its own model of capitalism and democracy. Indeed, each region will have to do so if one accepts the general idea of path dependency, i.e. the notion that the future is strongly influenced by the past. We do not live in a timeless, a-historical world. The world should gain from systematic diversity rather than suffer from the confusion and possible catastrophe caused by forceful applications of a universal model. Uniformity ultimately is impoverishing.

What is important here is to capture the totality of the system with diverse elements, in other words, globalisation with local differences. More and more developing countries argue that societies differ in their particular path of development; that each society has its own political and social structures and cultural values; that the role of the state and the substance of national policies vary according to the needs and requirements of each society's political and social structure and cultural values; and therefore that what is appropriate to one society may not be appropriate to another. The growing internationalism and globalisation will provide diversity at least as much as they impose uniformity.

Creativity, markets and cultural policies

The great diversity of multimedia producers in the educational and cultural fields, and the youthfulness of the market are extremely conductive to cultural encounters." The closing years of the twentieth century have been marked by an increasingly rapid rate of globalisation in world markets. As economic systems become more closely integrated, as financial markets transcend national boundaries and information exchange around the world becomes easier and faster, global markets have emerged for many of the goods and services that are bought and sold in every country every day by countless millions of people.

Although these rapid changes have expanded the range of choice available to citizens all over the world, they also bring with them a sense of insecurity. The cultural values which identify and link local, regional or national communities seem in danger of being overwhelmed by the relentless forces of the global market place. In these circumstances questions are raised as to how societies can manage the impacts of globalisation such that local and national cultures, and the creativity that sustains them, are not damaged but rather are preserved and enhanced. This is a central task for cultural policy.

In a rapidly changing world, there will be differences between countries and regions in the ways in which cultural policies can respond to the new challenges of the global market place.

Just as the arts lie at the core of the cultural sector, so too does the process of creativity lie at the centre of the arts. In a very real sense, then, cultural policy is about fostering creativity. How does globalisation affect the creative process? Perhaps there are opportunities here rather than threats. In music, in the visual arts, in literature, artists have responded to the stimuli provided by new technologies, new modes of communication and new aesthetic discourses.

Cultural industries within national boundaries are being increasingly caught up in global market processes. Although in most countries a local music industry emerges at a certain stage of development, serving a domestic market with home-grown cultural messages conveyed in musical form, it is not long before the international music industry begins to have an impact, both on the type of music available for consumption and on the conditions of production of music by local individuals and groups.

As the role of cultural industries becomes more sharply defined at both national and international levels, so the need to protect and reward creativity grows more urgent. In the age of new communications technologies, problems of copyright regulation are multiplied many times, and it is essential that more rapid progress be made, both within and between countries, in designing effective means of copyright protection in the digital era. Growth of trading relationships between countries brings with it greater opportunities for illicit trade in cultural property. Heritage management is being increasingly affected by transnational economic forces as new players (corporations, foundations, NGOs) enter the market-place.

Access to cultural heritage is changing too. Cultural policies dealing explicitly with new communications technologies are appearing in some countries, but overall policy development in this area is still embryonic.

Building cultural indicators

Before one can construct cultural indicators, it is necessary to have at least a tentative definition of culture. Both McKinley and Pattanaik settle for rather broad notions of culture. For McKinley, culture refers to the way that people live together, interact, and co-operate together with how they justify such interactions through a system of beliefs, values and norms. For Pattanaik, the cultural determinants of human well-being include political and social factors (e.g. participation in communal and political life and immunity from discrimination) as well as intellectual and aesthetic factors.

Cultural indicators of human well-being can serve different purposes. First, there is the purely descriptive purpose. Like any indicator, cultural indicators give information about societies, which may be interesting even when one is not trying to evaluate the cultures of these societies from any normative point of view. Cultural indicators may also have an evaluative purpose involving explicit or implicit normative criteria. The choice of indictors is obviously determined by the purposes which the indicators are intended to serve.

Aggregation

Aggregation is not an all-or-nothing affair. Some amount of aggregation is desirable so as to avoid the lack of focus and coherence that may result from a very large number of separate indicators. If, on the other hand, correlation between different indicators is low, one would wish to know, for many purposes, why this is so and therefore separate them. Separation permits one to investigate the relationship between different indicators, e.g. freedom and crime or democracy and tolerance of minorities or diversity and the number of patents registered. The three papers often differ in their approaches to cultural indicators of human well-being. However, there is one point that clearly emerges from all these papers : whatever approach it is decided to follow, we need more data than are available now before we can construct a satisfactory set of cultural indicators of well-being. Future progress in this area will depend as much on the compilation of more factual information as on further exploration of the conceptual foundations of cultural indicators of human well-being. Several countries have already initiated serious and systematic attempts to extend the range of statistical information on culture.

Policy implications

Globalisation and growing international interdependence present new challenges and opportunities for culture and cultural policies throughout the world. These challenges are environmental, political, social, human and cultural (in the narrow sense).

The role of culture will be seen to be of increasing importance in the discussion of development policies, especially of alternative approaches to development and its different styles. Culture is frequently invoked to explain both the successes and failures of development. For example, some have attributed the economic miracle of East Asian economies to Confucian culture and Asian values and asserted that cultural diversity is not merely useful but essential for development. It has been established beyond doubt that the Protestant ethic is not the only source of thrift and hard work.

At the same time, the recent turmoil in these economies has also been attributed to certain features of local cultures. Both positive and negative traits of economic development are said to be linked to culture. Neither view is fully persuasive. The discussion calls for a deeper analysis of the links between culture and development, as between culture and development crises.

Although we argue that diversity contributes to creativity, it is not enough to advocate diversity in the abstract. Our task now is to go beyond this and show precisely how diversity enhances economic success, social opportunity, political stability and conflict resolution, besides being valuable, beautiful and delightful in itself. The evidence suggests that democracy draws strength from certain cultural conditions. Yet it is by building democratic institutions that a more participatory culture evolves, and this in turn strengthens democracy. The direction of causality is mainly from social and political institutions to political values and practices.

The existence of democratic institutions is not associated with culturally-defined differences implies a clear signal: policy-makers cannot refuse democracy on the grounds of their own culture; they cannot use cultural traditions and features as an excuse for not institutionalising participatory and democratic political structures of decision-making, open to diverse voices and interests.

Cultural policies should be integrated with economic and political policies, so that national and local cultural values are recognised in the management of the economy. There is much room for experiment with creative forms of conflict resolution that foster equality instead of discrimination and conviviality instead of violence.

The growing risk of violent ethnic conflicts arising from the arrogant and intolerant assertion of cultural, indigenous, ethnic, racial, religious, linguistic or minority rights is apparent in many places. Isolating linguistic or cultural groups and 'drawing the borders in blood' reflects not only a misapprehension of the nature of culture and the evolution of history, but is doomed to fail in societies that are becoming increasingly interdependent and multicultural. Indigenous and culturally distinct groups, and ethnic, racial or religious sub-groups that demand rights to express and continue to develop their cultures, deserve to be supported, but their relationships with the wider societies, nations and world community in which they are embedded should also be recognised in thought and action. The cure for separatist, exclusive ethnicity is multicultural ethnicity. In the global system of cultural exchanges some cultures are disappearing. But as some forms of culture disappear, new forms appear locally. The disappearance of old cultural forms is entirely consistent with a rich variety of new forms of human life. Attitudes should be encouraged and laws and institutions established that recognise multiple voices and actors and provide ways of handling differences and plural, partial interpretations of the world. We should learn to value the variety of human forms of social and cultural life; and so long as these differences meet the constraints of a global ethics, in particular the respect for basic human rights, we should celebrate and rejoice in cultural variety.

Policy-makers have to rethink state, community and international institutions and policies to permit local populations to choose their languages, allegiances and ways of life, provided that the implementation of these choices is taken up by the local or micro-regional communities themselves. At the same time, institutions should be created that encourage a dialogue between leaders of different cultural groups to negotiate exchanges and promote a better mutual understanding. Intercultural dialogue becomes a prime policy line of action which should be implemented according to local ways of management and organisation. The important thing is that local communities and their administrative arrangements, and municipal, provincial and departmental or state governments should take on the main responsibility for this dialogue and ensure that no artificial walls are erected to stop the flow of intercultural discourse.

This is especially relevant for the young generations who, in their hearts and minds, are open to many cultures from which they take symbols, icons and customs that allow them to rejuvenate their traditions, thereby making them better adapted to the relentlessly changing conditions of a telecommunicated, globalised and shrunken world. Policies to encourage intercultural productions in the arts, especially by the young and by women, should be given priority. Women, where they are allowed to participate fully in social and cultural life, will contribute in large part to creating the new societies of the twenty-first century.

Cultural policy should look beyond a purely national emphasis and take, in addition, a broader, inter-national, inter-regional and global perspective. New partnerships between governments, corporations, private voluntary associations and other stakeholders should be developed. The positive impact of globalisation on local creativity, in that it opens up markets, should be identified and encouraged. The effects of global markets on local cultural industries, both good and bad, should be more clearly recognised, so that policy can protect and enhance their cultural and economic flowering.

Policies that favour the expression and development of cultural potential will also have repercussions on how people relate to their physical environment. Achieving environmental sustainability calls for democratisation of expertise and participation of local communities.

Global problems give rise to pessimism on the part of the public, yet it is local problems that are their main concern. Cities, the most multicultural sites of the future, should evolve ways in which people who speak different languages and have different loyalties can live together in peace. Urban squalor, violence and crime are not the result of urbanisation, but of inadequate incomes, unemployment, poor education, overcrowded housing, insecure tenure, homelessness and lack of social support. City governments and municipalities can encourage peaceful and prosperous urban communities by strengthening their support for local initiatives. Artists everywhere wish to express their personal and cultural identities, and in doing so they create global trends. The new site for the creation of art is the global market-place. Policy-makers should ensure that artists are able to participate in the expanding global markets.

Globalisation and Virtual Transformation in Cities

Globalisation can be considered as a consequence of the mathematical properties of the shape of the earth's surface. Taken at face value, globalisation is primarily a spatial metaphor (the socio-cultural implications of the mathematical properties of the earth's surface, notably the fact that from any spot on that surface any other point can be reached, while (provided the journey is continued for long enough in the same direction) the ultimate destination will be the point of departure, ultimately in other words the entire surface will be covered.

Yet it is important to also investigate the temporal dimension of the globalisation metaphor: the compressing of time and of time costs in relation to spatial displacement, as well as the meaning and the effects of such displacement. It is the interplay between the temporal and the spatial dimension which allows us to pinpoint why globalisation has taken on a substantially new shape in the last few decades. The shape of the earth has not noticeably changed over the few million years of man's existence on earth, and therefore human culture, or cultures, could perhaps be said to have always been subject to globalising tendencies.

But before the invention of the telegraph, the railroad, and the aeroplane the technology of time and space was in most parts of the world so limited that the effective social and cultural life world tended to be severely bound by geographical propinquity. Most people would thus live in a world where localising tendencies would greatly outweigh whatever globalisation took place or came along. People, ideas, and goods did travel, and often across wide distances, as the archaeological and historical record demonstrates.

If writing and effective imperial organisation then created a continuous and more or less stable orientation across space and time, the conditions would be set for early or proto-globalisation, characteristic of the communication technology of the mounted courier and the sailing boat. Where no such conditions prevailed, movement inevitably meant dissociating from the social setting of origin, and establishing a new local world elsewhere — a world usually no longer connected, through effective social interaction, with the one left behind, initially strongly reminiscent of the latter but decreasingly so — even in the case of nomadic cultures whose persistence in the face of spatial mobility has depended on their comparatively low investment in spatial attachment as an organising principle.

If today we have the feeling that globalisation expresses a real and qualitative change that uniquely characterises the contemporary condition, it is because of the hegemonic nature of capitalist technology, which has brought about unprecedented levels of mastery of space and time. When messages travel at light speed across the globe using electronic media, when therefore physical displacement is hardly needed for effective communication yet such displacement can be effected within one or two days from anywhere on the globe to anywhere else, and when the technology of manufacturing and distribution has developed to such levels that the same material environment using the same objects can be created and fitted out anywhere on the globe at will — then we have reduced the fees that time and space impose on the social process, to virtually zero. Then we can speak of globalisation in the true sense.

Globalisation is not about the absence or dissolution of boundaries, but about the dramatically reduced fee imposed by time and space, and thus the opening up of new spaces and new times within new boundaries that were hitherto inconceivable. Globalisation as a condition of the social world today revolves on the interplay between unbounded world–wide flow, and the selective framing of such flow within localising contexts; such framing organises not only flow (of people, ideas and objects) and individual experience, but also the people involved in them, creating more or less enduring social categories and groups whose collective identity as supported by their members' interaction creates an eddy of particularism, of social localisation, within the unbounded global flow.

The terms virtual and virtuality have a well-defined and illuminating history, which in its broad sweep of space and time, its multi-lingual aspect and its repeated changes of meaning and context, reminds us of the very globalisation process we seek to illuminate by the use of these terms. Non-existent in classical Latin (although obviously inspired by the word virtus there), they are late-medieval neologisms, whose invention became necessary when, partly via Arabic versions of Aristotle's' works, his Greek concept of du\na±mi? ('potentiality, power, quadrate') had to be translated into Latin. While the Scholastic/ Aristotelian philosophy, with its emphasis on general potential to be realised in the concrete, gradually retreated from most domains of North Atlantic intellectual life, the terms found refuge in the expanding field of physics, where virtual velocity, virtual moment, virtual work became established concepts around 1800.

This was a century after optics had formulated the theory of the 'virtual image': the objects shown in a mirror image there do not really exist, but they are merely illusory representations, which we apparently observe at the end of the light beams connecting the object, the surface of the mirror, and our eye. In our age of information technology the term 'virtual' has gained a new lease of life which takes its cue from the meaning given to the term in optics.

In the globalisation perspective we frequently refer to products of the electronic industry, and the furtive, intangible projections of texts and images on electronic screens is an obvious example of virtuality. Virtual reality has now become a cliche of the post-modern experience: computer games and simulations which — with extreme suggestions of reality — conjure up, for the consumer, vicarious experiences in the form of illusions. As electronic media, like television and video, march on in contemporary Africa, it is also in that continent that we can make out this form of virtuality in the context of the globalisation process.

But the applicability of the concept of 'virtuality' extends further. Drawing on a notion of 'virtual discourse' which while inspired by Foucault is in fact equivalent to that of performative discourse in analytical philosophy. Jules Rosette in a splendid recent paper reserves the notion of virtuality for a specific discursive situation: the 'symbolic revindications of modernity's broken promise', which play a central role in the construction of postcolonial identity:

> 'When a virtual discourse becomes a master cultural narrative [e.g. authenticite, negritude] , individuals must accept it in order to validate themselves as members of a collectivity'

This allows her to link the specific form of postcolonial political discourse in Zaire to the macro-economic predicament of Africa today, of which the elusive magic of money then emerges as the central symbol. Inspiring as this is, it is not necessary to limit the concept of virtuality to that of explicit, verbal discourse, and there is much to be said for a much wider application, encompassing implicit beliefs, the images on which the electronically-inspired use of the concept of virtuality would concentrate, and object. Here we may allow ourselves to be inspired by a recent paper by Rudiger Korff even if our emphasis is to be on the cultural and symbolic rather than — as in Korff's case — on the technological and economic side:

> 'Globalisation is accompanied by virtuality. The financial markets gained autonomy by producing the goods they trade among themselves and thereby developed into speculators' 'Monopoly'. Virtuality is well shown by the information networks in which the hardware determined the possibilities for person to person interaction. This allows an anonymity in direct interaction. All personality features are hidden, and virtual personalities take over the conversation. Even the world of commodities is virtualised. While for Marx a commodity had two aspects, use- and exchange value, today a 'symbolic' value has to be added. Traditions and cultures are created as virtual realities and states offer imaginations in their search for political subjects. This indicates a new stage in the dialectic of disenchantment and mystification. While capitalism disenchanted morality and substituted it with the magic of commodities and technology (Verdinglichung), today commodity fetishism is substituted by post-modern virtual realities. (...) Appadurai (1990) mentions in a similar vein ethnoscapes, mediascapes, technoscapes, financescapes and ideoscapes. (...) As with commodities, these 'imagined worlds' and virtual realities develop their own dynamics and start to govern their creators for whom it is impossible to distinguish reality from virtuality. Just like Goethe says in the Magician's apprentice: 'Die Geister, die ich rief, die werd ich nicht mehr los.'

Ultimately, virtuality stands for a specific relation of reference as existing between elements of human culture.

Before the development of contemporary communication technologies (which also includes such inventions, already more than a century old, as the telephone and the motorcar, and railway which is even considerably older) the coincidence between interactive, social space and geographical space could conveniently be taken for granted for practical purposes. If horse-riding and the talking drum represent the paroxysm of technological achievement, the effective social horizon coincides with the visible horizon.

It is only the invention of modern technologies which has revealed this time-honoured coincidence as accidental and not inevitable. For complex reasons which indirectly reflect the state of communication technology by the end of the nineteenth century, anthropology in its formative decades concentrated on social contexts outside the industrial North Atlantic, where such technologies was not yet available so that social space and geographical nearness continued to be two sides of the same coin.

For the geographically near to become the local in the classic anthropological sense, we need to add an appeal to the systemic nature of local culture. This refers to the claim that its elements hang together systematically, so that it is possible to reduce the culture to a far smaller number of elements and informing principles than the astronomical number of separate cultural events that take place, and material cultural objects that exist, among the set of people involved within a fairly limited space and time.

Creolisation then means, not that the systemic nature of local culture has been abandoned by the actors or destroyed by the onslaught of outside influences, but that it only accounts for appreciably less than the entire culture: a considerable part falls outside the system. Such creolisation can be argued to be merely a specific form of virtuality: as a departure from the systemic nature of local culture. If culture produces reality in the consciousness of the actors, then the reality produced under conditions of such departure is, to the extent to which it is virtual, only... virtual reality.

This is ground covered by Appadurai in his well-known paper on The production of locality. A merging of two notions of locality ('geographical space of nearness, neighbourhood' versus 'social space of identity, home') was an ingredient of earlier versions of Appadurai's argument but fortunately he has dropped that element in the final, published version, in favour of a view of locality not only as social space regardless of geographical contiguity, but also as problematic, as to be actively constructed in the face of the standard situation of non-locality.

Under modern conditions of both communication technology and the social engineering of self-organisation for identity, the socially local is not any longer, necessarily, the geographically near. We need a concept of social, culture and identity space which is carefully distinguished from geographical space — even although even the latter is, like that other Kantian category time, far less self-evident and unchangeable than Kant, and naive contemporary consumers of secondary school physics, would tend to believe.

In the same way as the Euclidean two-dimensional geometry of the flat plane can be demonstrated to be only a special case of the immense variety of n-dimensional geometries which modern mathematics has come to conceive, the insistence on geographical propinquity as a prime determinant of social relations is merely a reflection of the state of communication technology prevailing, during much of man's history, in the hunting and herding camps and the farming villages that until only a few millennia ago were the standard human condition.

As such it has been built into classic anthropology. Meanwhile, the distinction between social space and geographical space does not mean that the material technologies of geographical space have become irrelevant or non-existent in the face of the social technology of locality construction — a prudent approach to globalisation has to take account of both.

We have to study in detail the processes through which localisation as a social process takes place. The local, in other words, is in itself a problem, not a given, let alone a solution. We need to study the process of the appropriation globally available objects, images and ideas in a local contexts, which more often than not constitutes itself in the very process of such appropriation. Let us take our clue from the history of a major family of divination systems found throughout Africa, under conditions of 'proto-' globalisation.

This history is basically that of localisation processes involving astrological and numerological interpretational schemes as current in the medieval Arabian culture of North Africa and the Middle East, where they are known under the name of geomancy or Ailm al-raml ('the science of sand'). This process produced the interpretative catalogues for all African divination systems based on a material apparatus producing 2n different configurations, such as Fa, Ifa, Sixteen Cowries, Sikidy, Four Tablets: illiterate African versions so elaborate and so saturated with local African imagery that they would appear to be authentically, autochthonous African.

In the same way it can be demonstrated that the actual material apparatuses used in this connexion, although ultimately conceived within an African iconography and carving techniques, and clad in awesome African mystery and imputed authenticity, in fact are extreme localisations of the intercontinentally mediated scientific instruments of Greek, Arabian, and Chinese nautical specialists and scribes. The example has considerable relevance, because here some of the main factors of globalisation and universalism, have rather ironically ended up as forms of the most entrenched, stereotypical African localisation and particularism.

The hardest analytical nut to crack is to explain why, and as a result of what ideological, social, economic, and technological mechanisms, such extreme localisation seems to be more typical of sub-Saharan Africa than of other parts of the Old World in the second millennium CE. Whatever of the original, distant contexts still clings to these localised African precipitates amounts to virtuality and probably adds much to these systems' charisma.

Such extreme localisation of outside influences, rendering them practically imperceptible and positioning them within the rural environment, although typical for much of Africa's history, is however no longer the dominant form globalisation takes in Africa. Present-day virtually manifests itself through the incomplete systemic incorporation of cultural material which is both alien and recognised by the actors to be so, and which circulates not primarily in remote villages but in cities.

Examples of this form of virtuality are to be found all over Africa today, and in fact they constitute the majority of cultural expressions: from world religions to party politics mediating world-wide models if formal organisation, development and democracy; from specialist production of contemporary art, belles lettres and philosophy inspired by cosmopolitan models, to the production — no longer self-evidently but, self-consciously, as a deliberate performance — of apparently local forms of music and dance during an ethnic festival like Kazanga in western central Zambia; from fashionable lingerie to public bodily prudery demonstrably imposed by Christianity and Islam.

These symbolic processes are accompanied by, in fact carried by, forms of social organisation which create the socially local within the global. Such categories and groups are no longer spatially localised, in the sense that they do no longer create a bounded geographical space which is internally homogeneous in that it only inhabited by people belonging to the same bounded organisation.

We have to think of such organisations (whose member-ship is typically geographically dispersed while creating a social focus) as: ethnic associations, churches, political parties, professional associations, schools, hospitals, etc. If they are geographically dispersed, this does not mean that their membership is distributed all over the globe. Statistically, they have a fairly limited geographical catchment area commensurate with the available transport technology, but within that catchment area, the vast majority of human inhabitants are non-members — it does therefore not constitute a contiguous social space.

Virtual Villages of African Cities

The classic anthropological image of 'the' African culture as holistic, self-contained, locally anchored, effectively to be subsumed under an ethnic name, was deliberately constructed so as to constitute a local universe of meaning — the opposite of virtuality. For such a culture was thought to form an integrated unity, so all its parts were supposed to refer to that same coherence, which in its entirety gave the satisfactory illusion of localised meaningfulness.

It is necessary to dwell on this point, since it is capable of producing considerable confusion. Although there are notable exceptions, and although the research programme of which the present book is a first product is prompted by the determination to change that situation, it is true to say that most of the existing literature on globalisation was not written by established ethnographers of rural life.

The typical focus for globalisation studies is the metropolis, the self-evident access to international life-styles mediated by electronic media, with a dominant presence of the state and the culture and communication industry. However, people born in villages are now also being globalised, and an understanding of their experiences requires an analytical and descriptive grip on rural social formations. Not infrequently, Marxist studies of the 1970s and '80s, including my own, are claimed to have demonstrated the deficit of earlier mainstream anthropology. This is largely a spurious claim. Modes-of-production analysis, as the main contribution of Marxism to contemporary anthropology, has done a number of essential things:

— reintroduce an emphasis on material production and appropriation;
— dissolve the assumed unitary nature of the local rural society into a handful of subsystems 'modes of production') , each with their own logic of exploitation and ideological legitimation, and linked together

('articulated') within the 'social formation', in such a way that the reproduction of one mode depends on the exploitation of another mode; and finally,

— provide a theoretical perspective which could account for the persistence and relative autonomy (also as 'logics' of signification and legitimation) of these various modes and their articulations, even under conditions of capitalism and the colonial or post-colonial state.

This revolutionary reformulation of the classic anthropological perspective therefore could accommodate internal contradictions, multiplicity of fields of symbolic reference notably: as many fields as there were modes of production, while the articulation process itself also generated a field of symbolism of its own and outside functioning within the world system; but it did not discard the essentially local nature of the social formation, nor its systemic nature even if the latter was no longer conceived as unitary, holistic integration, but came to be represented as a dialectic composite of contradictions between the few specific 'logics', each informing a specific mode of production.

The Marxist approach did not render the notion of local integration obsolete: to the extent to which the articulation of modes of production under the hegemony of one dominant mode has succeeded, the resulting social formation is effectively integrated by its very contradictions.

So even from a Marxist perspective it appears to be true to say that historic societies in the present millennium have invariably displayed cleavages in terms of gender, age, class, and political power, while containing only partially integrated elements deriving from and still referring, beyond the local society, to other cultural complexes which were often remote in space and time. Yet they have offered to their members a fairly coherent universe, in which the human body-self, interpersonal relations, the landscape and the supernatural all featured in one composite, comprehensive world-view, whose symbolism and ritual elaboration was to reconcile and conceal, rather than articulate, such internal contradictions as constitute the whole and render it dynamic.

In this context, the meaning of an element of the local society and culture consists in the network of referential relations at the centre of which such element is perceived and conceptualised by the participants; through this relational network the element is taken, by the actors, and explicitly or implicitly, as belonging to that general socio-cultural order, cognitively and emotively linked to many other aspects of that order — a condition which produces a sense of proper placement, connectivity and coherence, recognition, identity as a person and as a group, aesthetics, bodily comfort and even healing.

In Africa, village society still forms the context in which many present-day urbanites were born, and where some will retire and die. Until recently, the dichotomy between town and village dominated Africanist anthropology. Today we have to admit that, considering the constant movement of ideas, goods and people between town and village, the dichotomy has lost much of its explanatory value. In terms of social organisation, economic and productive structures, goals and evaluations town and village have become complementary, even converging options within the social experience of Africans today; their difference has become gradual, and is no longer absolute.

However, while of diminishing value in the hands of us analysts, the dichotomy between town and village remains relevant in so far as it informs African actors' conceptualisations of their life-world and social experience. Here the idealised image of the village stands for an imaginary context where production and reproduction are viable and meaningful, pursued by people who — organised along the lines of age and gender divisions, and historic ('traditional') leadership — are turned into an effective community through an un-eroded kinship system, symbolism, ritual and cosmology.

Vital in this set-up is that — typically through non-verbal means — ritual manages to construct the bodies of the members of the residential group as charged or inscribed with a shared meaning, a shared identity, and while the body moves across time and space this indelible mark is carried to new contexts yet remains.

Even in the village context the effective construction of community cannot be taken for granted. Central African villages, for instance, have been described as the scene of an uneasy truce between strangers, only temporarily constructed into community — at the expense of kinship rituals which take up an enormous part of available resources and even so barely conceal or negotiate underlying contradictions among the village population. Such rituals of kinship (those attending pregnancy, birth, adolescence, marriage, and death) not only transform biological human individuals into competent social persons with a marked identity founded in the local community (or in the case of death transform such social persons in the face of physical decomposition); such rituals thus construct, within that overall community, specific constituent identities, e.g. those of gender and age. They refer to, and to a considerable extent reproduce and perpetuate, the productive and social organisation of the village society. Perhaps the central characteristic of the old village order was that the construction of community was still so effective that in the villagers' consciousness their actual residential group self-evidently appeared as the realisation of that ideal.

It is crucial to realise that in the twentieth century, even with reference to rural settings, we are not so much dealing with 'real' communities, but with rural folks' increasingly problematic model of the village community. Perhaps we could say that the village was becoming a virtual village. Rural ideological change in Africa during the twentieth century can be summed up as a process of people actively confronting the erosion of that model, its becoming irrelevant and impotent in the face of political economic realities.

Throughout the twentieth century, rural populations in Africa have struggled, through numerous forms of organisational, ideological and productive innovation combining local practices with outside borrowings, to reconstruct a new sense of community in an attempt to revitalise, complement or replace the collapsing village community in its viable nineteenth century form.

In fact the entire ideological history of twentieth century Africa could be written from this perspective. Peasants have been constantly engaged in the construction of new, alternative forms of community on the basis of rather new principles as derived from political, cultic, productive and consumerist ideas introduced from the wider world. Many of these movements have sought to re-formulate the notion of the viable, intact village community in new terms and with new outside inspiration and outside pressure.

Ethnicity, healing cults, prophetic cults, anti-sorcery movements, varieties of imported world religions and local transformations thereof e.g. in the form of Independent churches, struggles for political independence, involvement in modern national politics including the recent wave of democratisation, involvement in a peripheral-capitalist cash economy with new symbols of status and distinction, — these have been some of the strategies by which villagers have sought (often against many odds) to create and bring to life the image of a new world, and a continued sense of meaning and community, when the old village order was felt, or said, to fall apart. And that old village order, and the ethnic cultures under which it was usually subsumed, may in itself have been largely illusory, strategically underpinned by the ideological claims of elders, chiefs, first-generation local intellectuals, colonial administrators and missionaries, open to the cultural bricolage of invented tradition of the part of these vocal actors.

If the construction of community in the rural context has been problematic, the village yet represents one of the few models of viable community among Africans today, including urbanites. It is the only model which is part of a collective idiom pervading all sections of contemporary society. As such it features massively as a nostalgic reference in ethnic identity construction. Whatever alternative models of community are available, are shallowly rooted and reserved to specific sections of the society: Christians or Muslims (the local religious congregation as a community; and by extension the abstract world-wide collective of co-religionists), cult members (the cultic group as a community), members of a specific ethnic group, the elite.

Problems in virtual towns

Globalisation theory has stressed the paradoxical phenomenon that, in the world today, the increasing unification of the world in political, economic, cultural and communication terms does not lead to increasing uniformity but, on the contrary, goes hand in hand with a proliferation of local differences. It is as if myriad eddies of particularism (which may take the form of ethnic, linguistic and religious identities, consumerist life-styles etc.) are the inevitable accompaniment of the swelling stream of globalising universalism.

Anthropologists have — in theory, that is — long ceased to define their research object primarily by reference to a more or less demarcated part of the global landscape assumed to be the habitat of a bounded, integrated 'culture' supposedly shared by a people, tribe or ethnic group.

While the time-honoured technique of participant observation still favours their focusing on a set of people who are more or less tied together by enduring social relations and forms of organisation, such a set need no longer be localised (for modern technology— not just fax machines and E-mail, but also simple telephones and rural buses — enables people to effectively maintain relationships across wide distances: as members of the same ethnic group, as employees of the same multinational corporation, as members of a cult, as traders etc.)

nor do the individuals which constitute that set (as a statistical conglomerate, or a social network of dyadic ties) necessarily and as a dominant feature of their social experience construct that set as an ideal community with a name, an identity, moral codes and values. Fragmentation, heterogeneity, alienation and cultural and organisational experiment are characteristic of the global condition, not only in North Atlantic urban society but also, for much the same reasons, in the rapidly growing towns of Africa today.

In essence, the aspect of globalisation which we seek to capture by concentrating on virtuality, revolves around issues of African actors' production and sustaining of meaning. The notion of virtuality is hoped to equip us for the situation, rather more common than village anthropology prepared us to believe, that meaning is encountered and manipulated in a context far removed, in time and space, from the concrete social context of production and reproduction where that meaning was originally worked out in a dialectical interplay of articulated modes of production; where, on the contrary, it is no longer local and systemic, but fragmented, ragged, virtual, absurd, maybe even absent.

The study of such forms of meaning is of course doubly problematic because anthropology itself is a globalising project, and one of the first in western intellectual history. African towns, with their usually recent history, heterogeneous migrant population, and full of social, political and economic structures apparently totally at variance with any village conditions in the surrounding countryside, are laboratories of meaning.

To what extent has the contemporary urban environment in Africa managed to produce and nurture symbols which selectively refer to the state and the world economy, yet at the same time negotiate dilemmas of rural-derived identity and of urban-rural relations? It is here that one can begin to look for the stuff that African urbanism is made of. Is it true to say that these towns have engendered collective representations which are strikingly urban, and which offer partial and tentative yet creative solutions to such typically urban problems as incessant personnel flow, ethnic, class and religious heterogeneity, economic and political powerlessness, and the increasing irrelevance, in the urban situation, of historic, rural-derived forms of social organisation (kinship, marriage, 'traditional' politics and ritual)?

Mitchell's Kalela dance still offers a classic paradigm, stressing how at the city boundaries elements of rural society and culture may be selectively admitted onto the urban scene, yet undergo such a dramatic transformation of form, organisation and function that their urban manifestations must be understood by reference to the urban situation alone. Or, in Gluckman's famous words, 'the African townsman is a townsman'In other words, the African townsman is not a displaced villager or tribesman — but on the contrary 'detribalised' as soon as he leaves his village. These ideas have evidently circulated in African urban studies long before 1960.

Statements of this nature have helped to free our perception of African urbanites from traditionalist and paternalistic projections; for according to the latter they continued to be viewed as temporarily displaced villagers whose true commitment and identity continued to lie with their rural societies of origin. The stress on the urban nature of African urbanites even amounted to a radical political challenge, in a time when the colonial economy was largely based on the over-exploitation of rural communities through circulatory migration of male workers conveniently defined as bachelors while in town. We can therefore forgive these authors their one-sidedness, but there is no denying that they failed to address the fundamental problems of meaning which the construction of a town-based culture in the new cities of Africa has always posed.

But what happens to meaning in town? It is particularly in the context of meaning that we see African towns as the arena where a migrant's specific, disconnected and fragmented rural-based heritage is confronted with a limited number of 'cosmopolitan' socio-cultural complexes, each generating its own discourse and claiming its own commitment from the people drawn into its orbit in exchange for partial solutions of their problems of meaning.

Before discussing these complexes, it is useful to realise that, as a source of meaning, the historic rural background culture of urban migrants is not necessarily as fragmented as the multiplicity of ethnic labels and linguistic practices in the town may suggest. Ethnic groups have a history, and while some ethnic groups can be said to be recent, colonial creations, underlying their unmistakable differences there is in many cases a common substratum of regional cultural similarities and even identities: continuities such as a patrilineal kinship system, emphasis on cattle, similarities in the marital system, the cult of the land and of the ancestors, patterns of divination and of sacrifice, shared ideas about causation including witchcraft beliefs, converging ideas about conflict resolution and morality.

The result is that even urban migrants with a different ethnic, linguistic and geographical background may yet find that they possess a cultural lingua franca that allows them to share such historic meanings as have not been mediated through the state and capitalism. Sometimes specific routinised modes of inter-ethnic discourse explicitly mediate this joint substratum.

Traditional cults and independent Christian churches in town, which tend to be trans-ethnic, derive much of their appeal from the way in which they articulate this historic substratum and thus recapture meanings which no longer can be communicated with through migrants' direct identification with any specific historic rural culture. Moreover, partly on the basis or these rural continuities, urban migrants creatively develop a new common idiom not only for language communication, but also for the patterning of their everyday relationships, their notions of propriety and neighbourliness, the interpretation and settlement of their conflicts, and the evaluation of their statuses.

After this qualification, let us sum up the principal cosmopolitan complexes:

— The post-colonial state: a principal actor in the struggle for control of the urban space; a major agent of social control through its law-and-order institutions (the judiciary, police, immigration department); a major mediator of 'cosmopolitan' meaning through the bureaucratically organised services it offers in such fields as education, cosmopolitan medicine, housing, the restructuration of kinship forms through statutory marriage etc.; a major context for the creation of new, politically instrumen-tal meaning in the process of nation-building and elite legitimation; and through its constitutional premises the object of modern political organisations.

— A variety of manifestations of the capitalist mode of production, largely structuring the urbanites' economic participation and hence their experience of time, space, causation, personhood and social relations; involving them in relations of dependence and exploitation whose ideological expression we have learned to interpret in terms of alienation; but also, in the process, leading on to modern organisational forms meant to counter the powerlessness generated in that process; and finally producing both the manufactured products on which mass consumption as a world-wide economic and cultural expression depends, as well as the financial means to participate in mass consumption.

— World religions, which pursue organisational forms and ideological orientations rather reminiscent of the post-colonial state and the capitalist mode of production, yet tending to maintain, in time, space and ideological content, sufficient distance from either complex to have their own appeal on the urban population, offering formal socio-ritual contexts in which imported cosmopolitan symbols can be articulated and shared between urbanites, and in which — more than in the former two complexes — rural-based historic symbols can be mediated, particularly through independent churches.

— Cosmopolitan consumer culture, ranging from fast food shops to hire-purchase furniture stores displaying the whole material dream of prospective middle-class life-style, and from video outlets and record shops to the retail shops of the international ready-made garment industry, and all the other material objects by which one can encode distinctions in or around one's body and its senses, and create identity not by seclusive group-wise self-organisation but by individual communication with globally mediated manufactured symbols.

These four cosmopolitan repertoires of meaning differ considerably from the ideal-typical meaning enshrined in the rural historic universe. While historically related, they are present on the urban African scene as mutually competitive, fragmented, optional, and more or less anomic or even absurd. Yet together, as more or less elite expressions, they constitute a realm of symbolic discourse that, however internally contradictory, assumes dominance over the rural-orientated, local and historic repertoires of meaning of African migrants and workers.

The ways in which African urbanites, in their interactions and conceptualisations, construct, keep apart, and merge as the case may be, cosmopolitan and rural idioms, are ill understood for several reasons. Those who, as social scientists, are supposed to study these patterns of interaction are, in their personal and professional lives, partisans of cosmopolitan repertoires and are likely to be identified as such by the other actors on the urban scene.

Much of the actors' juggling of repertoires is evasive and combines the assumption of rigid subordination with the practice of creative challenge and tacit symbolic resistance in private spheres of urban life where few representatives of the cosmopolitan repertoires have access. And whereas anthropology has developed great expertise in the handling of meaning in one spatio-temporal context whose wholeness and integration it has tended to exaggerate, the development of a sensitive approach to fragmented and incoherent multiplicity of repertoires of meaning, each assaulted and rendered more or less meaningless by the presence of the other, had to wait till the advent of Postmodernism as an attempt to revolutionarise, or to explode, anthropology.

The classic predecessors in African urban studies worked on the assumption that the African urban situation was very highly structured — by what they called the 'colonial-industrial complex' imposing rigid segregation and class interests, by voluntary associations, by networks.In the contemporary world, such structure is becoming more and more problematic, and the town, especially the African town, appears as the post-modern social space par excellence. Our greatest analytical problem here is that as a social space the town lacks the coherent integrated structure which could produce, like the village, a systematic repertoire of meaning ready for monographic processing; but this may not merely be one researcher's analytical problem — it appears to sum up the essence of what the urban experience in Africa today is about, in the lives of a great many urbanites.

Postmodernism is not the only, and deliberately unsystematic, analytical approach to multiplicity of meaning within a social formation consisting of fundamentally different and mutually irreducible sub-formations. As a paradigm that preceded Postmodernism by a decade in the circulation of intellectual fashions, the notion of articulation of modes of production is in principle capable of handling such a situation. However, the emphasis, in this approach, on enduring structure and a specific internal logic for each constituent 'mode of production' renders it difficult to accommodate the extreme fragmentation and contradiction of meaning typical of the urban situation.

The work of Ulf Hannerz is exemplary for the kind of processes of cultural production, variation and control one would stress when looking at African towns from the perspective of the modern world as a unifying, globalising whole. However, it is significant that his work, far from problematising the concept of meaning as such, takes meaning rather for granted and concentrates on the social circulation of meaning, in other words the management of meaning. Hannerz's position here is far from exceptional in anthropology, where we theorise much less about meaning than would be suggested by the large number of anthropological publications with 'meaning', 'significance', 'interpretation' and 'explanation' in their titles. Also for Hannerz the African townsman is truly a townsman, and even the analyst seems to be entirely forgotten that 'many' of these urbanites, even today, have been born outside town under conditions of rural, localised meaning evoked today, and that this circumstance is likely to be somehow reflected in their urban patterns of signification.

In certain urban situations rural models of interaction and co-residence tend to be more prominent than in others. We need to remind ourselves of the fact that urban does not necessarily mean global. For instance, as a fresh urban immigrant one can take refuge among former fellow-villagers, in an urban setting. The vast evidence on urban immigration in Africa suggests that the rural-orientated refuge in a denial of globalisation tends to be partial and largely illusory, in other words towns precisely in their display of apparently rural-derived elements tend to high levels of virtuality/ discontinuity/ transformation.

6

Complexity in Urban Life

Urban streets are probably a key element of a humane city with encounters among strangers in public space and with differences, as well as the possibility of unforeseen events taking place. Modernist urban planning and architecture wanted to get rid of the urban street in favour of cars and a floating open space. Since 1980s, western countries have seen a renewed interest in planning and design of urban streets. The understanding of humane aspects of street life has been hampered by fear of urban complexity.

Role of Street in Urban Life

The street appears in sociological thinking as a type of place and as a type of social relationship, as well as a metaphor for thinking about life in urban settings. Although there is a variety of ideas about what the street is, if you think about all the ideas listed above and your own ideas, apart from descriptions of a place, they are probably about what people do there, and the social actions that take place in the context of the street; they are also a mixture of real experiences and images from the media of streets we may not have experienced but which are real to us. It also suggests that confining our attention to 'streets in themselves' won't be sufficient, that we need to think about the social context of 'the street' and what it means in terms of social space more generally. In order to understand and know what the street is as a feature of everyday life, we have to look at wider ideas and concepts: about the city, about social groups and structures, about the imagery of the street.

The street is an important 'locus of everyday life'. Yet compared to even twenty-five years ago, we are now more likely to encounter it in a car than by walking or using public transport. An increasing number of city centres have been pedestrianized, and the out-of-town shopping mall is now a common feature of urban areas not merely in the UK but in Europe and the USA too.

Some writing about everyday life and ordinary people that has been influential in sociology has at its centre the Marxist notion that 'the everyday' -particularly where it denotes repetition and 'dull routine' - is little more than a synonym for the alienation and oppression of the working class in a capitalist society. We find this view well-expressed at certain points in the writings of the Hungarian literary critic and philosopher Georg Lukacs, the French existentialist philosopher Jean-Paul Sartre and Henri Lefebvre, for instance, who identified the everyday as the separation of work, household and leisure. Indeed there has been a tendency to view the everyday in negative terms on both left and right, to see the apparent banality and routine of everyday life as oppressive, a symptom of the alienated nature of the life of the working class under capitalism.

The concept of 'the everyday' may often be used pejoratively. But this is not the only way in which it enters social thought, and especially not in relation to 'the street'. Others - sociologists, writers and artists - have taken a converse view of everyday life. They have tended to be open to, and to promote, value or romanticize the everyday existence of ordinary people, and in particular to look upon 'the street' as a place where a sort of theatre or spectacle of everyday life can be seen. A plethora of examples abound in the visual arts, from the Flemish painters of genre scenes of everyday life in the sixteenth century, the caricatures of Hogarth in the eighteenth century, to the surrealist movement of the 1920s and 1930s and documentary photographers and film-makers from the 1930s to the 1960s. The presence of ordinary people and their everyday life, especially on the street, seems to have been a major and constant element of European culture since at least the 1500s.

Sociologically, the street is primarily a space where a complex set of social relationships occur. We walk through it, negotiating our passage with the other people on the street, stopping to enter a shop or to visit a market stall. We encounter others there. We shop. We show off our clothes. We wear the appropriate sort of clothes - street fashion. Some might even play 'street-games' there. There may be street-crime. There are often street-traders. Amongst this evident diversity something in common is happening: we all know the where and what and how of the street.

It is on the one hand a type of social relationship with others in public spaces - with social rules about how we should behave with those others which we don't need to think about but are nonetheless, once we start to think about them or bring them into the open via one of Garfinkel's 'breaching' experiments, still there quite clearly in our minds. In this context, the street is, as a place and as a metaphor, a moral locale, a place where social order is displayed, where sociability is transacted. On the other hand the street is also, for our purposes, an idea or image, an imaginary place which we invest with different sorts of meanings via the particularistic imagery of culture. At the same time, the actual streets of our everyday lives are spaces we can only visualize through the memories, pictures, films or descriptions of actual, particular streets. Some of these images might be positive: the well-stocked fruit stalls of a street-market, for instance. Others might be negative: a street-fight, for example. But each of these images contributes to how we 'imagine' the street as a social space.

With the extension of a successful and powerful capitalist economic system of industrialization and commercial expansion, Europe and North America experienced a massive expansion of their towns and cities in the latter half of the nineteenth century. The great concentrations of population within these rapidly emergent metropolises created new social conditions which had not been seen before. New housing and other forms of urban development created, often within a few decades, massive conurbations of 500,000 persons and more.

Urbanization, then suburbanization, followed the development of new transport infrastructures such as the railways - and by the beginning of the twentieth century the emergence of motor transport - which began to extend the limits of the modern city far beyond its medieval confines. Where hitherto cities had been small, often compact, entities constructed on a relatively narrow social base, they now had to contain an increasingly diverse range of social groups: an urban proletariat of wage labourers; a new and burgeoning middle class of commercial and industrial entrepreneurs; between them in the social hierarchy the small shopkeepers, traders and artisans on the one hand and professionals and administrators on the other; and still powerful but of declining social importance, the remnants of the old landed aristocracy and gentry which maintained its presence in the cities, in the opulent mansions that had been their bases of urban power in pre-industrial society.

It is against the backdrop of such a fundamental set of transitions in the patterning and ordering of everyday life that sociology itself, as a distinctive intellectual discipline, began to emerge. Among the most significant features of early sociology are its concerns with understanding the impact and consequences of urban-industrial social change. In particular, many writers wanted to know why city life seemed to be so different from life in the country. Although not the only writer to direct attention to these shifts, the German sociologist Ferdinand Toennies is widely recognized as giving them a conceptual shape when he described them as the change from Gemeinschaft (community) to Gesellschaft (association).

For Toennies, the characteristic feature of urban, industrialized societies was their increasing reliance on a new, rational and contractual type of relationship between individuals and a new mode of social organization, rather than the closer ties and shared values that existed previously. Toennies was to argue that the motives people have for acting together, for relating to each other in social relationships, collectives and social organizations or corporate bodies, depend upon whether they are based on what he termed 'natural will' or on 'rational will'. He saw that 'natural will' (by which he meant the more habitual and emotionally based types of relationships to be found in traditional village and small town communities) tended to give way to 'rational will' in urban settings, where contractual relationships founded on a rational calculation of their outcomes tend to predominate.

The idea that new forms of economic relationships are bound up with the emergence of a distinctive way of life for people in the modern city seems obvious to us now, yet we must also be aware of the context in which sociologists such as Toennies were writing towards the end of the nineteenth century, when other types of explanation might have commanded more attention. For the creation of the vast new modern city seemed also to have brought with it everywhere, in Europe as much as in the New World, a myriad of modern ills: disease, crime, prostitution, civil unrest. Conservative and progressive writers alike viewed the city as a dysfunctional, oppressive entity. Here is Marx's colleague and friend, Friedrich Engels, writing about London in his The Condition of the Working Class in England:

> Only when one has tramped the pavements of the main streets for a few days does one notice that these Londoners have had to sacrifice what is best in human nature in order to create all the wonders of civilization with which their city teems, that a hundred creative faculties that lay dormant in them remained

> inactive and were suppressed ... There is something distasteful about the very bustle of the streets, something that is abhorrent to human nature itself. Hundreds of thousands of people of all classes and ranks of society jostle past one another; are they not all human beings with the same characteristics and potentialities, equally interested in the pursuit of happiness? ... And yet they rush past one another as if they had nothing in common or were in no way associated with one another.

The fascination with new forms of social relationship which are consequent upon changes in the economics, technology, demographics and settlement patterns of their societies, thus produced a common interest in identifying how and why people had begun to think and interact in different ways. The city, and the new patterns of life which it imposed on its denizens, especially in their interactions on the street, thus appeared symptomatic of an emergent modern society.

Sociological thinking about the street as a distinctive locale of modern life does not get into its stride until the latter part of the nineteenth century and the early years of the twentieth century. Georg Simmel was one of the first to attempt to analyse the social dynamics of street life as typifying modernity. Simmel's work may seem distant from us, but it underpins much contemporary thinking about everyday life on the street, and has had a major influence on post-modern conceptions of the city.

Georg Simmel spent most of his academic life in Berlin, which by the end of the nineteenth century was regarded as one of the leading cities of the modern era. In 1896 he wrote a brief essay on 'The Berlin Trade Exhibition' of that year, an event widely held to have marked the beginning of Berlin's status as a 'world city'. In this essay, Simmel uses metaphors for the street, and concentrates on the ways in which the spectator, walking through the exhibition's aisles, is constantly shown commodities arranged so as to give them 'new aesthetic significance'. The aisles of the exhibition are akin to the streets of the new 'world city', a place where department stores, shops and arcades offer a constantly changing 'exhibition', in which the modern life of 'exchange' and 'social distance' predominates.

Although Simmel wrote very widely on philosophy, sociology, psychology, art and aesthetics, it is in his analysis of city life, and especially the characteristic behaviour of people in the street, the 'quality' of its nervous energy, that a sociology of modernity begins to emerge for the first time. Simmel himself was urbane and cultured, yet also, as a Jew, manifestly a marginal stranger in the society in which he lived, and thus ideally placed to sense the fleeting and momentary nature of relationships, the ways in which the life of the streets typifies a new and modern form of social existence. One of Simmel's interpreters describes him as 'a modern urban man ... an alien in his native land. Like the stranger he described in one of his most brilliant essays, he was near and far at the same time, a "potential wanderer"'.

Prefiguring what has become almost a cliché of modern urban sociology, Simmel emphasized that the city is not something that emerges independently of social relationships, but is something that is consequent upon changes in their very nature: the City is 'not a spatial entity with sociological consequences, but a sociological entity that is formed spatially'. In one of his key essays, 'The metropolis and mental life', Simmel develops his analysis of the mechanisms whereby the personality of the individual accommodates to the external requirements of the new urban social structures.

Simmel emphasizes the 'neurasthenia' characteristic of city existence, the 'vibe' of street-life as we might now call it. He describes the almost neurotic sense of anxiety and stress which surrounds the urban way of life. Simmel argued that 'the deepest problems of modern life derive from the claim of the individual to preserve the autonomy and individuality of his existence in the face of overwhelming social forces' that are to be found in the metropolis.

At the same time as Simmel insists on the social construction of the modern way of life of the metropolis, he also makes clear that the city itself, as a largescale social organism, does have major consequences for individuals within it. Their reactions to the metropolitan way of life, to the 'modernity' of the city, require that individuals have to 'resist being levelled down and worn out' by this 'social-technological mechanism'. One characteristic form of this resistance is to be found in the search for ways of emphasizing social difference. This concern with distinctiveness, a need for separation from the social mass, is a key feature of modernity, and may even take the form of 'the most tendentious peculiarities, that is, the specifically metropolitan extravagances of mannerism, caprice, and fastidiousness.

Now the meaning of these extravagances does not at all lie in the contents of such behaviour, but rather in its form of "being different", of standing out in a striking manner and thereby attracting attention'. In this prediction of the importance of street-fashion, it is hard not to see in Simmel's analysis a cogent explanation of why metropolitan cities all have a vibrant and aesthetically dominant fashion culture. Simmel came up with an interesting explanation for the considerable attention paid to fashion in modern cities, with his argument that attracting attention on the street and in public places is essential because 'the brevity and infrequency of meetings' necessitates coming to the point as quickly as possible and making a striking impression in the briefest possible time. Simmel's ideas about the city, and in particular the everyday life to be found in the streets, thus operate with very similar notions about fundamental shifts in the way of life of modern, urban people as appear in Toennies' famous distinction between Gemeinschaft and Gesellschaft:

> The trend of modern history appears to Simmel as a progressive liberation of the individual from the bonds of exclusive attachment and personal dependencies in spite of the increasing domination of man by cultural products of his own creation. ...

> The principle of organization in the modern world is fundamentally different: an individual is a member of many well-defined circles, no one of which involves and controls his total personality.

Many of Simmel's ideas that bear upon issues about sociability, social distance and social interaction, about the nature of the street, the modern city and its characteristic way of life, were taken over by the Chicago School of sociologists, and applied in interesting and instructive ways to the smaller-scale analysis of often unregarded features of everyday life. A characteristic feature of the Chicago School was its concern with treating the city itself as a sort of 'social experiment' . In 'The city: suggestions for the investigation of human behaviour in the urban environment', a seminal essay written in 1916, Park argues strongly for the idea that sociology must 'take to the streets' to study urban problems and social processes:

> The city, in short, shows the good and evil in human nature in excess. It is this fact, more than any other, which justifies the view that would make of the city a laboratory or clinic in which human nature and social processes may be most conveniently and profitably studied.

Like the emergent patterns of life on the streets of the modern city of Chicago itself, it was concerned with those aspects of life we find most contingent, particular and fugitive in social interaction. It was greatly influenced by the philosophy of 'pragmatism' developed in North America in the second half of the nineteenth century. The main thrusts of pragmatism are:

(a) that it is important to deal with the concrete and particular rather than the abstract and universal;

(b) that there is no absolute truth, but that the search for meanings and truths is both necessary and possible; and, finally,

(c) that it is anti-dualistic in the sense that it does not separate 'the knower from the known, the subject from the object, or the creative from the determined'.

Pragmatist thought was perhaps most clearly expressed in the Chicago School sociologist W.I. Thomas's famous aphorism, 'when people define a situation as real, it becomes real in its consequences for them'. What pragmatism brings to sociological thinking is precisely the concern with looking closely at the particular and the everyday as ways of understanding social processes, rather than attempting to understand what people really do by deducing their behaviour from large-scale processes or the standpoint of a grand and abstract theory such as Marxism or Social Darwinism. A later commentator on this work suggests that it emerged in an 'attempt to create a unique philosophic rationale for the finer aspects of American society ... characterized as it is by respect for the individual and a belief in gradual change to meet society's fluctuating needs'.

Symbolic interactionism developed out of the work of the Chicago School and especially that of the social psychologist G.H. Mead. He argued that social behaviour depended on a complex system of agreed meanings that are learned through the process of symbolic interaction, that is of seeing yourself as others see you. This involves role-playing, and the play-acting of children is a way of learning how to live in society and to use appropriate actions and words to be understood and to behave appropriately in particular roles and situations.

The Chicago School sociologists used this approach to understand the everyday relations of people in modern urban settings. They were concerned with the way in which understanding social interaction requires sensitivity to its 'fluidity and its accent ... on flexible interpersonal relationships as a basis for an understanding of the working of society'. Because of this concern with the pragmatic nature of life in the US city, great attention was paid to the life of the streets themselves. Robert Park told his students researching in the city of Chicago to look for their subjects on the street corners, in the dance-halls and bars, in the immigrant ghettos, among the flop-houses (cheap hotels), and in the 'hobo' (homeless persons) areas which had become a feature of the city.

The Chicago School generated an enormous range of social studies of everyday life, producing a rich and highly detailed analysis of the minutiae of everyday life, much of it conducted in the public and semi-private spaces of the street and its locales. As the symbolic interactionist approach emerged in the 1930s and 1940s it became clear that it understood the urban street as a primary site of, and even in some senses a synonym for, the social life of the street.

Chicago sociologists argued that by observing the ways in which 'normality' is constructed in public spaces, we can begin to understand how deviant behaviour can occur. Indeed, normality itself becomes something to be explained. The emphasis on the symbolic meaning to the individual of his/her actions that was introduced by the Chicago School sociologists led directly to studies of groups and their deviation from this 'norm'.

Normality of Street Life

Racial, class and gender divisions are features of the social order of 'the street' as experienced by people in most societies. This may be more acutely felt by young people, because of their more intensive use of 'the street' as a locale for leisure activity, and as a geographical space defining identity. The study by Watt and Stenson of a town in south-east England examines young people's uses and perceptions of public space in relation to issues of safety and danger. Following on from Whyte's 'Cornerville', this study calls two of the areas studied 'Streetville and 'Workville'. It compares the views of urban and suburban youth, reflecting the typical spatial division of working and middle classes, and also introduces the different experience that young women have of public space.

Watt and Stenson emphasize the basic similarities in the ways in which people from different social, gender and ethnic groups negotiate the public space of the town which they studied. As their work shows, a complex set of interactions emerge that enable residents and visitors to negotiate the threats and dangers posed by the street. In short, they become 'streetwise', because the street itself is perceived as dangerous - and racial or ethnic labelling of an area is often enough to reinforce this perception.

The best adaptation for successfully negotiating street encounters appears to be to develop 'street wisdom', to become, in other words, street-wise. It would be possible to see this street wisdom as a key feature of modern life in the city, and indeed Simmel's analysis of the effects of the city in 'The metropolis and mental life' is an early suggestion of some of its components. To be 'street-wise' is to possess a particular knowledge of social relationships in order to survive in the social environment of the street, to negotiate its dangers and present social identity in a non-threatening manner, to 'normalize' the situation.

The street may be seen by many people as a space in which the construction of sociability is problematic and fragile, ready at any moment to break down under the threat of social disorder. Only by creating communal structures, or though systems of surveillance and control, can social order be maintained. The 'normality' of street life, its potential for social cohesion, can thus become a problem requiring external agencies such as the police.

'Normality' is not really a problem for classical social theory: the 'everyday' or quotidian is simply subsumed within a totalizing picture of how society operates, and is not assumed to require any special attention. Yet, to be 'street-wise' is to normalize relationships in a deviant setting, and there surely must be a way in which we can relate such seemingly random and personal encounters to a sociological understanding of the street. The social construction of 'normality' thus becomes something to be explained. If 'normality' is indeed something that has to be explained, then one of the most interesting approaches is that of the Canadian sociologist, Erving Goffman.

Goffman was a central figure of the 'second Chicago School' trained in the decade after the Second World War, and his writings represent the more radical approach to the mechanics of everyday life - and in particular the construction of normality - that is characteristic of this new phase of symbolic interactionism. His 'dramaturgical' perspective is a highly influential interpretation of the ways in which social interaction occurs in public places. Goffman paid particular attention in his work to what goes on in public spaces between individuals, and to what marks off strangers from those who have some prior acquaintance with each other. For Goffman, as for symbolic interactionism generally, people are social actors who construct appearances to perform the roles they must play in everyday life.

As the term 'dramaturgical' implies, Goffman's perspective is one which uses the metaphors of play-acting on the stage to describe how meaning is constructed in any social situation. Performance, impression-management, roleplaying and so on are terms which describe the 'artifice' with which the routine of everyday life is maintained. The simple activity of walking down the street to visit a local shop becomes a complex set of staged performances which require us to behave appropriately towards the other people we encounter, and even to manage the interactions involved in queuing to buy our bread. For what is queuing but a complex set of social rules about how to take turns? A classic example of Goffman's approach is his analysis of how couples demonstrate, publicly, their 'couple-dom': by what Goffman calls 'couple tiesigns' such as hand-holding, and the social 'norms' or rules which dictate when and how these tie-signs can or cannot be displayed:

> There is a rule in formal etiquette that it is improper for couples to walk down the fashionable shopping streets of a city holding hands. There is another rule that married couples at social parties are supposed to 'mix', that is, to lay aside their excluding relationship temporarily so that they can be active simply in their capacity as members of the party. A corollary of this rule

> is that they are not supposed to hold hands. (They may hold hands on the way to the party and back from the party but not during the party.) It is also the case that although college students can walk on the campus holding hands - in fact that seems to be one of the special places for this sort of activity - they ought not to listen to lectures thusly encumbered. Furthermore, in some social establishments holding hands even outdoors is forbidden.
>
> ... The significance of this discipline will be emphasized if we look at situations where hand-holding seems to be approved and even idealized. In our pictorial world of advertising and movies - if not in the real world - vacationing couples are featured walking down crooked little streets in foreign places holding hands. At issue here is the fact that tourists often feel they do not owe the business streets of foreign societies the deference these places often demand from locals; tourists can therefore withdraw, just as they can wear informal clothing. Further, the very foreignness of the place suggests a slight exposure, if not fear, and, for the woman at least, holding the hand of the one she is paired with is a pictured source of support.

Goffman's work attracted very considerable attention in both the sociological world and the wider media, for it seemed to capture the very essence of existence in modern societies. He focused on the type of social behaviour that can be observed in public locations such as the street, and many of his theories relate to the maintenance of social order in such settings. Being 'street-wise', for instance, involves what Goffman called 'successfully staging a character', or in other words normalizing the way in which people present themselves to others.

There are many connections which link Goffman's dramaturgical approach to the study of everyday life with the 'impressionistic' sociology of Georg Simmel. In both, the emphasis is very much upon the contingent and 'emergent' nature of social relations, the idea that normality has to be continually 'made' by symbolic interaction, and that the everyday life of the streets is something that allows us to observe universal characteristics of social behaviour from smallscale, particular 'snapshots'. But unlike many of their contemporaries who were concerned with creating abstract theory, neither Simmel nor Goffman sought to build a theoretical system from their 'snapshot-like' observations.

Both avoided large-scale theorizing about the social organization of everyday life. In that sense, their work concentrates on the individual's experience of life, on the street and in the modern city, and in modern society generally, to the exclusion of generalized assumptions about how society organizes those experiences. And, in large part, both Simmel and Goffman refer to the 'symbolic' construction of everyday life, to the ways in which the 'interaction order' is made meaningful to individuals. And perhaps this idea that everyday life is itself a sort of mental construct, a set of rules about social performance which all of us have to carry around in our heads, in other words a form of new 'imagination', connects us to the second way of understanding the street.

Imaginary City and its Streets

Georg Simmel taught Robert Park that 'The city is a state of mind'. The city is more than a physical presence, a mass of people and buildings; it is, as Simmel suggested, also an experience. The way in which individuals negotiate the city and its streets requires it also to be seen as 'an abstraction from the material', the imagined environment where we actually live:

> It is true that what we experience is never the city, 'the thing itself'. It is also true that the everyday reality of the city is always a space already constituted and structured by symbolic mechanisms. But representation does not quite get the measure of the relationship between the two realities, for it implies that one reality must be the model for the other, or a copy of it ... If it is not quite a representation, maybe ... it would be more accurate to think of the city as an imagined environment. This environment embraces not just the cities created by the 'wagging tongues' of architects, planners and builders, sociologists and

> novelists, poets and politicians, but also the translation of the places they have made into the imaginary reality of our mental life. ... The city in our actual experience is at the same time an actually existing physical environment, and a city in a novel, a film, a photograph, a city seen on television, a city in a comic strip, a city in a pie chart, and so on.

Charles Baudelaire has come to be seen as a seminal figure for the way in which his ideas express a critical shift in how the city and its streets are imagined. Just as Simmel saw something distinct in the modern city and its effects on the mentality and behaviour of its occupants, Baudelaire is seen as expressing one of the first definitions of modernity, writing in about 1859-60:

> By 'modernity', I mean the ephemeral, the fugitive, the contingent, the half of art whose other half is the eternal and the immutable.

Baudelaire was commenting on 'modern' art rather than modern society - or at least about the modern art of his time. The quote comes from an essay on Constantin Guys, whom Baudelaire idolized as 'The Painter of Modern Life', but who is now not considered as significant. However, Baudelaire has come to be seen as a seminal figure for a number of reasons, and these are tied up with the way in which his ideas have come to express a critical shift in how the city and its streets were imagined. This might be best understood as the imagination producing images of the street and its life. Put in another way, ideas drawn from the modernist aesthetic influence the way in which social relations in the modern city have increasingly come to be conceptualized, and to be understood as sights. Baudelaire was known as a writer until the 1930s, but as the genealogy of modernity itself began to be conceptualized he emerged as a source of key ideas about modernity and its images.

Modernity was 'both a "quality" of modern life as well as a new object of artistic endeavour. For the painter of modern life, this quality is associated with the notion of newness. Thus it is the very novelty of the present, its tawdry fascination with the here and now, rather than the ideals of classical beauty which had so marked earlier conceptions of art, that Baudelaire prizes. He wants us to glory in the juxtaposition of ancient and modern, the setting of timeless ideas of value against the ephemerality of the present.

Baudelaire's ideas are concerned with how an artist might imagine and translate into images the modern city and the life of its streets: what he terms a 'phantasmagoria' of modern life. It is something produced by 'a perceptiveness acute and magical by reason of its innocence' . This is clearly not intended as, nor should it be seen as, an objective description of a city or of the modern way of life to be found in it. Baudelaire is above all interested in establishing a basis for his aesthetic theories.

The ideas about modernity which Baudelaire developed were taken up again in the 1920s and 1930s by Walter Benjamin, a German intellectual working in Paris, who found in them a fruitful source for thinking about the nature of the modern city. For Benjamin, as a Marxist writer, was concerned to link the emergence of modernity with the advance of commodity capitalism and the 'commodity fetishism' (the investment of value in objects) that drives it. Baudelaire's ideas offered the key to the essential motor driving capitalism: as Benjamin notes, he saw the modern as not merely an epoch, but an energy. Benjamin projected (but never completed) a vast work about modernity itself; it was later reconstructed from the fragments left after his death in 1940 and published as Die Passagen-Werk (The Arcades Project). Benjamin finds Baudelaire's theory of the flâneur to be one of the keys to understanding how modern capitalism developed through the emergence of the fascination with novelty.

Benjamin's uses of Baudelaire in his writings - despite being often fragmentary and incomplete - have become highly influential in understanding how we can imagine the modern city and in particular the dynamic driving the life of its streets. They also symbolize an increasing fascination with the cultural dimension of everyday life, as viewed through the output of artists, writers, film-makers, photographers and so on, that has come to be known as the 'cultural turn' in sociology. A much greater attention is increasingly given to the cultural products themselves as indicators of modernity, and the open interpretation which might be accorded to the unfinished nature of Benjamin's work has helped that process to develop.

Walter Benjamin's fascination with the dynamic of modern capitalism as expressed through the life of the streets was not unique in the 1920s and 1930s. Across Europe, young artists and intellectuals were fascinated by the city, by the new spaces and forms created by modern architecture, by the 'machine age' which promised to transform the world of work, and create new products that would answer every conceivable need. Following the First World War there was a widespread desire to look forward. Nowhere was this clearer than in the 'new media' such as film and, especially, photography:

> Dizzying views up to skyscraper peaks, close-ups of gleaming machine parts, anonymous split-second dramas glimpsed on city streets, landforms revealed as near-abstractions from far aloft - such images suggested the impressions that might have been collected by a mobile eye nervously scanning the surfaces of contemporary life.

In France, however, the machine-age optimism of the 'new vision' was tempered by another movement which also gave considerable attention to images of the streets of the modern city: surrealism. The surrealists, in part inspired by the persuasive character of Freudian pyschoanalytic theory, did not rely on reasoned analysis or sober calculation; on the contrary, they saw the forces of reason blocking the access routes to the imagination. For the surrealists, the street became the place where the imagination, the unconscious, was constantly lurking - ready to jump out at any moment from the seemingly ordinary. Photographs, in particular, were able to convey this radical coupling of the unconscious and the 'quotidian' - the everyday. Surrealism thus celebrated the intoxicating, disruptive forces that the image might unleash.

Louis Aragon, in his 1925 novel Paysan de Paris, remarked: 'The vice called surrealism is ... the uncontrolled provocation of the image for its own sake, and for the element of unpredictable perturbation and metamorphosis which it introduces into the domain of representation. [For] each man there awaits ... a particular image capable of annihilating the entire universe'. As a result, the surrealists searched among the most ordinary and 'documentary' of images to discover the dynamics of urban life and in particular its key imaginary elements. They discovered the street images made by Eugene Atget. In his photographs of the deserted streets of old Paris, of shop windows haunted by elegant mannequins, of the gaze of a young prostitute, the surrealists recognized their own vision of the city as a 'dream capital', an urban labyrinth of memory and desire.

Walter Benjamin, too, writes about Atget's Parisian work: for it deals with the new spaces of modernity in a fashion that allows him an insight into the motors of commodity capitalism. But Benjamin's purposes are different from those of Aragon and Breton, whose fascination with the 'intoxicating reveries about a sort of secret life of the city' are in distinct contrast with his desire to 'waken the world from its dream' or in other words the fantasy life of commodity fetishism. Especially for those beginning to explore the world outside the studio with unobtrusive handheld cameras, the surrealist model of an urban flâneur, a wanderer open to chance encounters, was crucial. Aragon believed that if one were attuned to the fleeting gestures, enigmatic objects, and veiled eroticism glimpsed in the street, an unsuspected pattern of affinities - a new kind of poetic knowledge - might be revealed.

In the late 1920s and early 1930s the belief that the camera could snare and fix these moments of instantaneous, lyrical perception had many important adherents among young photographers in Europe. Their images, which found scenes of great interest and beauty in the theatre of everyday life to be found in the streets of great cities such as Berlin, Paris and London, were widely distributed to new mass audiences via the media of the popular illustrated magazine, which emerged in Germany in the 1920s and was to be taken up in the rest of Europe and the USA in the 1930s. They helped in the process by which the everyday life of the streets came to be thought of as important and celebrated as part of popular culture -i.e. the culture of the mass of ordinary people.

In the late 1920s the French poet and novelist Pierre Mac Orlan proposed that the camera could open a window onto the realm of another aspect of the everyday, what he termed the 'social fantastic'. Mac Orlan was no surrealist; nor was he a comprehensive theorist of photography. He was, however, perhaps the most perceptive French photographic critic during this period, and he developed what amounted to a modern poetics of the medium.

Taking his cue from the painter Fernand Léger, who had noted the 'shock of contrast' provided by a modern billboard set in the countryside, Mac Orlan reflected at length on the collision between technological civilization and the remnants of a popular culture rooted in the past. His notion of the 'social fantastic' referred to the frequently bizarre juxtapositions of the archaic and the modern, the human and the inanimate, glancingly encountered each day in the streets of the modern city - as, for example, in André Kertész's perception of the uncanny correspondence between anonymous passers-by and the cut-out figures of an advertising display. This mysterious new dimension of social reality could, according to Mac Orlan, be best explored by photographers, the most 'lyrical, meticulous witnesses' of the present. Mac Orlan too recognized Eugène Atget as the precursor of a new photographic sensibility which is rooted in the life of the streets. Such imagery has fed into the public subconscious and influenced how 'the street' is perceived. It will be evident that the 'imagined city' that emerges from the minds of Benjamin, the surrealists and Mac Orlan in the 1920s and 1930s is increasingly a place of poetic or dramatic images, rather than of an apparently 'objective' social observation.

Life and Complexity in Urban Space

What happened to the city streets until 1973 seems reasonably easy to understand, although the story above is fragmentary and merely indicated. The development since is not possible to see as clearly yet, but that something happened to urban planning and design around 1980 is obvious. The growth of Northwest European metropolises had come almost to a halt. Gentrification processes were going on in some older inner city districts. The aesthetics of modernist architecture and modernist space was heavily criticised, and new kinds of projects - seemingly built on ideas of pre-modern urban streets - saw the light of day.

While in Europe the re-introduction of the idea of city-streets was carried out as part of a public enterprise, in the US the re-introduction had mainly a commercial background, most clearly expressed in some of the Festival Markets, and earlier in parts of Disneyland. On both sides of the Atlantic the interest in the traditional city street was simultaneously promoted by efforts of building heritage preservation, which, beside all its merits, also have a tendency to turn old city parts into the rigor mortis of outdoor museum areas.

The renewed interest in the traditional city street did not last long, with the exception of streets in the old urban commercial cores, where pedestrianisation and growth of street life take place. In 1987, it was clearly not the new city streets that interested the avant-garde architects any more. This street interest became even more short-lived than the post-modernist interest in the aesthetic language of classical architecture.

In the last couple of years avant-garde architecture has gone trough a period of "de-construction", experimenting with contradictory and sometimes aggressive new combinations, where the major purpose seems to be experiments of pure form, and the self-expression of the architect, though not without the creation of a bit of mystery and astonishment. While this might contribute to the diversity and complexity of cities, if related to the question of city streets and human life in urban space - that is to the context of the city - this has not been the case.

The results, that are most often seen in the academies and schools of architecture, are often at the same time confused and full of aesthetic hubris - a large number of visually artistic but abstract drawing-board projects, disconnected from local context and empty of life. At this point the architecture of avant-gardists like Tschumi, Libeskind and Eisenman, and smaller mind followers, would be dangerous, was it not for the deep crises of the financial sector and the construction industry, that saves us from large scale experimenting with cities and the lives of people.

Abstractness and Inwardness of Urban Space

If we go to other professions than architects and planners to search for a deeper understanding of the lack of street life in most parts of contemporary cities, there is generally not much interest in the question. In North America, if asked, many would blame it on poverty, drugs and crime, the homeless and the gangs: in short the undesirables. In North Western Europe the weather would get part of the blame, although this is only partly true, as is shown by the growth of downtown street-life here in the last decades. Many would also blame it on the car. Others would blame TV, the average American watching more than 30 hours a week, the Europeans not quite reaching this level yet, but catching up.

Only a few would see the lack of street-life as a symptom of deep structures of modern society. Two intellectuals that have done it since the end of the 1960s - are the French philosopher Henri Lefebvre and the New York sociologist Richard Sennett. Both struggle to get street life back not only in sheer defiance of deep social obstacles, but to get rid of the roots of these obstacles themselves. Together they show, that to get life back on the streets we have to deal with forces as strong as Capital, God and Enlightenment.

Lefebvre and Sennett see the problems of modern urban space on two different polar axes. Lefebvre focuses most heavily on the contradiction of abstract space versus differential space, Sennett most heavily on the contradiction of spatial inwardness versus spatial outwardness. These spatial contradictions - if crossed - can define different aspects of the our city of interest, and state our problem of street-life in general terms.

According to Lefebvre we live in a capitalist society, that has a general tendency to turn the formerly absolute space of nature and early human culture into abstract space. Capitalist space is produced as commodity and as distribution networks. Therefore, seen from an exchange point of view, it should be as "general" as possible. The right-angle repetitious geometrical grids of the North American city can partly be seen as an example of this tendency.

Industrialised mass housing and mass office building are other obvious examples. But over and over again, economic competition and political struggle create a contradictory space, adding new differences to the original differences of space given by nature and history that so far have not been completely "neutralised". In this way, according to Lefebvre, spaces of difference are produced to some extent, although the general tendency is the production of abstract space. Since the 1960s differential space is also to some extent produced as a result of the growing importance of leisure and non-labour - a tendency of growing importance that may lead to a paradigmatic change in the concept of space.

According to Sennett, we also live in a capitalist society, but as he does not believe in Lefebvre's political ideas of great political revolutions, Sennett has to focus differently in his spatial analyses. If the capitalist economic "mechanisms" cannot be basically changed within a reasonable time, or without too large human costs, then the struggle for a better city has to be primarily cultural - not primarily political-economical.

This interpretation of the differences of Lefebvre's and Sennett's basic points of view has to be included in the understanding, why Sennett has to fight God and Enlightenment instead of Capitalism as such. That the struggle for a better city is in vain without a cultural perspective, is also Lefebvre's point of view, as he sees no attractive cultural quality in socialist city building so far, but the cultural perspective is not the starting point of his analyses.

The statement of God and Enlightenment as the main villains in Sennett's universe must be further explained though, if we are to understand him right. The God in question is the Christian God, and the problematic aspect of Enlightenment is its quest for a Grand Unity of everything. For Sennett, the common denominator of Christianity and Enlightenment is the perversion of the relation between inside and outside in a way that promotes inwardness and cripples outwardness. The problem of Christianity goes all the way back to the early middle ages, as expressed by Augustin's rejection of the worldly city in favour of the city of Heavens.

The problem of secular Enlightenment, on the other hand, is its attempt to overcome contradictions by escaping them in the name of unity, or by trying to brutally enforce a non-contradictory unity. This, of course, is doomed to fail. Inwardness continues as a result. To Sennett, the inward-outward axis of orientation is related to the questions of relations between private and public life, as well as to the relations between the Self and the Others in more general terms.

Sennett wants to turn people outward instead of inward - towards the streets and the encounter of human differences - instead of towards the home and the psychoanalyses with or without professional help. You could say that Sennett think it is both necessary and possible to break out of the mutual contradiction and unity that is a driving engine in most of Woody Allen's films - the alienating metropolis and a growing need for psychoanalyses.

But to turn outward, Lefebvre would say, is extremely difficult in a society based on private ownership to capital and land, and in a society dominated by large corporations and public bureaucracy. In spite of that, Lefebvre would agree that every possibility to turn outward should be cared for. In the end of The Production of Space he actually mentions the possibility of a reformist strategy towards differential space and a new society. In a moment, we will get back to Lefebvre's and Sennett's conceptions of the city to fight for, but before that let us look at the diagram 1.

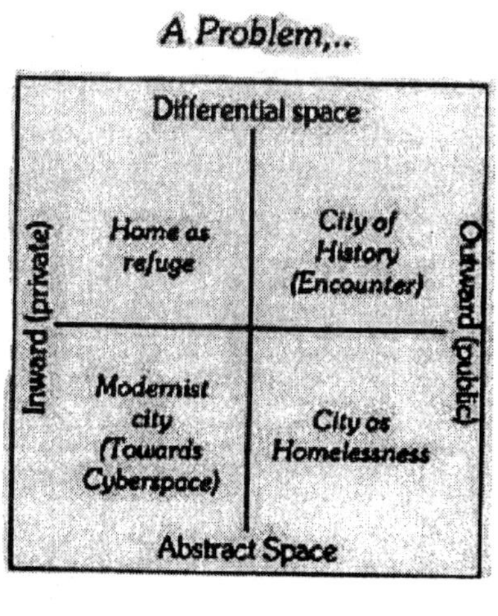

Diagram 1

The abstract space/differential space dimension can be seen as an axis of spatial production, the inward/outward dimension as an axis of spatial orientation. The crossing gives us four quadrants:

The first quadrant of "Diagram 1" can be interpreted as the "City of History" in a double sense - both as the historical pre-modernist city of streets and squares, which is as old as the preserved history of human societies (about 10000 years) - and as the city, where time makes a difference. This is the city of human encounter of other humans in real life, and the encounter of culture of different times.

The third quadrant - the diametrically opposite - can be interpreted as the "Modernist City". This is the city of advanced capitalism: an urban anti-space of isolated and inwardly oriented built objects sprinkled in a technological landscape, interwoven with distance-keeping lawns to look at, simulating naturalness and simple countryside pleasures. Although this city is heavily focused on time - trying to catch up with time all the time - it kills time, as it can only develop through the destruction of history and through repetition. This is the reason, why Berman's book on modernity got its title from Marx' and Engels' Communist Manifesto: All that is solid melts into air.

Modernity is the new as ever the same. In this "City of modernity", there is not much encounter of real and different human beings. On the contrary it becomes increasingly clear, although Lefebvre and Sennett do not say much about it, that the ultimate "Modernist City" is an electronic network. Skyscraper areas are still being built in the image of downtown Chicago, Manhattan and le Corbusier's "Plan Voisin", but the true modernist city of today is the electronic portable office of combined mobile-phones and portable computers, including portable fax-machines and networked modems, connected to satellite-based world wide services 24 hours a day. If You want to, You can even include global satellite navigation systems with a guarantied accuracy of 18 meters. If You have the right equipment, it does not matter where on the globe You are, and at the same time You can be sure that You cannot get lost, except in the electronic networks themselves. We now begin to see, that the ultimate modern city is made up of virtual realities located in cyberspace: the anti- space of real experiential space.

The second quadrant of "Diagram 1" can be interpreted as the "Indoor Private Home", where we can escape to the safety of the familiar, our personal things and the shallow depths of spatially and socially contained intimacy. This is not to say that we do not need homes, or that the heavy focus on housing in the modernist city has been all wrong. On the contrary: the home is necessary for the development of individual human beings. At the same time though, it is to state that the home is a trap, if it is not complemented by a city of encounter. Today, the threat to the family is not located as much in the streets, as it is in homes of isolation.

The fourth quadrant can be interpreted as the "City of Homelessness" - in the double sense of an outside world that we do not care about, and a home for the really homeless - the backside of the coin of the modern City, exploding in the face of us all over the Western industrialised world.

Why do abstractness and inwardness contradict urban possibilities and urban life? This should be a little more clear by now:

— Abstract space is intended to generalise exchange value. As a consequence space is planned in a way that contradicts the promotion of difference. Town planning and building codes contribute to enforce homogeneity to a large extent.

— As for inwardness: as long as we focus too much on inwardness, people are separated from the differences of other people, and in the end they get alienated to themselves. We get lack of solidarity and psychological problems. If we do not experience ourselves in direct relation to others, the others get unreal to us and we get unreal ourselves too.

It is a big problem, that our society has been extremely afraid of difference in real life. At the same time the large need for difference is shown by the obsessive focus on difference in entertainment and sports through various kinds of media.

Much urban sociology and urban geography have spread confusion on the urban question, not only World War II regionalists like Mumford, but also left-wing intellectuals of the last two and a half decades. Manuel Castells killed the city as a theoretical object in the beginning of the 1970s. But it turned up again in the form of "collective consumption", then metamorphosed into the question of spatial and social practices of "everyday-life" routines, and a female perspective on the role of the local community.

Lefebvre was there all the time, taking part in the discussions, but not very many listened and even fewer understood what he tried to say. Admitted, he was difficult, tried to cover vast areas and was French. He wrote on "everyday-life" already in the 1950s. From 1968 to 1974 he took up questions of the city - not on1y in relation to different modes of production as seen from a Marxist "systemic" point of view, but also as an urban experience of humans living in the city - the city as lived space. He even claimed the city a human right. Later he had to focus on the role of the modern state.

In his last book on the city - The Production of Space - Lefebvre heavily states the human need of difference as counter-weight to everyday routine, and the decisive role of difference in opening up new social and political opportunities. As capitalism creates contradictions in urban space, spaces of difference emerge, that can be transformed into counter-spaces of new human possibilities. If we cross-read his books on the city and on space thoroughly, we will find that the important qualities of differential space and counter-space have to do with aspects like:

> social and other human differences, the meeting of strangers, play and eroticism, human works as unique objects, possibilities

> for the unplanned, unpredictability, inter-change and inter-active communication, as well as the use of all senses. All this should be human rights in urban space, according to Lefebvre! There is not much to learn about an urban design of difference in Lefebvre's books, though. He also thinks that architects and especially urban planners normally do more harm than good.

Sennett's characteristics of his urban spaces of interest resemble those of Lefebvre's in many ways but Sennett explicitly mentions the street, as the most important general aspect of the city. When it comes to the question of urban design, Sennett is also as negative about the professionals involved, as is Lefebvre. Although Sennett tries to find the keys to an urban design that makes a difference, he does not come up with very much of direct practical use either. He clearly is in favour of discontinuities and non-linearities in social space as well as in physical space, but nobody can learn how to build cities from his book. The distance from theory to practice is either too far, or his advise are already better described elsewhere in some of the more practical urban design literature.

Anyhow, the facts remain that the urban spaces of encounter, difference and possibilities which Lefebvre and Sennett have pointed to need to be further investigated, as well as the knowledge and the design practices that can promote them. To focus on the city of encounter is to focus on strangers, randomness, chance, the unexpected, discovery, adventure, etc. - and it is to focus on the space outside, that is to focus on the streets of cities.

Issues of Urban Complexity

Cities, as physical entities, are often seen in opposition to nature, but in nature, as well as in the city, both ordering and chaotic processes are at work. And both develop through time. The result is complexity. Today there is almost no nature, that has not already been altered by man. Man does not live in first (not manmade) nature any more, but in a second (manmade) nature. The city can in fact be seen as the most complex part of this second nature. First nature, as well as second nature, starts off from rather simple forms, and develops towards the more complex. The same is true of the capacity of the individual human being in his or her development from childhood to maturity. As human beings with roots in nature, we can't live with pure order. We can't live with chaos either. We can only thrive in complexity. Both first nature and second nature need a differential space for complexity to develop and to remain. It is at the edges of difference, that life develops most intensely, whether that is e.g. the edge between a forest and a meadow or the edge between private and public space, buildings and street.

The transitional part of nature bridging the gap of first and second nature is the human body itself. The body is the key to humanity, to human complexity, and human space. Whatever mental differences between people - based on different social and economic conditions, culture, individual differences, preferences, etc. - we all have bodies and understand, more or less consciously, that this is the starting point for all of us. Further we all have had a childhood, that in the beginning was body without consciousness. Our ability for sympathy and empathy is basically related to the body. To accept our bodies and wish the best for them is the key to humanity. The body is itself very complex, and includes rhythm, symmetry, front-back, left-right, up-down, body and limbs, warm-cold, colours, growth, ageing, sub-consciousness, etc. - and it directly affects clothing and housing as well.

The latest knowledge on the information-handling of the human brain- and nerve systems show that the capacity of our bodies is far larger than our consciousness. Our senses receive millions of bits every second, but our consciousness can only handle about 16 bits a second. The rest of the information-handling is subliminal. The question of subconsciousness is thus much greater and far more general than Freud thought.

human beings are only partly in control of their bodies. Much philosophy and religion have therefore denied the body, often with disastrous results.

Our understanding of space has to start from the body, because this is from where our human experience starts. Space gets its qualities and quantities through the body. Our body is not like that of a bird, a snail or a fish. Therefore our spatial experience is not related to being in general, but specifically to human bodily being.Concepts of thought and the uses of language are developed in relation to bodily practices as well. Lakoff and Johnson have shown, that metaphorical language is the vehicle of consciousness and builds on elementary bodily experiences. This is why it is possible to say that the body is in the mind. Experiences that we can not handle directly, we understand and express through metaphor (and metonymy), and this at the same time constitutes a common basis for creativity applicable to both science and art. That is to say, we handle complexity through metaphor, and by metaphorical creativity human reality grows ever more complex.

A Perspective..

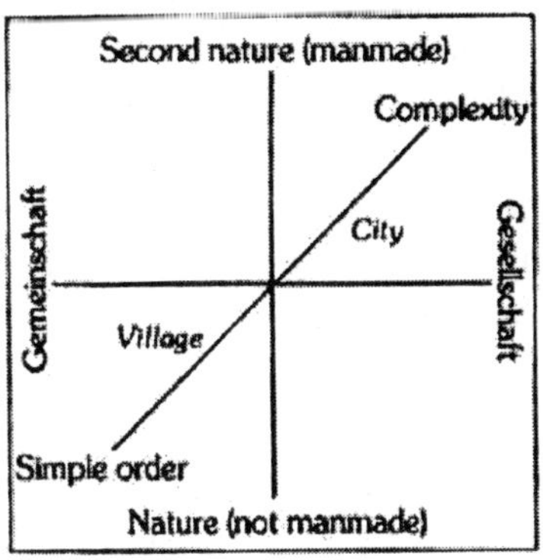

Diagram 2

Society includes the question of complexity too. Tönnies' concept of a polar axis of society as expressed in the opposition of Gesellschaft to Gemeinschaft, is here an especially interesting one, and it has recently been discussed by Asplund. To explain it very shortly, Gemeinschaft is the traditional kin-based village society, while Gesellschaft is the money based society of strangers in the City.

The bridges between Gemeinschaft and Gesellsehaft are money and the individual. Both take on new importance at the end of the Middle Ages through the growth of trade and the division of labour. The individual is a phenomenon related to the development of a money economy. Money makes the free individual possible, which in turn further promotes the money economy. This adds a new level to complexity. Not only is there a personal history behind every individual a history that is partly unique - but individuality as a general category is in itself historical. It emerged with historical time in antiquity, almost vanished in early Christianity, reappeared in the late middle ages and was reinstituted with the birth of the Renaissance.

In the 1960s the transformation of industrialised western man to individuals had come so far, that almost every child had a bedroom of their own, i. e. a built space of their own - a situation unprecedented in human history. From this stage the question of individuality increasingly becomes a double one - from basically depending upon growing separation to the double question of separation and relation - from the focus on the "I", to the focus on the relation between "You" and "I". In the city this question necessarily have to include the question of people, that You do not know: people from other city districts, anonymous people, strangers, foreigners, great numbers of people and differences of culture too large for anyone ever to get to know them all. In this situation of Gesellschaft humanity and humane development is related to the acceptance of strangers, not only to keep up peace, diversity and creativity, but as a condition for the further development of individuality as well.

Simmel already understood almost a century ago that an important part of urban social relations has to do with strangers, but 20th century sociology has focused almost entirely on interaction between and inside groups and classes as collective phenomena and not very much on the interaction of individual strangers. Psychology on the other hand has focused on the single individual either in dose relation to family experiences or on the relation between the single individual and the physical environment. Therefore the meeting of strangers in urban space has been a field of only sporadic attention. Asplund has recently pointed to the importance of "elementary social life" and elementary social responsiveness which can take place also among strangers. He has further noted, that randomness and coincidence has become an integral and essential part of the urban conditions of life, that is of Gesellschaft.

The perspective on social relations has been too narrow also in other ways. Beginning in the 17. century, a mechanistic world view developed. Although this world view started to disintegrate with early 20. century physics, it continued to influence society. It so happened, that the mechanistic perspectives of modernist architecture and city-planning reached its full development at the very moment when the mechanistic perspective broke down in modern physics. Within the mechanic modernist view the city could best be compared to a machine, and as a consequence urban development had to be looked upon as strategic planning, where one decision-centre knows what is best for people and therefore can plan for them. Habermas' critical discussion of modernist rationality has a lot to do with this, and he now favours a theory of communicative action.

Habermas' communicative actions originate in Gemeinschaft too, but first really become a problem in Gesellschaft, with its growing complexity. A focus on communicative action - contrary to strategic action - as a model of social development, has deep consequences for the understanding of cities, as has Habermas' complementary notion of system-worlds versus lifeworlds. The concept of communicative action makes it possible to take into account both normative and expressive social processes, as well as the socialisation and maturing from child-hood to adulthood of each individual.

During the last 25-30 years efforts have been made to understand complexity in architecture and urban development through analyses of languages, especially through semiotics. As language has to with communication, it is tempting quickly to go further into questions of language. Urban space is full of language: spoken language, written language, bodily gestures, fashion and personal expression of clothes and other attributes as well as of the body itself, pictograms, architectural language, etc. Languages enforce the notions of difference, as well as the possibilities of identification and encounter.

The different kinds of language add to the complexity of urban space. Although semiotics may have something to contribute to all kinds of language, it is important to note, that spoken and especially written language is only one part of the spectre of languages, and that different languages have different backgrounds and different rules. Visual and musical languages are quite different from spoken and especially written languages. As the city contains all kinds of language at once, a study of the city as language is an immense task, which is very difficult to undertake. This takes us straight back to the questions of complexity.

The notion of complexity is difficult to grasp in practical life, and even more difficult to handle theoretically. Or, properly, it has been until recently. Today information theory and "chaos" theory has a general understanding and definition of complexity, although there is no general way to measure or compute it in practical life.

Complexity is neither simple order nor a complete mess. It is something between order and chaos, and it grows at the edge of chaos. A complete mess or chaos cannot be represented in any shorter or more compact way than the mess itself. A simple and static order on the contrary can be represented as a short formula. Complexity is different from both of these, and although it often is a result of rather simple formulas too, it includes iterations, the repetition of patterns - taking part of the result of the former round as the input to the next - and most often also adding some randomness to the process. This means that complexity is a result of a process unfolded in time. From the point of view of information theory, complexity is the result of information that has been discarded. Only in special cases is it possible to figure out the kind and amount of discarded information. This is why there is no general way to measure or compute complexity in practical life.

The new theories of chaos and complexity, which has been developed since the late 1970s and with the necessary help of computers, are changing our view of the world and the view of ourselves. They show that complex patterns can grow from simple formulas, i. e. fractal patterns, and that many processes are non-linear, discontinuous and irreversible. The forming of structures or patterns over time that are neither simple nor completely chaotic, is the creation of depth. To humans this is related to meaning. This becomes important as the new theories cover several scales at once, also scales relevant to the size of man, unlike the theories of most modern physics that tend to concentrate on the scales of the atoms or the universe. Suddenly science is related again to immediate experiences of everyday life.

The social complexity of the city must basically be understood as Gesellschaft, not as a collection of Gemeinschaft. This is not easy to do right away, as urban planning in the 20 century has focused so heavily on the promotion of Gemeinschaft through the construction of family dwellings and neighbourhood units. Social complexity cannot be fought by making the city less complex though, as this will reduce outward activity and increase personal psychological problems. Lack of outward complexity will also hit the weakest groups hardest, because they will be left with the worst parts of abstract space.

The physical complexity of the city, first of all has to be seen as a street phenomenon. Streets are at the same time the general ordering structure of the city and the kind of space where urban encounters can take place on a wide scale in everyday life. Physically complex urban space in the form of urban streets increases outwardness: private services as well as out-ward oriented do-it-yourself activities, the meeting of strangers, coincidence of trajectories, etc. Urban streets of this kind, that at the same time contain the possibilities of incremental change, further the creative aspects of Gesellschaft, while abstract space or physical complexity understood wrongly will further the destructive aspects of Gesellschaft. In The Metropolis and Mental Life, Simmel has pointed to both the creative and destructive aspects of Gesellschaft, so this is nothing new - but, with a few exceptions, there has been no reasonably developed understanding of this in relation to the planning and design of cities.

The nature of complex geometrical pattern of urban space has a profound influence on the distribution of people's movement and the location of activities, most modern space being highly segregated, while older deformed street-grids normally integrate. Highly integrated outdoor urban spaces, containing people in a socially undifferentiated way, constitutes a virtual community of possible encounter. Urban streets are essential to Hillier's concept of urban life, but Hillier's theory does not include absolute population density, nor does it include what goes on in the city at heights above approximately 2 meters. Neither is he interested in what the facades look like, except the number of entrances. On the other hand Hillier's Social Logic of Space includes an understanding of the generation of complex social-spatial patterns from a combination of simple rules and randomness. In Hillier's theory depth of space is also very important. This spatial notion of "depth" is quite different from the historical notion of "depth" in the theory of complexity.

Modernity's relation to time often goes against complexity though. Modernity is the tragedy of destruction in order to create the new as ever the same. In this way, post-modernity has to run in front of modernity. It is inherent to modernity to try to reduce complexity, because modernity wants everything to be new. Sometimes it succeeds with devastating consequences. Through a developed notion of complexity, the questions of the theoretical status and usefulness of the concepts of human ecology and urban ecology may possibly also be interpreted anew. Maybe the decisive aspect that unites the general concept of ecology with "human ecology" as it was understood by the Chicago school of urban studies in the 1920s is complexity? And maybe the understanding and liking of complexity can save the "urban" in the "urban ecology" of today from being anti-urban from the outset.

Urban Design of Complexity

From a social point of view, the city of complexity is identical with the city of social diversity, interwoven with some social homogenisation in various areas. Diversity should be seen as the dominant aspect, homogenisation being accepted to some extent as a spatial expression of different subcultures of choice. Social homogenisation through standardised abstract citybuilding promoted by the state or by corporations should be avoided, as this will create an anti-city, which most easily can be compared to institutions like prisons or to company towns.

Social diversity has proved to be quite difficult to build into new city areas, although it increasingly has become a goal. Socially mixed housing is hard to achieve in practice for many reasons: a segregated housing market with several different financing and economic support systems, the scale of operation of public and private planning and construction agencies, publicly enforced penalties and premiums adversary to moving from one dwelling to another, and the lack of a unified taxation system in metropolitan areas, as they normally are split up into different communes with different taxation-levels, that has little to do with the level of services. Although it is not easy, large scale housing segregation can and ought to be countered. The means to do so have been described many times, and shall not be repeated here.

The question of integration of dwellings with services and places of work in new city areas has proved to be even more difficult, also where it has been programmatically wanted. The large size of many contemporary units of work is part of the problem. The difficulty to plan for them in advance together with housing is another. Services and places of work cannot be dictated to move into new buildings, unless they are all public enterprises. Public enterprises can be no general solution, though - only supplementary - as we need to stabilise the public sector from a taxation point of view, to release the potential creativity and activity in people, and to promote marked-based private services.

Large contemporary places of work kill street life. It should be remembered though, that the large corporations do not contain the majority of jobs in the contemporary city. Most of the jobs are to he found in middle- sized and small firms, and in the public sector. Although it is often true that the public sector also has a built in tendency towards hugeness and centralisation, this can be fought and changed politically. What is most important, the large numbers of new jobs are in very small firms, while the large private corporations lay off people through automation: the ultimate robotised corporate factory or electronic office having almost no people working there at all.

Today, many of the newly created jobs in small firms are invisible, as they often take place in inward-oriented homes. This may reduce the possibilities for their further development: for co-operation, for direct advertising in urban public space, for interplay with the public, and for activities that need shop or workshop kind of spaces. The only real advantages of dwelling-based small firms are reductions of costs of rent, less commuting, and the possibilities to overlap work with family duties. The last two could be taken care of in the traditional street-shop environment as well with shops at ground level and dwelling on the first floor. The main obstacle is the cost of renting floor-space for work.

If social diversity versus social homogenisation is the major issue of social complexity in the city, then the major issue of physical complexity probably is the axis of "Grand Unified Plans and Designs" versus "streets of incremental change". "Grand Unified Plans and Designs" has been the dominant tendency of city-planning and architecture since the beginning of the renaissance period. The Italian city of Ferrara of the 1490s is probably the first modern city in this sense and at the same time the first street-killing at a grand scale through the building of completely inward-oriented palaces at the most important street crossing of the new city extension.

The implementations of "Grand Unified Plans and Designs" have had their ups and downs since the 15th century, mainly as a consequence of economic ups and downs, and the degree of centralised government - the states of absolute monarchy and the 20th century corporative states being the most dominant promoters of these kinds of plans and designs. The more decentralised and democratic the state, the less "Grand Unified Plans and Designs" and the more incremental physical additions and change we will find - although it is not therefore true the other way around. One important reason, that makes the mixing of social groups and the mixing of activities, dwellings, services and places of work so difficult, beside the reasons mentioned earlier, is the way modern cities are planned and built as "Grand Unified Plans and Designs".

Streets can have two different basic kinds of character: The absolutist or corporate street on the one hand, with a strong will towards physical homogeneity, or at least with a strong will to decide almost everything about the street from one centre of decision-making, and on the other hand the democratic incremental street, accepting physical heterogeneity and decisions with many centres. In this way, there is a relation between the physical appearance of the street and the way in which the decisions about the street take place. Some corporations and public agencies want to build streets today that look physically complex, through decision-making at only one or at a very small number of decision centres. This may fool somebody for sometime, but not many for a long time, unless these kinds of streets are left to become more truly complex later on, and their spatial structure permits it.

The question of incremental additions has been raised before, e. g. by Christopher Alexander in his New Theory of urban Design, but it has not been done consequently from the point of view of the urban street. The city of true complexity has democratic incremental streets and a street pattern with a high geometrical integration. These streets create a virtual community of potential encounter of strangers. New York's Greenwich Village is an example, which shows that contemporary art and culture do not grow best in modernist space, but in old industrious streets.

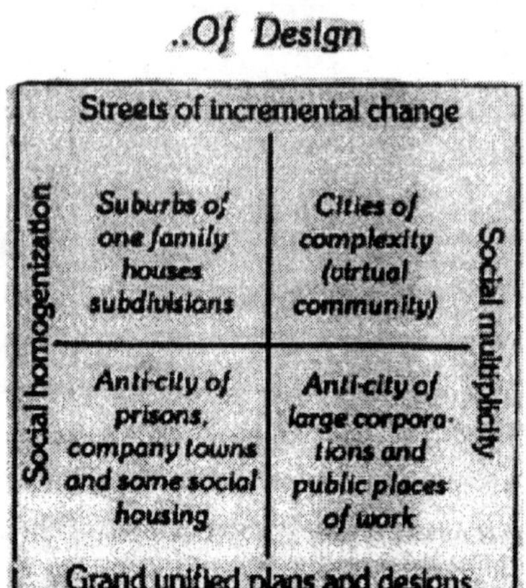

Digarm 3

The fourth quadrant of Diagram 3 - the possibility of simultaneous social diversity and "Grand Unified Plans and Designs" - was more difficult to label, than the rest. The only union of social diversity and "Grand Unified Plans and Designs" we immediately can think of, are in the built work-place structures of large corporations and large public administrations themselves - but here the free admission and initiatives of people are severely restricted. The functioning of these structures is also mainly inwardly oriented towards the organisations themselves. Therefore they are "anti-city". If it is true, that social diversity is impossible in "Grand Unified Plans and Designs" at the level of the city, then urban planning and architecture have to do serious rethinking.

In the end we find a new polar axis, a new overall contradiction that contains the essence of the urban question today. This is an axis between the 3rd quadrant of the first crossing (Diagram 1) and the 1st quadrant of the third crossing (Diagram 3) - or to speak out: between the modernist city and the real city of complexity. This, at the same time, is the axis of electronic virtual reality tending towards cyberspace, versus a virtual real world community in Hillier's sense of the outward, urban street-form of possible real encounter and open solidarity of strangers. This axis is not an axis that we can choose to have or not to have. As the coming of virtual reality is unavoidable - and it is almost already here - the only thing we can possibly do to create a balance, is to complement virtual reality, as much as we can, by building real city streets.

If complexity is a result of a historical process, it can be questioned if urban complexity can be designed at all. As the notion of "Grand Unified Plans and Designs" has pointed to, we very often think of urban planning and design as an all comprehending, integral and complete single project for a part of a city including several buildings, a part of a street network complete with furnishing, etc. These kinds of plans and designs most often reduce complexity, although some complexity can be included or added by keeping parts of earlier nature and/or buildings, or by having several architects working independently, but with some set of design rules for the project.

True complexity can not be designed in the form of an overall project, though. It has to grow piecemeal through gradual intervention of different actors representing different economic units. This raises the question, to the degree that urban planning and urban design can be avoided as overall integrated plans and designs: a difficult question in societies of rapid economic and technological change, paired with lack of cultural rootedness, and including cultural diversity. Beside, this question might threaten some established systems-worlds and professions as well.

Incremental and fragmentary streets need not necessarily be ugly. Harmony and homogeneity are to some extent necessary for an aesthetic experience to take place, but changes and breaks are necessary too. The question of ugliness - as of beauty - is a double question of aesthetic ideals and communicative action, including the question of languages of architecture and the character of the decision-making process. It also includes the question of time and the speed of change - as the dialogue of architectural expressions in real life streets takes place at the slowest of all paces in human society -some built individuals along the streets making statements and raising questions, that might first be answered with a delay of years, decades and even centuries. The question of architecture as language should basically be seen as a dialogue between buildings through time.

- more people are working extra jobs and women's 'second shift' gives them a 65 hour average work week
- inequality between skilled and unskilled workers increased
- unemployment was on average double that of the previous twenty-five years
- the volatility of employment (labour market churning) increased by over 40% between 1970 and 1987
- union membership declined from 35% in 1955 to under 15% in 1996
- strikes fell almost 90% from peaks in the 1950s, 60s and 70s to the doldrums of the 90s
- the wealth of the bottom 40% fell by half from 1983 to 1992 while that of the top 20% grew by one-fifth

The chief determinants of wages need to be laid out conceptually and weighed against the evidence. The first is the *productivity of labour*, or the state of production. Where productivity is high and rising, wages should reflect this over time — if the profit-wage split is constant. Long term improvement in production (technological progress) is the essence of industrialisation, the principal source of the wealth of the advanced capitalist nations, and the origin of favorable wages compared with the poorer regions of the earth. High productivity is a necessary but not sufficient condition for good wages, however.

Productivity only delivers good wages if the working class has the historic capacity to extract a good *price for its labouring power*, i.e., a fair share of the social product. Distribution of income depends first of all on the price of labour-power established in the labour market. Supply and demand conditions may be more or less favorable to workers and wages. They gain leverage against capital through their relative scarcity, unity and experience in the market(s) for labour; they usually lose where supply is too great, workers

7

Global Trends in Labour Markets

Today, working class around the world are confronting numerous challenges that they have never faced. Majority of them are no better off than they were a quarter century ago and many are much worse off. In the Northern Tier countries for the period 1973 to 1996, average rate of wage increase was only one-third that of preceding 25 years, while rate of unemployment was double that of the postwar era. On average, workers suffer greater job insecurity and more widespread unemployment than before.

The 'productivity wage' of the postwar era, when wages could be expected to rise in tandem with productivity and national output, is but a hazy memory of a Golden Age that lasted all of a decade or two in America and Europe. Workers also suffer the indignity of greater inequality as compared with the ballooning incomes and wealth of the rich, particularly the top 5% of people who own most of the capital in the world. The United States leads the way in most indicators of inequality and wage erosion among Northern Tier countries:

- real hourly wages for all employees fell by 12% between 1973 and 1990 and remained flat throughout the 'boom' of the 1990s.
- the median family of four earned the same in real income 1996 as in 1973, while working more hours
- the average working year was four weeks longer in 1990 than 1960

are inexperienced, or skills are few. Workers' bargaining strength is also undermined by the repeated restructuring of labour demand in the course of industrial change, brought about by new technologies and the search for higher productivity.

The first two factors, labour productivity and labour price, are the focus of conventional debates about the globalisation and the fate of workers. But the net of causality must be cast more widely in order to capture two other forces entertained begrudgingly, if at all, outside the chambers of organised labour or the academic left: politics and profits.

The third determinant of wages is the *politics of labour*, or what used to be called class struggle and is now politely called 'the social contract' or 'the labour regime'. Economies are not bare-bones systems of markets and prices, production and trade. They are political through and through, in two senses.

On the one hand, the contending classes are engaged in strategic action to improve their share of income (surplus value); that is, capitalists maneuver to strengthen their hand in bargaining and weaken labour; workers organise to increase their collective strength. On the other hand, classes seek advantage in the arenas of the state, which shape the operations of markets fundamentally, whether through taxes on incomes, tariffs on trade, the law of property rights, or rules governing union elections.

The last determinant is *profit on investment*, or the state of capital accumulation. Where capital is earning a good return and reinvesting briskly, productivity and wages ought to be rising. But this is not always so; profits may dip and crisis set in. This can reduce the supply of capital (investment) and the demand for labour. That, in turn, can undermine productivity gains and the strength of labour while steeling the resolve of capital to extract a higher rate of surplus value by reducing wages and other indirect strategies to weaken workers' power. Both the Bible and Karl Marx agree that 'the first shall be last and the last shall be first', and while neither the meek nor the proletariat may inherit the earth, capital has come as close as anything to doing so; therefore, we shall see that capital accumulation is very likely the most important condition for the well-being of labour today.

Finally, economics and political analysis of whatever stripe is not enough if it leaves out geography. We must, therefore, take into account a fifth dimension of the problem: the *conditions of place(s)* - regions, countries, continents — as distinct combinations of the previous elements of economy and politics, and how they interact in larger systems of spatial relations all the way up to the global scale.

One can therefore speak of the "five Ps of political economy": production, price, politics, profits, and place. Corresponding to each is a prevailing myth that clouds the issue and prevents clear understanding by workers of their situation. These myths are rampant in the labour movement of the United States. And in every case the trick of ideology is to turn the light of causality and blame toward the worker and away from the shadowy world of capital. The first is that productivity resides in the individual worker, not in the conditions of the social economy. The second is that excess labour supply is the critical weakness dogging workers' bargaining position. The third is that neo-liberalism is about freeing up markets rather than freeing capital from the shackles of labour's power. The fourth is that stagnant wages are due more to wage-competition than stagnant profits. The fifth and last myth is that globalism is a *fait accompli* that means 'the end of geography.'

Place and Globalism

The ruling myth holds that globalisation is no longer a trend in capitalist development, but a full-fledged reality. Capital flows are global, competition is global, manufacturing is global, and labour migration is global. This myth is joined at the hip with the myth of least-cost location, which says that the danger of industry fleeing to offshore sites is immediate and universal because capital is instantly fluid and utterly indifferent to where it operates manufacturing plants. It means that workers in all countries are in direct competition for the same jobs, and that the cheapest and most docile labour will be the winner in the capitalist beauty contest. It means that any government that taxes or regulates or otherwise pollutes the 'local business climate' will drive off investors to distant shores, hurting its own working people.

Globalism is thus the perfect excuse to do nothing — that inhibits the freedom of capital. We are helpless before it. It tightens the competitive screws and forces market discipline on the foolish ones who try to stand up to the dictatorship of capital.

In fact, there are still very definite limits to capital mobility, to the internationalisation of manufacturing, to the movements of people between countries, and to the boundaries of competition. Geography still matters enormously in the course of capitalist development. There may be a "world system" of the global economy, but there are also a host of "local capitalism's" with sharply different ways of doing things and divergent histories, or development paths. Mostly, these differences are associated with national boundaries, nation-states and national cultures. But the specificities of place apply at other scales as well, from the urban to the continental. Ironically, globalisation has been paralleled by the strengthening, in many areas, of regional and continental scales of economic integration.

Many commentators have noted what they call the resurgence of the region (or the local). Regions have weakly defined boundaries, by comparison to nation-states, and the term is often used rather loosely — as in the concentric circles one might draw around Hong Kong, Guandong Province, or the whole South China sea region — but they have an economic, social and often political integrity, all the same.

Most contemporary regionalists are referring to industrial districts at the scale of a city or small province, but the phenomenon of regionalisation is much more general. The United States, for example, has a long history of regional diversity, as do all other countries large and small.

Continental groupings are another important geographic unit of the world system, as emphasised by recent trends toward integration at this scale under the European Union (EU), NAFTA, and throughout East Asia. The EU in particular has closed its borders to the outside world, so that it now collectively trades less with the global economy than it did in the 1960s. NAFTA is a similar device to strengthen North American ties in the face of global competition; it represents as much a turning away from globalisation as a confirmation of it. Japanese overseas investment and trade are strongly regionalised in Southeast Asia and relatively minor in Europe.

In other words, globalisation has not eroded all shores on which local difference and competitive advantage are anchored. International trade volume in no way eliminates the points on the map between which trade takes place. Cross-border production systems may defy easy identification of national origins but do not erase the specificities of places in which various components are made. Internal flows of goods within multinational corporations do not eliminate the spatial division of labour, they simply alter its organisational form.

The specific qualities that confer productive competence and competitive advantage remain anchored to localities in a variety of ways, and the global economy — whether viewed as an international trading system, multinational corporate system, or a global joint-venture system of innovation — might best be thought of in terms of local nodes and distant networks.

The reason that nations and regional nodes can thrive in a global economy is that certain place-specific assets cannot be easily replicated. Classically, these have been seen as local "endowments" of natural resources and labour skills.

California, for example, waxed fat on its earthly riches, such as gold, silver, oil and soil. But more important, it developed some of the great concentrations of skilled labour (and capable firms) on earth. These constitute an exceptional production base, a localised network of thousands of workers and suppliers of every kind of product, skill and know-how there is. This is an essential feature of the fecund industrial districts of Silicon Valley, Hollywood, or the aerospace crescent of Los Angeles. And to this mix add the great pools of capital, especially the foremost venture capital funds in the world, and the great research centers in and around the universities and medical schools. Here lie the foundations for sustained economic growth.

The curious thing is that California is thought of as one of the most placeless societies on earth, one known for its endless in-migration of people from somewhere else, yet its peculiar character as a place has been reinforced by this very feature. More broadly, the United States has been the world's leading example of a large free-trade zone for almost 200 years, and yet even here regional differences have still not disappeared, even in something as theoretically fungible as technology. This ought to serve as a warning against glib pronouncements about the 'end of geography'.

The demise of the nation-state in the face of capital mobility is a recurrent theme of the globalisation myth. But this erosion of boundaries must be carefully assessed. The most striking examples of border reduction are in Europe, a place of small nations that embarked long ago on a political mission to overcome its internal fragmentation and propensity for internecine warfare. Large countries such as the United States, Japan and China remain remarkably insular in their political and social development by contrast. Russia and Central Asia have moved in the opposite direction of Europe, of course, fragmenting into more isolated nation-states with the break-up of the Soviet empire and economic trade bloc.

The United States remains less open to international trade than most nations. US import-export exposure remains around one-fifth of Gross Domestic Product (GDP), up from 14% in 1976 to 21% in 1996 (manufacturing is two-thirds of foreign trade, however). And some smaller nations often thought to be heavily reliant on global exports, like Korea, are much less so than traditional traders like Britain. Paul Krugman has been the most prominent voice among international economists asserting the continuing vitality of national economies against the prophets of globalisation, and he has scored many a point against his opponents on the relative openness of national economies. The whole world is not Hong Kong or Britain.

Nonetheless, the expansion of global investment, manufacturing and trade over the last fifty years has been striking. The stock of foreign direct investment (in productive capacity), which accelerated dramatically in the 1980s and 90s, had reached $2 trillion by 1992. Merchandise trade expanded at four time the rate of manfuacturing output over the entire period 1950-94, with a steadily widening gap between rates. Today, close to one-fourth of global manufacturing output is traded. Services are less readily traded, but even so volume of global trade is still up from 8% of world GDP in 1900 to 15% in 1992.

The case for globalisation is most striking in the realm of money and finance. This is where the figures stretch credulity. There was $1.2 trillion in currency exchange and $500 billion in bond transactions per day in 1992, 25 times the amount of commodity trade. Certainly, money capital is vastly more mobile than it was a generation ago, thanks to an electronic and institutional revolution in finance, and it puts the monetary policy of every country in jeopardy to the forces of the market and financial speculation.

Yet three things need to be kept in mind about this phenomenon. The first is that money is by definition the most fluid form of capital and the most abstracted from the grit of production, goods and everyday life; we should expect it to be the most placeless element of the modern economy. The second is that has been a general shift of capital out of production and into the financial sphere, much of which is unproductive and speculative; money can slosh about the globe often with little connection to trends in real output and trade. The third is that despite the international mobility of money, the biggest financial crises of the last two decades — the US Savings and Loan debacle ($250-500 billion in bad debt) and the Japanese banking fiasco ($1 trillion in bad loans — equal to almost one-quarter of GNP) — were almost entirely internally generated.

The resilience of place-based, circumscribed economies plays an important role in determining the well-being of workers. Economic territorialisation — meaning greater internal integration than global exposure — has the effect of binding together the fate of capital and labour within a single country or place, and differentiating it from those beyond the pale. The same is true of the less fully integrated but still distinctive economies of regional clusters such as Silicon Valley or Greater London or continental spheres like the EU and NAFTA.

Within any bounded locale, the productivity of industry and the prevailing wage tend toward an average. This occurs partly because of the equalising effects of capital flows and labour migration; but factor supply adjustments are not the whole story. Rather, both labour and management are caught up in a web of common circumstances that ties together their performance and productivity levels; these include, on the one hand, generalised basic levels of education, work discipline, technical competence and standards of living among managers and workers and, on the other hand, a thousand threads linking together the social division of labour from the highest to the lowest ends of performance and return. While high-grade, well educated, and experienced workers are the principle asset of any advanced industrial cluster, even those with low skills will be sucked into the vortex of activity and end up as links in the chain of collective labour and benefit from higher average wages than a similar worker labouring in a poor country or backward area.

Productivity

The principle condition for a high-wage, high-income labour force is a high-productivity economy. The 'secret' to the wealth of nations, as Adam Smith pointed out a while ago, is the cumulative achievements of industry over long periods of time. Where productivity is rising, wages should reflect this over time, as they did in postwar Europe and Japan, or have in the newly industrialised countries of our time, such as Singapore and Hong Kong. This effect is likely to be lagged by several years even in the best of circumstances, but it has held across a remarkable number of countries over the last two centuries. Other considerations may enter into the actual wage rate, as we shall see, but for the moment let us focus on this central fact of modern economic growth.

A dominant myth — held by labour's enemies and friends alike — ignores this most basic fact of long term growth through the expansion of labour productivity in order to focus on labour *cost*. The myth is fundamentally geographic: it says that industrial location is driven by the cost of labour, hence employers will move away from high wage areas to places where lower wages prevail. If this were true, however, all industry would have moved to Mississippi or Haiti long ago. On the contrary, most of the world's industry is found in the advanced capitalist countries (and within them in the principle urban centers, such as Chicago, Detroit or LA) where costs, including wages, are generally the highest, not the lowest.

The Northern Triad nations of North America, Northern Europe and Japan still command over 70% of the world's output, employment, investment and income, and the ongoing complaint of most of the world is the difficulty of ever catching up. Those who have done so, like the Four Asian Tigers, are much studied, discussed and emulated today. A global economy is still a geographically concentrated economy.

Behind this myth lies the whole edifice of conventional economics, which says that capitalists make optimising calculations based on market prices under conditions of perfect competition and constant returns; thus the chief dynamic of production is the drive to minimise costs, including those of hiring workers.

Neo-classical theory is fundamentally unable to cope with the central fact of modernisation and the unending industrial revolution unleashed by capitalism: technical progress in products and production methods. After Marx, no economist grasped this fact until Joseph Schumpeter, and even he was marginalised by the discipline for being too much the 'bourgeois Marx'.

By the 1950s economic historians had blown the empirical lid off the neo-classical idea of growth via capital deepening alone, yet technological change and increasing returns to scale have only become legitimate topics for mainstream theorists in the last decade. Even so, the leading proponent of the New Growth Theory, Paul Romer, can still claim naively that US technical leadership is due to the scale of this country's internal market!

Technical progress and rising productivity clear the path for the high-road of capitalist development — meaning steadily rising wages and incomes. The high wage economies of Europe have been growing more or less steadily for 100-200 years at compound rates of at least 1.5%. In the United States it has been 2-3%. In the postwar Golden Age of prosperity, the advanced capitalist countries of the OECD grew at an average rate of 4-5%. Japan grew at astounding double-digit rates through the 1950s and 60s. In all these countries, average incomes have risen dramatically as well over the long term. Despite the wreckage of World War II, wages and income per capita in Japan and Northern Europe (excluding Britain) are now higher than in the United States.

As a nation or region takes the high road to development and its industries expand, it takes on a distinctive geography, as well. Industries (and not just manufactures) tend to grow in clumps, like bacteria on a nutrient medium. Firms and factories (and offices) cluster together in areas such as Birmingham, Chicago or Paris to enjoy agglomeration economies, or increasing returns brought about by spatial concentration. They share an experienced labour force within commuting distance, they buy and sell specialised inputs from each other, they are served by local financiers, attorneys and traders who are knowledgeable in the business, they spawn new firms and specialties as the collective enterprise expands, and they share knowledge of the 'industrial arts' of what they do. That knowledge is embodied in workers, managers, investors, councilors, machinery and production practices, and the collective accomplishment of all concerned is greater than the sum of the parts.

Moreover, as industries produce, they learn, and as they learn, they improve their products and methods; learning becomes central to the whole dynamic of industrialisation, along with investment, competition, and advances in general education and science. This is a collective process which generates a higher productivity of social labour generally and belies the Liberal myth that productivity lies in the individual worker alone. Curiously, Alfred Marshall recognised all this without incorporating into his marginalist economics, the foundation for Anglo-American theory for the last century.

This is a dynamic geo-industrial process — the production of industrial places — by which industrialisation builds upon itself and, in so doing, builds up the locale of which it is a part. Workers are drawn in, new firms begun, new capital generated, and new machines put together on the spot. Industrial development is a 'bootstrapping' process to a large degree because of the revolutionary expansion of human capacities unleashed within industrial systems. That is why virtually all industrialised nations are more prosperous than non-industrial ones, why there is a developed world and an underdeveloped world, why there are rich cities and poor countrysides. This tendency is only partially opposed by the 'spread effects' of trade, decentralisation away from high cost locations, and the appearance of new centers of activity away from older cores.

Growth thus generates high employment and labour demand in the long run, and sufficient returns to pay good wages. A high wage economy is a product of development, not a barrier to it. Indeed, wages are a spur to growth, if they attract more high-quality labour, provide incentives for labour to contribute, expand the local market, and keep capitalists and workers on their technological toes. On the contrary, low wages, cheap labour and weak unions are frequently a sign of national or regional economic failure, forced by poor returns, low growth and pinch-penny employers.

At the sectoral level, the high road means innovation to lower costs through mechanisation and automation *and* innovation in products that find a market by virtue of what they do for the price (i.e., generate a consumer's surplus that can be converted into surplus profits); niche markets, barriers to entry and monopoly pricing can also create surplus profits, but are not the sole basis for them. A low-wage road to development may be expected in those industrial sectors (and segments) where technical change is difficult, skill is not exacting, and entry barriers are low, such as costume jewelry and light bulb manufacture.

At the firm level, companies that perform well over time do so principally by keeping on top of technical change, product màrketing, and organisational improvements. In short, labour's remuneration and competition between groups of workers are mediated by the performance of nations, regions, sectors and firms — and the capitalists who preside over these economic levels.

Of course, not every sector, workplace or job is at the upper end of the scale of productivity, innovation, skill and wages. Workers in such favored locations in the division of labour will fare better than those in stagnant sectors, backward factories, declining companies, and crummy jobs. Mostly forgotten in present-day paeans to high-tech and high skill, of information age and symbolic analysts are the great swaths of ordinary jobs held by ordinary people without much claim to modernist fame. Such breadth of occupations lies deep in the nature of the division of labour, and still operates with force within companies, factories, regions and national economies. The fully-skilled national economy is even more unlikely than the oft-predicted, but little realised, fully-robotic factory. So we must speak of averages in high-productivity, high wage economies — although the variance may shrink or expand.

The high road of capitalism is the world of Paul Krugman and his neo-Ricardian fellows among the New Trade Theorists. The United States and its workers are not threatened by global competition, they argue, because they remain relatively insulated from foreign trade and secure on the high road of increasing returns (productivity growth). For Krugman, only 10-20% of US manufacturing wage erosion is due to global trade, and this mostly at the low end. Moreover, for him the phenomenon of increasing returns in perfectly general, spreading from one country to another by virtue of specialisation and increasing size of the global market, i.e., through comparative advantage in trade.

As new countries enter onto the high road, they jostle for position but do not displace those already lodged at the top of the industrial derby; indeed, everyone is better off for engaging in international trade. It is, in fact, the high-productivity, high-wage economies that engage in most of world trade and international competition. Here, argues Krugman, the playing field is relative level and growing larger all the time. In fact, the average wage of US trading partners in 1990 was 88% of the American wage. Cheap labour competition is a minor issue, in his view.

Globalisation is not a zero-sum game, according to trade theory. And why should it be? Why should economic growth in one country hurt another? Why shouldn't rising imports be matched by rising exports? To deny this is analogous to saying that California's expansion has come at the expense of Michigan's, when the United States as a whole is richer for having both. Thus, Krugman is right, as far as he goes -- which is to say an argument for the benefits of rising productivity in a world of robust profits, full employment, and a fair division of the spoils. Yet all has not been rosy in Michigan nor in California of late, so something may be wrong with Krugman's assumptions.

In fact, a lot can go wrong for workers in favored locations in the global economy; their high road can begin to erode. Three reasons for this are:

1) productivity may not grow as expected due to failures of investment;

2) competitors with rising productivity may whittle away the advantages of former leaders; and

3) gains in productivity may throw more workers onto the streets.

Average productivity growth may fall off, as it did in the United States after 1973, declining to an average of just over 1% per annum. This would explain sluggish wage growth in the same period — an explanation favored by Krugman and Robert Lawrence. Still, one would need to explain why productivity growth fell off as it did — an historically unprecedented slackening of performance by the American economy after two centuries.

A possible account is the neo-Schumpeterian one that technical change was exhausted within the old Fordist paradigm. This is hard to swallow for two reasons. Productivity collapsed suddenly after 1973 to half its former rate of expansion. Why not a gradual diminution? And how could technical change slacken so much in an era in which computerisation and the information revolution are being proclaimed from the mountain tops? In fact, these technologies *have* yielded a suitable rate of productivity improvement — but only in manufacturing. In the United States, manufacturing productivity gains since 1979 have averaged around 3%, above historic trends. But in non-manufacturing, technology has been nearly stagnant. Evidently, the new technologies have not been adopted as widely as is often thought. Why not? Because of a low rate of capital investment. But why low investment? There's a puzzle for Mssrs. Krugman and Lawrence, which we cannot answer until we consider profit movements in the final section.

Competition from highly productive labour abroad can begin to pinch domestic companies and workers, as it did in the United States. While the Myth of Cheap Labour holds that capital will seek the lowest wage workers regardless of their capabilities, what really matters is unit costs. Overseas labour becomes a competitor — either for traded goods or plant relocation offshore — when it reaches relatively high levels of productivity. That is why the greatest challenge to US industry has come not from low-wage countries like Mexico and the Philippines but from First World trading partners such as Japan and Germany.

This high-productivity challenge began in the 1960s and had its most devastating effects in the 1980s. The American share of world exports started falling by the late 1950s and the trade deficit pushed the US into dollar devaluation by 1970, which spurred a short recovery. By 1980, however, Germany had passed the US in share of world exports and the Japanese had unleashed a barrage of high quality, lower cost exports.

Manufacturing is the part of the economy most exposed to international competition by virtue of the fungible nature of its products (today it makes up two-thirds of US trade, one-sixth of US domestic sales). Manufacturing imports hit almost 40% of US manufacturing output, and trade deficits peaked at over $150 billion per year before the dollar was devalued again through the Plaza Accord of 1985. US basic industries were clobbered and an era of deindustrialisation set in train. During the recession of 1979-82, output and employment in manufacturing fell by over 10%. Of the more than two million jobs lost, about one million can be attributed to imports.

What competing countries had at the time was a killing combination of rising productive capabilities as they rushed to catch up with American levels of efficiency, and lagging wages — which had hit bottom in the ruins of World War II and had not yet attained the level of the United States. As a result, unit costs were very favorable compared to American companies, which suffered accordingly. Productivity in German and Japanese manufacturing was 50% and 75% of US levels by 1970, while wages were only 60% and 25% of American workers, respectively, leaving unit costs at 80% and less than 50% of American industry. This was achieved through massive capital investment through the postwar era over 10% in Germany and more than 15% in Japan — double the US rate.

That the game of catch-up would come in part at the expense of the United States is to be expected, since its absolute domination of world trade and manufacture after World War II was a unique circumstance. Complacency of American corporations made things worse as the world caught up with flaccid companies and oligopolistic sectors with bloated management structures, deadening control systems, declining records of innovation, high executive salaries, and so forth. One could attribute all this to the natural growing pains of the postwar world, but still see long run gains for all participants through the rebuilding of the global economy to new levels of output and prosperity. So why the persistence of competitive difficulties for American industry and American workers?

After all, even though Japanese industrial wages are now 125% of US wages, it still runs a trading surplus with the US of around $50 billion per annum. Another effect is the permanently higher elasticity of demand for American labour (i.e., substitutability of US workers for high productivity foreign workers), especially in sectors facing global integration. There is still too much competition from too many productive companies and workers in the Northern Tier, let alone the Newly Industrialised Countries (NICs) of the Southern Tier. Here's another puzzle for the New Trade theorists.

There is a supply effect when companies downsize, factories shut, or redundancies occur, releasing workers into the labour market. While this raises average productivity by removing the least efficient units, it creates a labour surplus that can depress wages. This happened in the United States in the deep recessions of 1980-82 and 1990-92. Conversely, as companies successfully raise productivity to meet the challenges of competition, they may also shed workers, with the same effects on labour markets. Thus, even industrial success can have its cost for labour.

Capitalist dynamics and competition, which demand recurrent innovation and restructuring to stay up with the pack, will undercut every fixed position in time. Put geographically, no factory, town or region, however successful in its times, can keep the wolf from the door indefinitely; the inconstant geography of capitalism has left many a vacant lot, deserted boomtown, and forgotten industrial center. In a Krugman world everyone would still be better off if the market adjusted smoothly to changes in competitiveness and divisions of labour. But, of course, it does not. In fact, the evidence is that US labour markets became less stable after 1980, making workers subject to a greater chance of being rendered unemployed, sometimes repeatedly. This churning of the labour market came from the demand side.

In short, rising productivity is central to long-term economic growth, which tends to concentrate in the most favored places in the global system. There, wages have climbed behind the advancing front of industrialisation. Trade among favored nations ought to propell them forward not drag them down — all other things being equal. But productivity may fall off in one place and accelerate in another, cutting into wages in the former. The puzzle is why did productivity-inducing investment slacken and excess competition persist over the last quarter century as never before?

Supply and Demand in Labour Markets

High productivity only means high wages if the working class has the historic capacity to extract a proportionate share of the social product and to keep the rate of surplus value (roughly, value added) from rising. Even if we assume that all is well with productivity and that output markets clear (no excess competition), it is by no means given that workers should enjoy the fruits of their labour. That all depends on the state of labour markets, and whether excess supply presses down on wages. Thus, wages may *not* track productivity gains everywhere or over long periods of time.

In treating the wage-profit split, we need to overcome the mythology of conventional economics that the operations of perfectly competitive, fluid markets assure that workers get what they deserve. The neo-classical orthodoxy asks us to believe that there is a seamless web connecting the marginal productivity of labour to the wage rate. If wages are low, it must be due to low productivity at the workplace.

Most neo-classical theorists go farther, holding that productivity inheres in each individual worker and his or her 'human capital'. Hence the widespread myth that wage stagnation resides with the undereducated worker who cannot keep up with a technologically progressive world economy, evident in the soft neo-liberalism of Robert Reich, former Secretary of Labour. Another variant is that wage troubles are due to the inflexibility of workers who stubbornly resist flexible work rules and reassignments that allow management to keep up with a changing world economy.

But the price of labour is *not* determined simply by the productivity of the worker or the job. Labour (whether organized or not) must bargain for a piece of the economic pie from the corporations who take in revenues from the sale of their products at home or abroad.

Labour's ability to bargain is strongly constrained, however, by the workings of labour market, that is, by conditions of supply and demand. If demand outruns supply, generating a condition of labour scarcity, it gives workers greater leverage in bargaining (even more so if the sector enjoys surplus profits which can be converted into higher wages). If demand is slack or supply excessive, capitalists tend to gain the upper hand.

A neo-classical economist would say that disequilibrium and rents are temporary states that should pass away as capital and labour adjust to changing circumstances in the long run. But one is wise to recall Keynes famous retort that, "in the long run we are all dead." Marx went farther in arguing that capitalism creates its own labour surplus — an industrial reserve army — as a condition of accumulation, which constitutes a permanent drag on labour's bargaining power. Today, Keynes' and Marx's warnings merit a further look.

In the Northern Tier, the bargaining position of workers might be diminished by a labour surplus coming from any of three directions:

1) workers in low-wage economies exporting cheaper goods;

2) immigrants arriving from poorer countries competing for domestic jobs; and

3) surplus labour generated inside the country.

This is what most people mean by the spectre of 'cheap labour'. It is the world depicted by many friends of labour, as well as by conservatives who hail the weakening of labour's 'monopoly' power by newfound competition. In the American case, commentators such as William Greider or William

Wolman paint a stark picture of job-flight and overseas competition from low-wage nations from Thailand to Mexico. Others such as George Borjas and Allen Scott worry about the flooding of domestic labour markets by immigrant workers from the Southern Tier countries, especially Mexico. Still others see surplus labour coming from technical unemployment as automation and lean production are adopted to meet stringent overseas competition. Let us consider each facet of cheap labour for the United States.

The greatest peril of labour surplus, or cheap labour, appears to come from overseas competition in low wage countries. Historically, these nations presented little threat to the advanced capitalist world's advantages, including higher wages. They were usually far behind in technology, capital investment, work discipline and a whole set of institutions and practices needed for capitalist success. What raises the spectre of 'cheap labour' today is the challenge from an expanding set of NICs with rapidly improving technologies and labour forces, especially in Southeast Asia and Latin America. This might be called the Third Wave of postwar global development, the industrialisation of an ever-wider circle of nations beyond the Northern Triad. It is an extension of the high-productivity competition discussed above, but with a greater lag between rates of growth of productivity and wages.

What has workers in the United States worried is not the mythic Mexican 'peon' or Chinese 'coolie' toiling for pennies in sweatshops, but the discovery of new Mexican, Indonesian or Malaysian worker toiling factories with productivity levels equal to domestic plants, but earning wages one-tenth of American levels (e.g., the $.85 average in Mexican maquiladoras). This we can call the 'Shaiken effect', after the influential work of Harley Shaiken on automobile plants in northern Mexico. A crucial fact in the Mexican case is that wages have fallen dramatically along the border while productivity has continued to rise. It is an exemplary case of divergence between productivity of labour and return to labour — a 'short run' adjustment problem lasting twenty years and sure to last another generation under the best of conditions. Both Mexican and American workers, argues Shaiken, are put in jeopardy by the ongoing integration of the two national economies under NAFTA.

An assessment of the global challenge from the Shaiken Effect turns on how much of current US foreign trade is with the Southeast Asian NICs and Mexico, how big is the (merchandise) trade deficit with those countries, and rates of investment. By 1990, East Asia accounted for 13% of world exports, the same as Germany and more than either Japan (9%) or the United States (12%). Of the total US trade deficit of $132 billion in 1993, the Asian NICs, Mexico and Brazil accounted for $23 billion (compared to a $7 billion surplus in 1980). These figures were rising fast in the 1990s until the Asian crisis struck. By 1995 the US trade deficit was up to $180 billion and low wage country trade had, by one estimate, reached 20% of imported manufactured goods to the United States and Europe and a striking 33% to Japan; another estimate puts the low-wage country trade deficit at $55 billion in 1995.

Meanwhile, maquiladora employment increased from 500,000 to over 1,000,000 between 1994 and 1998, for example, and Mexico now runs a trade surplus with the US. Internal savings and investment in East Asia were running at double the rates of North America and Europe, while net capital flows to the whole Southern Tier reached $110 billion by 1993, over half the rate of foreign direct investment in the Northern Triad itself.

China looms even larger than the New Wave NICs. The US trade deficit with China was an astounding $57 billion in 1998. Investment in China 1991-95 was $120 billion (compared to foreign investment in the United States of $200 billion). China might be the ultimate cheap labour country of the world, given its vast population, low income level, and tightly controlled politics. China has experienced a phenomenal expansion of its industrial base, with growth rates of over 10%, but still has many workshops competing by means of sweated labour. With a GDP less than that of California, it will take a long time for China to enter the first rank of industrial nations and even longer for its workers' incomes to approach First World levels.

Krugman tries to mask the impact of low-wage competition abroad by saying that in 1990 imports from low-wage countries (below one-half US wages) were only 2.2% of US GDP (about the same as in 1960); but the share of *trade* not output also counts. Most studies show a substantial loss of US manufacturing jobs to imports, and a lesser effect on wages. Losses are skewed toward the lower segments of unskilled work and low-wage manufacturing industries, like textiles. After an exhaustive survey, Cline estimates that globalisation was responsible for about 20% of the growth of wage inequality in the 1980s.

The second source of cheap labour is immigration. Hiring lower-wage immigrants can function as a simpler alternative to offshoring factories. Why go abroad when the world is beating a path to your factory gate? The substitution of immigrant labour for US-born labour has occurred in many American workplaces and industries. But to what effect? We know that millions of new entrants came into the United States after the immigration laws were relaxed in 1965. What began as a trickle in the 1960s surged in the next decade and peaked in a great wave in the late 1980s. But did this adversely affect American workers? That is not easily answered, and we should not be ready to damn immigrants. Their arrival can be correlated with almost any significant social change over the last quarter-century, but that does not necessarily make them causal agents in any of it.

Immigration is driven, above all, by economic demand for labour. The clearest indication is the way migration responds to geographic differences in job creation and to long waves of business activity. Major immigration cycles are triggered by upswings in accumulation at poles of attraction and peter out when growth in those places declines. California was the largest recipient of immigration to the US in our time because it was the greatest job generator, and the rising curve of migrants roughly tracked the curve of job creation. This close relation between labour demand and supply of in-migrants has been true over a long a succession of mass migrations to the state following the Gold Rush.

Every wave of in-migration corresponds to an epochal boom in the state's development. In fact, the migration of the last quarter century was no greater in mass than that of the previous quarter-century, the great postwar flood; the main difference was that the first group were largely US-born and the latter foreign-born. Immigration finally overran demand between about 1988 and 1991, as the economy collapsed, then fell in response to a sharp decline in jobs.

There is nothing to the reactionary claim of a labour glut because the world's poor are flooding our shores in a mad scramble to escape their misery. With few exceptions, the segment of emigrants from any poor country is quite small. The exception is mass displacement due to warfare, as in El Salvador in the 1980s, but such political refugees made up less than 10% of immigrants to the United States in 1990. Altogether, international migrants are on the order of 5% of the global labour force, and most of these move within the Third World.

In the United States, immigrants constitute less than 5% of the labour force; it is very hard to see how this highly mobile margin could bring down wages and employment rates so severely as has occurred. If immigrants are to blame, why did average wages continue to rise through the much larger influx to the US in the early 20th century? Why is unemployment higher in the rural confines of Northern California, where the populace is largely white, than in Southern California? Why is European unemployment double that of the United States in the 1990s, when immigration restrictions have been more draconian there?

The job competition between foreign-born and US-born workers is less than it might seem, in any case. While immigrants are often portrayed as poverty-stricken, they come with a whole range of skills, from medical doctors to engineers. The modal immigrant is not a Mexican farm worker. Different skill groups (often of different national origins) compete with quite different segments of the domestic labour force: Mexicans with African-American janitors, Salvadorans with Japanese gardeners, Iranis with Jewish realtors, French engineers with Berkeley-trained Chinese-Americans, and so forth.

It is impossible to make a simple claim about immigrants glutting one big labour market and dragging everyone's wages down. In many cases surplus immigrants glut segments already occupied by their countryfolk who arrived earlier. Conversely, skilled immigrants are the lifeblood of high technology in places like California, which is why Silicon Valley employers have fought vigorously for exemptions to bring in more foreign engineers — while unskilled Salvadorans hang out on street corners waiting for day jobs.

Why aren't immigrants a blessing? This is the same puzzle that faced us in terms of international trade: why is the labour market a zero sum game? If labour demand is sufficient, immigrants ought to add to the productive labour force and to the mass of surplus value (profits) in the economy. They also represent additional consumers. Did the Irish of the 1840s and 50s ruin Britain and the United States? Nativists arguments of the day are now forgotten. Mass immigration at the end of the 19th century did not keep the US from becoming the leading industrial power. And it corresponded to a rise in labour militancy not a decline up to World War I. Conversely, the cutoff of immigration in 1923 came *after* the historic defeat of the unions and radical parties after World War I, and was followed by a shrinkage of the wage-share of national income in the 1920s. Something has 'queered the pitch' in the international economy, but it is not global labour migration.

In a relatively self-contained economy such as the United States, the biggest source of surplus labour and cheap labour is still internal. This is often overlooked with all the fuss over globalisation. Capital has a lot of wiggle-room geographically and temporally within the confines of the world's biggest unified free-trade zone and uses it to good effect.

The United States has a huge reservoir of labour and of low wages regions outside the main urban centers and prosperous coastal areas. It is easy for mobile capital to find cheaper labour at the internal peripheries of the economy. Silicon Valley electronics firms have dispersed their operations all over the American West for the last 30 years. Auto firms (including the Japanese) have been clever at placing their newest plants along the rural fringes of the lower Midwest-upper South.

German investors love the Carolinas, with their lack of union traditions, as do the chicken and hog processors who have moved down from Delaware or Iowa. Indeed, the whole of American industrial geography has tilted toward the Sunbelt for decades, where unions are scarce and wages lower; this became a *cause-célèbre* in the 1970s before anyone worried about immigrants or globalisation. It has not resulted in a simple leveling up of wages, as neo-classical theorists hold, but more like a leveling down. Similarly, industry can draw on internal pools of surplus labour without going outside the cities: it only needs to employ women, young people, and minorities not previously fully part of the labour force. This has been the strategy of back offices, fast-food franchises, and big box retailers, for example.

In a period of slow and erratic accumulation, furthermore, the US economy has been unable to sustain a high level of overall labour demand, despite a great deal of palaver about the "Great American Jobs Machine." The unemployment rate has run at over 5% for the last twenty-five year stretch, twice the average of the preceding quarter-century.

Unemployment peaked at around 10% in each of the recessions of the period, in the early 1970s, 1980s and 1990s. This has been true in every region of the United States, including the fastest growing such as California and Florida and those with little immigration, such as the upper Midwest. This raises questions as to why recessions have been so severe and why employment hasn't rebounded during upswings to absorb surplus labour. The answers must wait until we consider profit movements.

Then there are the dynamics of technological improvement unleashed by capitalism. Automation and lean production have greatly reduced the labourforce in American manufacturing in recent years while output per worker has climbed, but the firestorm of technical change sweeps across many fronts, including the opening up of new product markets, the birth of new firms, and the shrinkage of once-leading sectors.

The advancing front of industrialisation sweeps factories, jobs, companies, and workers into the dustbin of history with disturbing regularity. We live in a world of unceasing change, of unyielding modernity or what is today called "restructuring", and it is a highly geographic process. Jobs lost in one place and labour force are unlikely to be replaced in the same place and by the same workers.

This perennial upheaval takes its toll on the working class. Militancy, unions, and bargaining strength have been deeply undermined by sectoral and geographic shifts. Steel is not the mass employer of thirty years ago, fast-food outlets are — but the latter are almost entirely beyond the reach of unions. Such shifts are not necessarily political in their conception by capitalists, who may be introducing the latest technology for purely economic reasons.

Neo-liberals argue that workers can and must adjust to industrial change by retraining, geographic mobility, and general 'flexibility', hence the Reagan Administration's call for laid-off auto workers in Detroit to migrate to oil-rich Houston in the early Eighties (not good advice, as it turned out, given the subsequent bust in Texas). But workers ability to adjust usually lags behind the pace of restructuring, which shakes the house of labour so fiercely that workers' organisations break apart and the high wage spots slide down to a level nearer the swamps of the poor and disorganised.

Another facet of industrial change is a shift in the kinds of jobs on offer to a greater proportion of 'contingent work'. The Great American Jobs machine has meant a lot of jobs for part-timers, short-timers and subcontractors — the bulk at poor wages. A striking feature is that this jobs growth has occurred almost entirely in the so-called 'service sectors'. Manufacturing has shrunken as a proportion of aggregate employment from 25% in 1960 to 22% in 1979 to 16% in 1996 (absolute numbers peaked in 1979). This is not simply a product of technical change to an Information Society, however. industrial exporters were forced to become 'lean and mean' by shedding workers, reorganising work and supply chains, investing in new machines and raising labour productivity. Because the American market share in tradables has been capped by global competition, manufacturing improvement has been largely jobless growth. By contrast, non-manufacturing sectors such as retailing and medical care are locally-based and suffer little from foreign competition. They have been able to keep profits up by raising prices and lowering wages, while still adding willy-nilly to their labour force.

The phenomenon of deterioration in wages and job quality with employment growth is much larger quantitatively than either immigration or maquiladoras (service jobs have increased by the tens of millions over the last two decades). It is independent of labour supply or wage rates in two ways.

First, employers have wanted to create contingent work (part-time, short-term, and contract) for reasons of flexibility and performance. Indeed, in the high skilled segments of business consulting, technical services, and design, performance is the dominant factor as US companies strive to meet higher standards of management and technology, and the wages for these jobs have remained high even as they became contingent.

Second, non-manufacturing employers have not deigned to invest in equipment to raise labour productivity, despite higher average profits than manufacturing. The Great Jobs Machine has meant jobs *without* machines. On the other hand, as basic industry shed jobs and workers, it generated a mass of surplus labour available to the service sectors, which picked up these workers (or their wives and children) at bargain prices. Because workers have been hard up for jobs and income, they have been willing to take part-time and short-term work, often for lower wages and no benefits. This is a sign of labour's weakness and oversupply.

In sum, the spectre of cheap labour competition is real — though apparently a good deal less devastating than the impact of Japanese and European competition. Low-wage imports from the third-waves NICs only became substantial by the mid-1990s, when US unemployment rates actually fell and wages began to inch up (but not by much). Low-wage immigrants peaked in the late 1980s and were suddenly conspicuous by their unemployment in the recession of 1989-92; but evidence for a major effect on domestic wages is scant, apart from the symbiotic effect their arrival has had on the capitalists' strategy of creating low-wage, contingent jobs.

Finally, the massive growth of second-rate jobs in the service occupations bears little relation to import competition and a tangential one to immigration; it would seem to have more to do with the massive release of workers from manufacturing that began in the 1970s and low rates of productivity growth in the service-sectors.

The most striking thing is that the long-term decline in US wages began in the 1960s, well before any of the global cheap labour factors kicked in and before anyone had dreamed of raising the spectre of mass Chinese imports, Mexican immigration, the Sunbelt shift, or deindustrialisation. Similarly, unionisation and working class power has been declining steadily since the 1950s, while unemployment jumped up to new levels after 1973. So cheap labour is not a very satisfactory explanation for the recent plight of American workers. How, then, do we account for the paradox of a system that has been able to absorb immigrants, technical change, westward expansion, and sectoral shifts for most of its history, but has failed conspicuously to do so over the last bleak quarter century? Let us now look to the dynamics of class struggle or capital accumulation rather than labour productivity and labour supply.

Politics of Labour Power

In the end, economics is not enough and a politics of labour — our fourth P-factor — enters into the equation of wage determination. The classes maneuver and struggle through administrative, legal, and even violent means, most of which are mediated by the state. This is a bare-bones definition of politics, even of labour-politics, but it will suffice for present purposes. Any notion of politics stands in opposition to the economistic myth that the condition of labour is determined solely by the impartial hand of global competition and the operation of labour markets. The surprising thing about this counsel of despair is that so many unionists and friends of labour buy into it.

The business class love it, of course, because it hides their active role in suppressing wages and increasing their profits and rents. It is the line espoused from the California State Chamber of Commerce to the French *patronate.* It is the logic behind the "structural adjustment" policies of the International Monetary Fund. It is the bankers' faith behind the Federal Reserve's rush to tighten interest rates whenever it detects a hint of "inflationary wage push". It is the world of neo-liberalism we inhabit.

The prevailing wage rate in any country or region is by no means determined automatically by the state of productivity, global markets and competition. The distribution of the social product (the rate of surplus value) depends on the bargaining power of labour and capital. There is room to maneuver on both sides in any company or place in the global economy, and the victories of the contending classes will leave workers better or worse off at the end of the day. Thus, the downward pressure on wages and labour conditions over the last quarter century in the United States, for example, is more than a reflection of greater competition, American decline, or glutted labour markets. It is in part the result of a concerted strategy of capital, government, and the political Right to roll back the gains of made by labour in the middle of the 20th century. The myth of neo-liberalism is that it is a policy to free capital from the shackles of government interference so it can compete more nimbly in global markets; the fact is that it is a strategy to liberate capital from the restraints put on it by the labour movement and social regulation. We talk all the time about competitive advantage and cheap labour competition, but who has the courage to speak about the politics of labour? The term 'class struggle' is today considered a sad relict of a communist system safely dead and buried.

Workers have been under attack all around the world, as the ideology and practice of Neo-Liberalism was exported by the Thatcher and Reagan regimes. The International Monetary Fund has been pushing draconian austerity policies on governments deemed too sympathetic to their people, while born-again neo-liberals like Carlos Salinas Gotari of Mexico and Fernando Enrique Cardoso of Brazil have eagerly applied the nostrum to their own countries. The Neo-Liberal package of reforms includes the weakening of labour protections, the removal of social subsidies to the poor, lower taxes on the rich, selling off state companies and assets, deregulation of financial markets, re-regulation of intellectual property rights, reductions of tariffs and quotas on international trade, and so forth.

In the United States, a long corporate offensive against labour and the rightward shift of politics since Reagan have taken a dramatic toll. Managerial and government aggression have contributed to a long steady decline in real wages, job quality and job security since at least 1975. Key moments in the attack on the working class can be easily flagged, beginning with the breaking of the PATCO strike in 1981. This was followed by a weakening of the National Labour Relations Act, mostly through appointments to the Board and to the courts. Along with this came a relaxation of child labour laws, safety regulations, and fire codes. The minimum wage languished, falling to half of its previous real level. Simultaneously, the rug was being pulled out from under the working poor by the reduction of social benefits paid out of federal, state and local funds.

The devastation of the mass production centers of the industrial heartland by the depression of the early 1980s and foreign competition did more than throw millions of workers onto the labour market, it badly weakened the unions in the sectors which the CIO had made the centerpiece of American unionism: autoworkers, steelworkers, rubber workers and the like. And as the economy recovered new growth sectors from high tech or fast food were unorganised. This not only reduced the percentage of unionised workers in the country but took away the leadership in national wage (pattern) bargaining, which had rested with the heartland unions since the 1940s.

At the same time as the unions were shrinking, companies became increasingly adept at using the threat of plant closure, relocation and global competition to extract concessions from workers. While corporations often had no intention of going anywhere, their threats were backed up by the evidence of massive foreign direct investment and some dramatic instances of moving factories abroad. Such relocation is highly political because foreign sites come with a very different and often lower standard of worker bargaining rights, protections and so forth, and the race-to-the-bottom has engendered deregulation as well as lower wages.

Less visible but equally corrosive in the long run have been the innumerable corporate subversions of worker's ability to organise and engage in collective bargaining. A new breed of management consultant and labour lawyer came into prominence to lead the corporate charge for union decertifications, take-aways of benefits, dual wage structures, no-strike contracts, lock-outs, replacement workers, etc. Another kind of new manager made it his specialty to 'downsize' supposedly overstaffed companies to please the wizards of Wall Street looking for high dividends and stock prices.

While all this was going on, the capitalist class rewarded itself with ample tax cuts of all kinds through the Tax Revolt — on property, capital gains, income, inheritance, corporate profits and so forth. As tax rates on capital have fallen, those on labour have continued to rise. Simultaneously, returns on financial assets (held chiefly by the rich) were raised through the elimination of single-digit limits on interest rates, removal of rent controls, insurance of large denomination bank deposits, fire-sale purchases of public companies, and so on. This expanded the bulging ranks of millionaires even farther.

The financiers have had the much more money to play with and better prospects of making money breed money without the bother of investing in manufacturing. Global financial assets were $35 trillion in 1992, or twice the GDP of the entire Northern Tier. Meanwhile, financial flows have gone from 10% to 95% speculative over the last thirty years. And the wreckage of financial speculation is usually laid at the feet of ordinary people: the estimated cost for saving Mexico's banking system is $60 billion, or two year's income for the bottom half of that society. Capitalist revanchism taken to extremes of deregulation and labour repression is a low-road to capitalist development. The low road rests on cheap labour, cost cutting and a repressive state to keep labour under control. How does a country get on the low road? In the Third World context, where underdevelopment, backwardness and industrial failure have been common, the question has been a pressing one.

Few in the advanced industrial countries have bothered to consider the variety of capitalisms, sure that there was only one capitalism with a smiling Social Democratic face. But this ignores the reality of place and the diversity of capitalist social forms and economic arrangements. The low road has made excellent political and economic sense to the ruling classes of many a country, most in the Southern Tier, where the peasantry is under the thumb of landowners, the working class is disorganised, or dictatorial terror is a long-standing practice — and where the United States and European colonialists have kept their thumb on popular revolt and national liberation.

Its long prevalence in places like the American South or Southwest, however, cannot be laid at the feet of dictators or imperialists, but to local histories of sharecropping, Dixiecrats, conquest, white supremacy, and Right to Work laws. Those who have taken this path have, on occasion, done well exporting primary commodities and attracting low-wage manufacturing, as in the Caribbean today; but none has a record of growth, innovation and prosperity comparable to high road industrial regions such as the Rhineland, California, or Tuscany.

It is a fearful prospect to see how much of a turn the Northern Tier countries, and especially the United States, have taken toward the low road under the goad of neo-liberal policy and a capitalist class aggressively rolling backs the gains of workers, organised labour, Social Democratic parties, Keynesian stimulation policies, and the social insurance of the welfare state. This is labour and class politics with a vengeance, and it has driven a sharp wedge between the rich and the poor, the Northern and Southern economies, and industrialisation (productivity gains) and wages. One might well ask if capitalism itself can prosper for long under such a regime? So far the answer is no, despite appearances to the contrary thanks to the rapid enrichment of the few in our times. We now turn to the overall performance of global capitalism, in all its fading lustre.

Profit and Capital

The last determinant of wages — the rate of profit, our fifth P-factor — is the most important of all. But it is the least discussed, especially in polite company and more particularly among economists. By rate of profit we mean not just the share of income going to capitalists, but the rate of return — the ratio of surplus value to invested capital. It is that which motivates capitalists to hurl their money into production and circulation in order to make more money. The investment of money to make more money, or capital accumulation, is, after all, the goal of the system, for which growth in other dimensions — output, total value (income), productive capacity, employment, etc. — is simply the means to an end. Even David Ricardo acknowledged this. Accumulation is the main driving force of the world economy, along with its correlates, capital-capital competition and capital-labour exploitation. This is why it makes more sense to speak of 'the capitalist system' than 'the global market'. The greatest economic myth of all is that the market has as its principle purpose the service of human needs rather than the aggrandisement of capitalists and their corporations.

Given the explosion of global investment and the collapse of Communism, capitalist triumphalism is in the air. Even among friends of labour, the mobility of capital is frequently held to be virtually infinite, and workers losers for it. The argument is that capital's global reach brings more working people into competition with each other, enlarges the global labour surplus and puts cheap labour in direct competition with expensive labour; this erodes wages in the Northern Tier (and even undermines rising wages in the older NICs by competition from the newer ones).

As we've seen, this sobering picture is by no means wrong. But it is misleading in so far as it partakes of the myth of capital's perfection and potency, and says nothing of capital's limits and contradictions. Geographers have been the first to resist this whitewash, by insisting that capital cannot be everywhere at once, ignore the assets of places, or move on a dime. Corporations are not omnipotent and often perplexed by change. Monetary flows are often speculative in the extreme and based on nothing more than collective madness. And capital's free-wheeling operations can impede its own further profit-making, both locally and globally.

Profit is the variable missing from the equation for wages. In our discussion so far, it has reared its head only to be sidelined as long as our focus was on labour, not capital. Yet profit rates affect the other P-factors (productivity, price and politics) decisively. Profit is the *raison d'être* of capital and profit rates are the key economic influence on investment, and hence on rates of accumulation.

On the positive side, a high average profit rate, i.e., a good return on capital investment in industry, tends to improve productivity, wages and class peace. When profits fall, however, productivity tends to slump, wage demands to be blunted, and class struggles to break out. The logic of this is simple — and the evidence surprisingly strong that this is what has happened over the course of the last fifty years.

First the logic: when capitalists are earning a good return they normally reinvest briskly in industrial production, purchasing new machinery and building new plants. Improved techniques are embodied in new equipment and layouts, so productivity should rise (it also tends to rise as capacity utilisation improves during an upswing). This depends, of course, on technical possibilities, good decisions, and practical experience; capital presses at the expanding industrial frontier but does not create it out of whole cloth. Still, investment is the prime mover in the adoption of new technologies. It is odd how much the literature on technical change these days glides over the role of investment in its obsession with networking and learning economies.

Second, where capital is doing well and investing in new plant and equipment, labour demand should be robust. With strong demand, labour is absorbed and wages should move upward as supply tightens. Cost-squeeze is a common occurrence in an era of prosperity, even though investment booms trigger supply responses, such as flows of migration, which counteract the development of shortages. This side of equation is sorely neglected by the prevailing focus on labour supply in the literature.

Third, labour politics has less of an edge when profits are good and capitalists feel they can yield more in the way of wages and benefits without jeopardising their rates of return. Tight labour markets tend to help unions organise, fill their coffers with dues, and make strikes more winnable (if capitalists feel the pinch of lost production in a robust market).

When profits go sour, the reverse will be true. Without adequate investment, productivity will not grow briskly. Without the effective demand for labour, labour markets go slack and wages stagnate. When capitalists feel the pinch of lower profits, they are likely to turn on workers and try gain by wage cuts what they cannot make through better sales. This is exactly what has happened over the last quarter century throughout the developed world, and particularly in the United States, which felt the profit pinch first and longest and whose industries and workers had the farthest to fall from their exhaulted position astride the globe in the immediate post-World War II era. Robert Brenner, in an exhaustive review of the evidence, calls the period of relatively poor growth "The Long Downturn".

Global profit rates on manufacturing fell by about half in the early 1970s, after a long run of good times in the postwar Golden Age. They stayed low into the 1990s, despite a modest rebound in the late 1980s. For the seven leading industrial countries, the rate of profit in manufacturing 1970-1990 was less than 40% of what it had been 1950-1970. The performance of the major economies reflects this decline and stagnation in profits. The global effect of lower profit rates was weaker performance in the key indicators of economic growth.

For the OECD countries from 1973 to 1996, the rates of investment and output growth were approximately one-third to one-half the rates from 1950 to 1973. Productivity growth slackened in like degree and wage increases fell off in proportion. As one would expect, weakening capital accumulation causes a productivity slowdown and wage stagnation. Weaker profits have also brought a pattern of business cycles with upswings tainted by speculative booms and deep recessions plagued with financial crisis, as well as volatile flows of investment from one sector to another, one country to another — in desperate search for better returns. This helps explain the churning of labour markets.

Profit and performance difficulties showed up earliest in the United States (along with Britain). By the mid-1960s US profits were declining and trade deficits ballooning; the dollar began to weaken as payments flows grew more imbalanced. The profit decline cannot be attributed to rising wages cutting into the rate of surplus value, however, because wage demands were already weakening in the early 1960s — before the rate of profit began falling.

While US workers tried to recover lost ground through a rash of strikes in the late 1960s, wages did not budge; meanwhile, German workers voluntarily held the line (improving German profits) and Japanese wages went up (but were easily accommodated by Japanese employers). In 1970 the situation hit a crisis point, and the US triggered a worldwide recession by devaluing the dollar to correct its yawning deficits.

European and Japanese profits fell precipitously with the slump of 1973-75. The US economy recovered but did not get back on the high road of investment and productivity gains. Instead, companies sought to raise their fallen profits through price increases, and inflation soared. The wolf came to the factory door in the early 1980s, when the Federal Reserve tightened the screws on inflation by raising interest rates.

Meanwhile, Japan came roaring back with even better mass production methods and Europe continued to close the productivity gap; US manufacturing companies lost market share rapidly and could no longer raise prices to make up for it. US manufacturing was swept away in a firestorm of recession, bankruptcy, and global competition. The catastrophic bulge in unemployment threw the working class back on their heels, gravely weakening key unions and their allies in the Democratic Party, and allowed Reagan's neo-liberal policies to triumph — particularly since he sugar-coated them with liberal spending on the military that revived the economy.

American productivity fared better after 1985, but financial instability and a new recession intervened. Only in the 1990s did the US economy begin again to outperform its Northern Triad rivals. By that time, overheated Japan and Europe hit the swamp created by falling profits themselves and became mired in low-growth (and bad debts) throughout the decade. Worse for them, American fiscal policy had turned conservative in the wake of the federal budget deficits run up by Reagan's military Keynesianism, and the US was no longer inflating its demand to help promote global development. Workers have suffered throughout the advanced industrial countries, as a result. Even with a strong recovery, American firms are shedding workers at a rate faster than the early Eighties and wages continued to stagnate until the labour market finally tightened circa 1996.

Meanwhile, the NICs began their miraculous climb into the ranks of industrial competitors to the Northern Tier countries. At first the United States welcomed the Four Tigers into the fold, leaving its markets relatively open and unprotected against their exports. But this added to the rising burden of trade deficits and manufacturing decline throughout the 1980s. The US tried to reverse its plight with the Plaza Accord of 1985, which devalued the dollar against the Japanese yen (tighter quotas on Japanese imports were also introduced). Japan's industries felt the pinch of higher costs and a reduced American market, and turned to Southeast Asia as an escape valve, investing huge amounts of capital in factories throughout the region. This threw gasoline on the growing fires of East Asian industrialisation. American corporations sent great floods of capital abroad, as well, as in the case of Mexico, spurring the export sector there, as well. Not surprisingly, a vast surge of exports came issuing forth from the Third Wave NICs, and this time imports caused significant manufacturing jobs losses in Japan as well as the United States.

Finally, the fallen rate of profit in manufacturing in the US and Japan led to a flight of capital out of productive investment and into other fields within both countries. In Japan the main outlet by the late 1980s was massive real estate speculation. In the United States, the main vent has been the stock market, which has charged upward at a double-digit rate for over a decade — a figure quite out of keeping with growth and profits (it is the most overvalued it has been in 120 years). Another response, as we've seen, has been the expansion of the service sectors. The reason? Because that is where the rate of profit held up best during the long downturn.

The rate of profit and capital's failure to accumulate thus account for the main features of labour's plight in the United States. But why did profits fall? The proximate reason is the pressure of competition from foreign imports, which hit manufacturing hardest because hard goods are the most fungible, tradable parts of national output. The onrushing centers of industrialisation — First Tier, then the Four Tigers and Third Wave NICs — were brought into a position to best American manufacturing in terms of unit costs, as we have noted.

Nonetheless, competition is not a sufficient explanation. It might account for the US losing its huge advantage, but why would profit rates have declined only slighter later in the miracle economies of Japan and Germany? And why would Southeast Asia hit the skids so dramatically in 1997 after a decade of intense industrialisation? Is it even cheaper labour in India and China? Or because the US States became competitive again? One circles around the problem but never lands. The puzzle of the zero-sum global game remains.

What we have seen, instead, is a frantic scramble by all parties to international trade to increase their share at the expense of everyone else. In the 1990s, the rate of growth of exports accelerated, as everyone desperately searched for new market share abroad. The ratio of growth of trade to growth of output hit a level twice that of any previous postwar decade. Is this due to a lack of global demand, in the Keynesian sense, as Greider and Glyn believe? In one sense, yes.

A regime of world austerity ushered in the 1990s, led by Clinton-Gringrich budget balancing, German bankers astride the European currency union, and Japanese deflationary policies. This kept demand growing more slowly than at any time in the postwar period. Yet austerity, for all its vices, was in part a response to excesses of deficit-spending in the 1980s; central bankers Meino and Greenspan were repeating the monetary purgatives applied by Volcker a decade earlier. Nonetheless, the real drag on the world economy is overcapacity — too many factories — rather than too few customers. There has been a sustained worldwide glut of capital stocks in basic industry. The cause is two-sided. New factories have been added and productivity improvements made without regard for the profitability of already-existing capitals, and this investment has proceeded extremely rapidly (double-digit rates) at the expanding edges (and deepening centers) of the world system.

Meanwhile, factories made redundant or obsolete by the new have not been closed fast enough to compensate for the gains elsewhere. That is, excess capital could not be, or would not be, written off in declining sectors, firms and countries as fast as new capital stocks entered the world market. Or, to put it in neo-classical terms, there has been a failure of adjustment — rate of entry exceeded rate of exit. But unlike the neo-classical story of market response and a tendency to equilibrium, there has been a long, persistent state of disequilibrium.

That disequilibrium made itself known with a bang once more in the Asian meltdown of 1997-98, which is still working its way back through the US and Europe. American companies, especially California ones, have began a new round of layoffs and poor quarterly reports, and the great stock run-up is careening over the mountain top into a recession. A US slowdown will reverberate through Europe, stanching its mild revival. But why the turnaround in American fortunes up to now? This might appear to contravene the gloomy picture of low profits. Indeed, US rates of profit improved in the late 1980s and 1990s, for good reasons.

First, a great deal of industrial capital was written off the landscape during the recessions.

Second, US companies restructured: new technology and lean production methods were brought on board as investment in new capital picked up; so productivity improved.

Third, currency devaluation after 1985 helped vis-a-vis Japan.

Last, but not least, business took its profit out of the hide of the workers: wages went nowhere while the economy picked up steam and productivity rebounded, hence a higher rate of surplus value.

In sum, a smaller capital base and a higher rate of surplus value means a higher rate of profit.

8

Urban Criminology

From the mid-1980s onwards 'globalisation' become increasingly the buzzword. Globalisation has many dimensions but two aspects can be identified as important for the increased crime rated in cities. Firstly, the world is becoming increasingly a single market place. Communications, including the internet and the mobile phone, rapid air transport, mean that goods and services can move rapidly around the world. In the legal economy this means that a leading bank in the UK can, for example, decentralise its customer care department to India, where labour is much cheaper. Legal capital can move around the world with increasing ease. Illegal activity is not far behind.

Secondly, global economic growth is uneven. No country is insulated from competition from some other part of the globe. Many agricultural products for example have suffered from falling prices over the last few decades. For example one of the big conflicts at present in world forums such as the World Trade Organisation is that poor countries complain their goods are being shut out of markets in the rich countries of Northern Europe and North America at the same time as the latter are ruining small farmers in the poor countries by dumping subsidised agricultural products. Under such conditions poor farmers whose livelihood has been undermined by these developments can hardly be blaming for turning to the production of raw materials for illegal drugs in order to maintain their incomes.

Meanwhile in the rich countries themselves, there are growing areas of poverty and deprivation, in inner cities and older industrial areas where jobs have been exported to low wage areas of the globe. The poor look desperately for money making activities and also for products that take their minds off their desperation. Meanwhile among the rich, rising incomes and the culture of urban life have massively increased the demand for illegal activities such as pornography, now widely available on the internet, drugs and sex, including sexual tourism.

In this context the growth of a number of flourishing illegal economies can be easily understood. These illegal economies have been estimated to account for about 8-10 percent of world trade. The main forms are

— *Illegal migration*: as people from devastated regions in the poor countries attempt to move to richer areas: from Mexico to the United States, from North Africa to Spain, and Europe, from war zones such as Iraq, Afghanistan, areas of the former Soviet Union to Western Europe etc. Criminal smugglers (using the same routes as for drugs trafficking) will assist this process for a price, often the life savings of the migrant and with no guarantee of safe arrival

— *The sexual trafficking of women*: specifically young women lured by tales of employment in glitzy western cities find themselves forced into prostitution after having given all their money, and usually their passports, to traffickers and pimps who organise the migration. Often they also function as drug 'mules' while in transit.

— *Arms smuggling*: many poor areas, particularly in parts of Africa, and Asia and the former Soviet Union, have become war zones, in which guerilla groups struggle for regime change or civil wars flourish. The collapse of the Soviet Union in the early 1990s, the subsequent conflicts in its former satellite colonies such as Yugoslavia and Chechnya have added to these conflicts. Such conflicts both increase the flood of refugees and migrants and the flood of illegal arms as United Nations, US and European governments attempt to stem the flow of weapons to these areas. We will focus more on these issues in a later lecture on terrorism

— *Drugs smuggling*: the growth of the global trade in heroin and cocaine although not necessarily more lucrative than migrant smuggling, has come to be regarded as the classic case of the new global illegal economy. About 5% of global population consume illegal drugs.

Causes and Kinds of Social Deviance

Deviance is generally defined as any act that violates a social norm. But the phenomenon is more complex than that. How do we know whether an act violates a social norm? Is homosexuality deviant—a violation of a social norm? Some people think so, but others do not. At least three factors are involved in determining what deviance is: time, place, and public consensus or power.

First, what constitutes deviance varies from one historical period to another. Nearly 2,000 years ago, the Roman Empress Messalina won a bet with a friend by publicly having a prolonged session of sexual intercourse with 25 men. At the time, Romans were not particularly scandalised, although they were quite impressed by her stamina. Today, if a person of similar social standing engaged in such behavior, we would consider it extremely scandalous.

Second, the definition of deviance varies from one place to another. A polygamist (a person with more than one spouse) is a criminal in the United States but not in Saudi Arabia and other Muslim countries. Prostitution is illegal in the United States (except in some counties in Nevada) but legal in Denmark, Germany, France, and many other countries. As a married man, former President Clinton got into hot water for having an affair, but married leaders in China are fully expected to have girlfriends.

Third, whether a given act is deviant depends on public consensus. Murder is unquestionably deviant because nearly all societies agree that it is. In contrast, drinking alcoholic beverages is generally not considered deviant. Public consensus, however, usually reflects the vested interests of the rich and powerful. As Marx would have said, the ideas of the ruling class tend to become the ruling ideas of society. Like the powerful, the general public tends, for example, to consider bank robbery a serious crime but not fraudulent advertising, which serves the interests of the powerful.

In view of these three determinants of deviant behavior, we may define deviance more precisely as an act considered by public consensus, or by the powerful at a given time and place, to be a violation of some social rule.

Most of the deviant acts studied by sociologists—such as homicide, robbery, and rape—involve violat-ing a criminal law; hence, they are criminal deviance. Some sociologists have, however, urged that more attention be focused on noncriminal deviance, such as homophobia, using pornography, and mental disorder. Here, we discuss both kinds of deviance. Common offenses punishable by fines or jail terms include:

— Gambling illegally, such as betting on a sport event or political election
— Evading taxes, such as failing to report or exaggerating deductible expenses
— Committing computer crime, such as copying software illegally
— Serving alcohol to minors
— Drinking in public, where prohibited
— Possessing marijuana in small quantities for personal use
— Committing adultery in states where it is illegal
— Patronising a prostitute

— Appearing nude in public, such as nude sunbathing, where prohibited
— Stealing TV signals, such as with a satellite dish
— Speeding or other moving-traffic violations
— Parking illegally
— Smoking in public, where an ordinance prohibits it
— Failing to recycle where required

Homicide

Homicide is mostly a personal crime, far more likely to be committed against acquaintances, friends, or relatives than against strangers. Swayed by common sense, we may find this incredible.

But as sociologists Donald Mulvihill and Melvin Tumin explained, "Everyone is within easy striking distance from intimates for a large part of the time. Although friends, lovers, spouses, and the like are a main source of pleasure in one's life, they are equally a main source of frustration and hurt. Few others can anger one so much." As a crime of passion, homicide is usually carried out under the overwhelming pressure of a volcanic emotion, namely, uncontrollable rage.

Homicide occurs most frequently during weekend evenings, particularly Saturday night. This holds true largely for lower-class murderers but not for middle- and upper-class offenders, who tend more to kill on any day of the week. One apparent reason is that higher-class murders are more likely than lowerclass homicides to be premeditated and hence are less likely to result from alcohol-induced quarrels during weekend sprees. Research has also often shown that most U.S. murderers are poor, including semiskilled workers, unskilled labourers, and welfare recipients

Whatever their class, murderers most often use handguns to kill. Perhaps seeing a gun while embroiled in a heated argument incites a person to murderous action. As

Shakespeare wrote, "How oft the sight of means to do ill deeds, makes ill deeds done." Of course, firearms by themselves cannot cause homicide, nor can their absence reduce the motivation to kill. It is true that "Guns don't kill; people do." Still, were guns less available, less dangerous weapons such as fists or knives might be used instead. Thus, many heated arguments might result in aggravated assaults rather than murders, thereby reducing the number of fatalities. But given the enormous number of guns in private hands, it is not surprising that far more deaths result from gun attacks in the United States than in Canada, Britain, and other industrialised countries, where there are considerably fewer guns per person.

The easy availability of guns has contributed to a stunning upsurge in killings by teenagers and young adults before the early 1990s. Bus since then, the homicide rate among young people has declined, largely as the result of increased economic prosperity, tougher law enforcement, and greater protection of domestic violence victims.

Rape

Rape involves the use of force to get a woman to do something sexual against her will. It is a common problem in the United States but exactly how common? And why is it common? Incidence and Characteristics Every year, about 110,000 cases of rape in the United States are reported to the police, but the actual number of rapes is considerably higher, running into the millions.

According to the most conservative estimate, at least 10 percent of women have been raped. Most of these rapes are not even legally defined as such, let alone reported to the police. A key reason is that the overwhelming majority of cases involve intimates such as lovers and close friends, whereas the popular perception of rape is associated with strangers or mere acquaintances.

In one survey, while 22 percent of the women said they had been forced to have sex, only about 3 percent of the men admitted to having committed forced sex. Why do the overwhelming majority of men fail to acknowledge what some women see as forced sex? The apparent reason, again, has much to do with the fact that most cases of forced sex involve intimates. Consider the following two scenarios given by Michael and his colleagues.

One involves a married man coming home late after drinking a lot of beer with the guys. He wants sex, but his wife cringes when he approaches. She obviously does not want sex. He does and has his way. He does not think it was forced, but she does. Another illustration involves two young people on a date. She touches his hand, his arm, and then even his thigh while they are talking at dinner. She thinks she is only trying to get to know him, but he thinks she wants sex. Later, when he makes his move, she says no. But he thinks she means yes. He believes the sex was consensual. To her, it was forced. But why do the males in such scenarios fail to see that they have committed forced sex? The reason seems to lie in the traditional patriarchal belief that a man should be aggressive to win a woman's heart. Resulting from such aggression gone out of control, forced sex is an extension of the traditional pattern of male sexual behavior. The belief about the importance of male aggressiveness is embedded in the culture that encourages rape.

The culture of rape reveals itself through at least three prevailing attitudes toward women.

First, women traditionally have been treated like men's property. If a woman is married, she is, in effect, her husband's property. Thus, in most countries and some states in the United States, a man cannot be prosecuted for raping his wife. The reasoning seems to be: How can any man steal what already belongs to him? The property logic may also explain the difficulty of getting a man convicted for raping a "cheap, loose woman" or a known prostitute. Such a female is considered every man's property because she has had sex with many men. If a "good" woman is raped, we often say that she has been "ravaged," "ravished," "despoiled," or "ruined," as if she were a piece of property that has been damaged.

Globally, when conquering armies commandeer the conquered population's property, they also tend to rape the women as if they were part of that property. During World War II, German soldiers raped massive numbers of Jewish and Russian women after occupying many villages and cities in Europe, and the Japanese army systematically raped women and girls as it invaded Korea, China, and various Southeast Asian countries. In today's armed conflicts, foreign soldiers continue to rape local women.

Second, women are treated as if they are objects of masculinity contests among men. To prove his manhood, a man is culturally pressured to have sex with the largest number of women possible. The pressure to play this masculinity game often comes from friends, who ask questions such as "Did you score?" "Had any lately?" If the answer is no, the friends may ask, "What's the matter? Are you gay or something?" Such social pressure tends to make young men want to show off their masculine qualities, such as aggressiveness, forcefulness, and violence.

Even without peer pressure, the popular belief in sexual conquest as a badge of masculinity encourages men to be aggressive toward women. If women say no, men are expected to ignore this response or even translate it into really meaning yes. Such lessons in sexual conquest often come from the stereotype of the movie or television hero who forcefully, persistently embraces and kisses the heroine despite her strong resistance, and who is rewarded when she finally melts in his arms.

In real life, such sexual aggression can easily lead to rape. This is why many sociologists regard rape as an extension of the socially approved conventional pattern of male sexual behavior. It is also not surprising that members of the Spur

Posse, a group of high school boys in California who compete with one another by scoring points for sexual conquests, were once jailed only for a few days on charges of molesting and raping girls as young as 10. It is also no wonder that other winners of the masculinity game, such as college men with considerable sexual experience, are more likely to rape their dates than are the so-called losers, who have little or no sexual experience.

Third, there is a popular myth that, deep down, women want to be raped. This myth is often expressed in various ways: "She asked for it"; "She actually wanted it"; and "She lied about it (or consented to sex but later decided to 'cry rape')." In essence, the victim is held responsible for the rape. The victim is assumed to have done something that provoked the man to rape her. That something involves being in the wrong place (walking alone at night); wearing the wrong clothes (short shorts, miniskirts, or some other sexy dress); turning the man on (letting him kiss or pet her); or having an attitude (behaving assertively or independently).

Because of this blame-the-victim assumption, defense attorneys for alleged rapists tend to portray the victim as a willing partner. In one case, the victim was accused of having a "kinky and aggressive" sex life. In another case, the victim was said to be "sexually voracious" and to have "preyed on men". The willing-victim myth is a major motivating force behind many rapes. In a study of convicted rapists, 59 percent denied their guilt and blamed their victims instead. They insisted that their victims seduced them, meant yes while saying no to the sexual assault, and eventually relaxed and enjoyed the rape. Not surprisingly, men who believe this dangerous myth about women are more likely to rape them.

Binge Drinking

In recent years there have been many cases of college students dying from binge drinking, which involves having at least five drinks in a row for men or four drinks in a row for women.

According to Dr. David Anderson, of George Mason University in Fairfax, Virginia, at least 50 college students throughout the United States drink themselves to death every year. While endangering their own lives, binge drinkers also tend to disturb or hurt their fellow students, such as causing them to lose sleep, interrupting their studies, and assaulting them physically or sexually.

Although binge drinking is a serious problem, it has long been a tradition on many U.S. college campuses. And despite the raising of the legal drinking age to 21 in all states since the late 1980s, binge drinking continues to be about as prevalent today as it was 20 years ago. According to a nationwide survey, some 44 percent of college students (50 percent of the men and 39 percent of the women) have binged at least once during the past two weeks. There is also a relentless quality to the pursuit of intoxication among many students who drink: About 40 percent of students intend to binge or get drunk every time they drink. Compared with their moderate or nondrinking peers, binge-drinking students are more likely to miss class, fall behind in schoolwork, have poor grades, engage in unprotected sex, get injured, damage property, fight, or get into trouble with the police. Binge drinkers are also more likely to be male, white, involved in athletics, or living in fraternity or sorority houses. Why, then, do they binge drink? The stress from having to work hard for good grades is one contributing factor. A more important factor is the social pressure to get drunk so as to fit in and not to be seen by others as uptight or antisocial. This may explain why a large majority of fraternity brothers and sorority sisters are binge drinkers. The social pressure to fit in can also explain the unusually high incidence of binge drinking among those who regard parties as a very important part of their college life.

Corporate Crime

Corporate crimes are committed by company officials without the overt use of force, and their effect on the victims is not readily traceable to the offender. If a miner dies from a lung disease, it is difficult to prove beyond reasonable doubt that he died because the employer violated mine safety regulations.

Corporate crimes may be perpetrated not only against employees but also against customers and the general public. Examples include disregard for safety in the workplace, consumer fraud, price fixing, production of unsafe products, and violation of environmental regulations. Compared with traditional street crime, corporate crime is more rationally executed, more profitable, and less detectable by law enforcers. In addition, crime in the executive suite is distinguished from crime in the street by three characteristics that help explain the prevalence of corporate crime.

Corporate criminals often see themselves as respectable people rather than common criminals. They maintain their noncriminal self-image through rationalisation. Violators of price-fixing laws, for example, may insist that they are helping the nation's economy by "stabilising prices" and serving their companies by "recovering costs." In their book, there is no such crime as price fixing.

The noncriminal self-image is also maintained through seeing oneself as a victim rather than an offender.

Corporate criminals argue that they were just unlucky enough to get caught for doing something that practically everyone else does. As a convicted tax offender said, "Everybody cheats on their income tax, 95 percent of the people. Even if it's for $10 it's the same principle"

The noncriminal self-image is further maintained through denial of criminal intent. Corporate criminals may admit that they committed the acts that landed them in prison, but they regard their acts only as mis-takes, not as something motivated by a guilty criminal mind. As a convicted tax offender said, "I'm not a criminal. That is, I'm not a criminal from the standpoint of taking a gun and doing this and that. I'm a criminal from the standpoint of making a mistake, a serious mistake" .

Primarily due to lack of caution or knowledge, many victims unwittingly cooperate with the corporate criminal. In a home improvement scheme, victims do not bother to check the work history of the fraudulent company that solicits them, or they sign a contract without examining its content for such matters as the true price and the credit terms. Some victims purchase goods through the mail without checking the reputation of the firm.

Doctors prescribe untested drugs, relying only on the pharmaceutical company's salespeople and advertising. It may be difficult for victims to know they have been victimised, even if they want to find out the true nature of their victimisation. Average grocery shoppers, for example, are hard put to detect such unlawful substances as residues of hormones, antibiotics, pesticides, and nitrites in the meat they buy.

Generally, little effort is made to catch corporate criminals. On the rare occasions when they are caught, they seldom go to jail or they receive a light sentence, if they are incarcerated. Their pleas for mercy are heard after they promise to repay their victims or to cooperate in prosecutions against others. They insist that a long prison term will do no good because their lives are already in ruins. Even when convicted of crimes that caused the death of many workers or customers, corporate offenders have never been sentenced to death, let alone executed, though numerous lower-class criminals have been executed for killing only one person.

Mental Problems

Mental problems are far more common than popularly believed. Every year, about 22 percent of U.S. adults suffer from a mental problem serious enough to require psychiatric help or hospitalisation, and the figure for adolescents is 10 percent. The most common problems are anxiety and phobia followed by depression and alcoholism. In fact, all of us have been or will be mentally ill in one way or another. Of course, most of our mental problems are not serious. We occasionally suffer from brief bouts of anxiety or depression, "the common cold of mental ailments."

This can be illustrated by what happened for a few days following the terrorist attacks on the World Trade Center and the Pentagon on September 11, 2001. After repeatedly seeing the horrifying images of death and destruction on television, Americans throughout the country suffered from anxiety, depression, and other stress-related symptoms such as fatigue and insomnia. These psychological complaints, in turn, led some to develop physical ailments including ulcers, hypertension, and irritable bowel syndrome.

For most people, though, these problems soon disappeared, thanks, in part, to the surge of social support from relatives, friends, and even strangers. However, the types of mental problems that sociologists and psychiatrists usually study are more serious and durable. They include psychosis, typified by loss of touch with reality, and neurosis, characterised by a persistent fear, anxiety, or worry about trivial matters. A psychotic can be likened to a person who thinks incorrectly that 2 plus 2 equals 10 but strongly believes it to be correct. A neurotic can be compared to a person who thinks correctly that 2 plus 2 equals 4 but constantly worries that it may not be so.

Sociologists have long suspected that certain social forces are involved in the development of mental problems. The one most consistently demonstrated by research to be a key factor in mental problems is social class: the lower the social class, the higher the rate of mental problems. The poor are more prone to mental disorder because their lives are more stressful: more family problems and unemployment, more psychic frailty and neurological impairments, and less social and emotional support.

Other social factors, such as gender, ethnicity, and culture, give rise to certain types of mental problems. Thus, women are more likely to experience depression and anxiety attacks while men tend more to have antisocial personality, paranoia, and drug and alcohol abuse disorders. Jewish and Asian Americans have a higher incidence of depressive disorders, usually in the form of anger turned against oneself.

Puerto Ricans and African Americans tend more to show paranoid and sociopathic propensities in the form of distrust and resentment against others. Finally, certain mental disorders take place in some cultures but never or rarely in others. In Latin America, for example, people experience susto, the pathological fear that their souls have left their bodies. In the United States, women get anorexia nervosa, an extreme fear of weight gain that is rarely found in other societies.

Suicide Bombings

Since the September 11 terrorist attacks, many in the West have assumed that so-called suicide bombers must be psychotic, or at least irrational, and that they must be poor and uneducated. But evidence seems to suggest just the opposite.

According to a study on the 149 Palestinian suicide bombers who tried to attack Israel between 1993 and 2002, the majority had about the same social background as the September 11 terrorists. They were young, male, and single. They came from relatively well-off, middle-class families, and they were better educated than most people in their countries. Thus, they were rational enough to know, for example, that they could resort to a suicide bombing as their ultimate weapon in perpetrating an asymmetrical war with Israel. They knew that, like the September 11 terrorists, they couldn't fight a conventional war with their enemy because they had no tanks, no artillery, and no air force, while their enemy had one of the world's most powerful and modern militaries.

Why, then, do these individuals choose to get themselves killed while most other terrorists do not? One apparent reason is the suicide bombers' Muslim religious belief that by becoming martyrs, they will be rewarded in heaven, which includes being greeted by virgins. But this may not hold true for most of the Muslim Chechen suicide bombers in Russia, who are women, nor for the bombers in Sri Lanka and other countries, who are not Muslims.

Again, what motivates not only the Palestinian terrorists and the September 11 attackers but also the female Chechen bombers and the non-Islamic terrorists to engage in suicide bombing? The answer can be found with the aid of the sociological concept of altruistic suicide. Individuals who commit altruistic suicide are so strongly tied to their group that they effectively lose their selves and stand ready to do their group's bidding. Examples from the past include the elderly Inuit and Hindu widows, who faithfully followed the tradition of their societies that encouraged people in their circumstances to commit suicide. Such suicide was relatively common in ancient societies, in which the group reigned supreme at the expense of the individual.Not surprisingly, the suicide bombers of today typically live in traditional societies that give priority to conformity over individuality. And like the altruistic suicides of the past, the suicide bombers are too deeply integrated into their groups—terrorist organisations — and identify completely with them.

A number of social factors support their all-consuming ties to these organisations. The candidates for suicide bombings are recruited and then subjected to intense spiritual and ideological indoctrination and terrorist training. In the Middle East, the bomber's surviving family is further provided with such rewards as cash bonuses, pensions, and health benefits. And the bomber is celebrated as a hero in the community. After a young man carries out a suicide attack, his parents may proudly announce his martyrdom in the newspaper.

Organised Crime

From the mid 1970s onwards the opportunities for the development of organised crime began to increase substantially on a global scale. newer activities such as the global market in illegal drugs give rise to new types of criminal organisation. Traditional organised crime groups may or may not become involved in such activity, and if they do, then their forms of organisation may tend to change.

The Italian sociologist Letizia Paoli has, for example, identified two 'paradoxes' of modern organised crime. Firstly, that markets in illegal activities such as drugs exhibit no immanent tendency towards the development of large-scale criminal enterprises on the model of the Sicilian Mafia, Japanese Yakuza or Chinese Triads. Secondly, that although these types of large-scale criminal organisations do exist, they are not exclusively involved in illegal market activities, and the type of organisational forms they have developed is not the result of their participation in illegal market dynamics. Indeed, as she argues specifically in the case of the Sicilian Mafia, such organisational forms may to some ex tent hinder participation in modern global illegal markets.

We shall explore some of these issues here. How far have traditional organised crime groups adapted to modern illegal markets and how far have they been left behind by newer, more flexible, groups better able to respond to market opportunities without worrying about power and status in local communities. We got a flavour of this change at the end of the previous lecture when we looked briefly at the changing circumstances of organised crime in Britain.

During the 1960s it was assumed by many commentators in Italy that the economic effects of the post war boom were finally bringing about the demise of the old Mafia groups, whose power rested on the weakness of the government and the old localised isolated family-centred communities of rural Sicily. It was argued that the power base of organised crime was crumbling. A number of specific factors were associated with the process of modernisation itself.

Firstly, the Mafia lost some of the functions it had played in traditional Sicilian society. Under the impact of agricultural modernisation, the disintegration of the large landed estates and land redistribution reduced the mediating role of the traditional Mafia between the big landowners and their tenants.

Secondly, the large scale migration, particularly of young men, to the expanding industries of northern Italy together with the expansion of public sector construction activity in Sicily itself weakened traditional sources of Mafia recruits and enforcers.

These economic developments in turn brought forth social and political changes. Modern forms of employment in Southern Italy fostered the growth of trade unions and workers' parties, in particular the Italian Communist Party which strengthened modern forms of the representation and mediation of interests. Such organisations, it was assumed, had no interest in Mafia methods. Likewise employers bidding for contracts in public sector construction, or in any other area of economic expansion, would have an interest in rational open and free competition and would constitute a growing force not only against the Mafia itself but the entire system of bureaucratic clientalism and favouritism which characterised traditional Sicilian society and within which the Mafia flourished.

Increased economic activity and public investment meanwhile brought a strengthening of the state apparatus and a withdrawal of toleration of any rivals to the state in the sphere of public order maintenance. Finally, at the level of popular culture these changes undermined the traditional symbols of social prestige and status. The old virtues of the Mafia man of honour – in particular respect flowing from the willingness to use violence – were undermined by the those of the accumulation of wealth and conspicuous consumption as symbols of social status. The old Mafia was, during the 1950s and 60s undergoing a profound crisis under the impact of industrialisation and modernisation. As Arlacchi puts it:

> During the 'fifties, and still more during the 'sixties the men of honour underwent a deep crisis: what was their identity, where did they fit in, if they were no longer official proxies in the mediation of conflicts and the repression of non-conformist behaviour, and if public praise and flattery from the authorities had given way to speeches at meetings and sentences in courts that denounced them as enemies of order and progress?

The old Mafia, it appeared, was relinquishing its connections to, and participation in, the central dynamics of power in Sicilian society. It was becoming weakened and marginalised. It was failing to reproduce itself as a social group as evidenced by the apparent ageing of the Mafia population as evidenced by court trials during the 1960s.Arlacchi concludes:

> During the 'sixties the Mafioso's role was becoming more and more nearly that of a mere common criminal, a modern urban gangster who had neither popular roots nor popular backing.

A not dissimilar dynamic was identified during the same period as signalling the coming demise of the Italian-American mafia. The postwar rapid economic growth was producing social mobility in the Italian-American community, the old ghettos were weakening, and with them the communities within which the Mafia had operated. Involvement in crime became less attractive as a source of wealth and status. The coming of the federally administered welfare, the expansion of state education and a system of social security payments to the poor had weakening the importance of the Mafia and similar ethnically based groups as 'fixers' and people you went to for help in sorting out jobs and other problems through political corruption and nepotism in city government. The American sociologist Daniel Bell summed the trend as early as the beginning of the 1960s

> With the rationalisation and absorption of some illicit activities into the structure of the economy, the passing of an older generation that had established a hegemony over crime, the rise of minority groups to social position, and the break-up of the

> urban boss system, the pattern of crime we have discussed is passing as well. Crime, of course, remains as long as passion and the desire for gain remain. But big, organised city crime, as we have known it for the last seventy five years... is at an end.

But, in Italy at least, the assumption of mafia decline was premature. It underestimated the capacity of the organisation to adapt to new circumstances and to integrate itself into and take advantages of the new forces of industrialisation during the post war boom. Furthermore it must not be forgotten that the Americans had in fact given considerable assistance to the resurgence of the Mafia in Italy both by deporting some leading Italian-American mafiosi (such as the New York boss, 'Lucky' Luciano) back to Italy, and also by using the Mafia during the closing stages of the second world war to assist the Allies landing in German occupied Sicily.

The Italian economic expansion of the 1960s to the 1980s, like that of other European industrial countries involved much expansion of welfare state and public services: local government was building roads and schools and hospitals etc. All this involved state contracts to building and construction companies. There was also a massive expansion in areas like private house building and tourism. The Mafia was able to integrate itself into these new processes and put its traditional resources and methods to the new activities of business enterprise and capital accumulation.

It was able to use, for example, threats of violence to secure building contracts for the companies it controlled. It was able to bribe or intimidate public officials to award contracts to those companies or to give planning permission to Mafia owned private construction companies to build houses, hotels and holiday accommodation. The Mafia was able to hitch itself to the new forms of power and economy, to avail itself of new opportunities and change the elites with whom it entered into relations of co-operation, intimidation and corruption.

The old agrarian landowner elites were replaced by the modern political party systems, in particular the Christian Democrat Party which ruled Italy almost continually until the early 1990s for whom the Mafia guaranteed votes in return for protection.

With the coming of the European Union (EU) this process intensified. The Mafia was able to use its influence to divert EU regional grants to poor areas in Southern Italy and Sicily to those interests that it controlled. Funds for the relief of Earthquake disasters were systematically diverted to corrupt politicians and business interests. Instead of modernisation getting rid of the Mafia, the Mafia was able to hitch itself to the process of modernisation and the expansion of industrial Italy. By the mid 1980s the leading Mafia investigator Giovane Falcone concluded that "We have reached the situation where any economic intervention on the part of the State only runs the risk of offering the Mafia further opportunities for speculation".

Much of the money that was invested in building construction by Mafia companies came from the expanding global drugs trade, and also with kidnapping for ransom. With the economic downturn during the 1980s which has intensified in all European industrial countries during the 1990s the access to alternative sources of credit, based on drugs money, has become an important way in which the Mafia and other Italian organised crime groups, like the Camorra of Naples, have increased their control of small business. Under conditions of economic instability such as at the present time, banks think twice about lending money to shaky small business – the small business sector is very large in Southern Italy. The Mafia will lend money at lower interests rates, but will seek a share in the control of the enterprise and will use violence to collect overdue loans. This is an elaborate form of what was defined elsewhere as 'loansharking'.

At the beginning of the 1990's according to a report by the Italian Financial police "the illegal economy is in a position to finance its operations through channels which parallel the traditional sources of bank credit. Illegal self financing, besides withdrawing some undertakings from bank tax, gives small concerns a strong competitive edge." This in fact drives many small firms to seek out the Mafia spontaneously, rather than wait for the blackmailers. Rather than pay 16-18 percent VAT or bank tax on credit, money was being borrowed from the Mafia at 4 percent interest. The other side of the coin was that the Mafia demanded control of half the assets of the company. By mid 1993 it was estimated in a report by Confcommercio–the Italian small business association that the Mafia controlled 50 percent of public works projects and building sites in southern Italy, 20-22 percent of building firms and 20 of restaurants.

So modernisation had not undermined at least this form of traditional organised crime, rather organised crime itself had modernised, and used its traditional power to capture an important role in the expanding economy particularly in Sicily and southern Italy.

Drugs Trade

Drug production acts as a social cushion against poverty for thousands of small farmers. For example in Latin America, in countries like Colombia, falling prices for textiles and of course coffee under the impact of global competition since the mid 1980s led thousands of small farmers to shift to the production of coca leaf from which cocaine is produced. Coca leaf is regarded as a traditional plant and its production carries no social stigma. Similar considerations apply to the production of poppys from which opium and then heroin is extracted in areas of Asia.

Drug consumption is not simply a result of poverty and deprivation but is also a middle class lifestyle choice in the urban north. The basic question we are interested in is this: what varieties of organised crime are involved in these illegal economies? How have traditional groups fared and what newer groups have arisen? When speaking of those involved in the illegal drugs trade we tend to talk of traffickers and dealers rather than gangsters, emphasising that what is taking place is above all an economic money-making activity.

It is obvious from the global nature of the drugs trade that the successful trafficker is someone who knows how to travel and negotiate state boundaries, can handle finance, can make deals with people whom he or she has minimal knowledge of, can perhaps speak two or more languages. A much more cosmopolitan person than the traditional localised, community based image of the mafioso that we have been dealing with up till now. However, a more detailed focus enables us to see that some diversity of types of entrepreneurs can be involved in this complex global illegal economy.

Producer Countries

These areas have a lot of fixed assets that need protecting: crops have to be protected from government attempts at eradication (e.g. by spraying from the air) producers have to be paid, the raw material has to be shipped to refining laboritories in secret locations, guards have to be paid, police and soldiers bribed etc.

These areas often involve something rather more like the situation that faced traditional organised crime. That is to say the control of territory is important. The production facilities may be located in areas in which the state is already weak or can be easily bribed. e.g. in Colombia in Latin America coca farmers may be in areas controlled by guerilla groups who protect them in return for a portion of the profits. Local warlords and chieftains in Afghanistan and adjacent areas may protect opium growers and then tax them as an important source of income.

But although territory is being controlled and occasionally organised criminals may be seen to invest in local communities to secure compliance, and need to corrupt state officials, police and politicians in order to protect their assets, their interest in territorial dominance stems mainly from the need to protect their economic interests. They have little interest in local status, power and presteige as such. Their main orientation is to the global illegal economy, how much money they can make through exports to consumer countries etc.

Nevertheless, in Colombia during the 1980s when about 80 percent of the cocaine export trade was controlled by powerful groups of criminal businessmen based in the cities of Medellin and Cali, a few of the leaders, in particular Pablo Escobar, achieved a sort of social status. When he was shot in 1993 many poor people came to Escobar's funeral. It is alleged that he had invested money in housing and social amenities for poor people in his area and given money to the church. This is also true of criminal organisations in other parts of the world, in South Africa for example.

Global distribution

Global distribution of the finished product is handled by a diversity of different groups who are globally mobile. In many cases these traders come from ethnic groups which are settled in more than one country. For example Turkish traders bringing in heroin from Afghanistan overland through Turkey will profit from the existence of a Turkish community in say, London or Frankfurt. This may enable them to more easily conceal their drug smuggling in the guise of legitimate importers of turkish foodstuffs etc. Similar examples could be given for other groups. One factor which enabled Sicilian Mafiosi to get into the drugs trade, which we shall discuss presently, was the presence of an Italian-American community in the United States.

But not all distributors necessarily have a settled community in the destination country. The ease of travel around the world makes this less necessary. Colombian traders began operating effectively during the 1980s in the United States for example, in the absence of a settled Colombian community in US cities. Initially they traded through the Cuban exile community in Florida but then set up on their own. These are businessmen pure and simple, they have no aspirations to local power and prestige. They are small groups of highly mobile and flexible entrepreneurs.

The people employed by these entrepreneurs consitute a very flexible workforce people who also move accross state boundaries: truck drivers, ships captains, young women being trafficked into the sex trade. Journalists and police talk about traffickers drawn from a variety of ethnic groups and regions such as: Turkish, Albanian, Russian, Colombian, Chinese (Triads), Nigerian, Italian, Caribbean (Yardie), Japanese (Yakuza) gangs

Consumer countries

These international traders then sell on to a diversity of local groups of various sizes and forms of organisation whom in turn, sell to street dealers. This can easily be handled by small firms. Thus according to Paoli in Germany, during the 1990s, figures from the Federal Criminal Office shows the small size of criminal groups revealed in police investigations:

— 54% of investigations unearthed groups of less than 10 people
— 39% involved groups of 11-49
— 7% involved groups of over 50

An outfit can be as small as two or three people who, for example, go to a bar in Rotterdam, make contact with a trader, buy drugs, arrange a shipment, collect at the other end and then sell on to lower level street dealers. This sort of organised crime has come to be termed 'disorganised organised crime.' It is much more like project crime: small groups, combination for a time, and only difference is that it takes a bit longer to organise regular drug shipments than a one-off bank robbery, though the same people may be involved in both activities.

But basically the forms of organisation are based around the telephone rather than the mafia family:

— the armed robber will have a list of contacts who specialise in certain activities: safebreaking, driving cars at high speed, firearms, money laundering.

— the drug dealer will have a similar list: people who own boats, and vehicles, street dealers in various cities, various bars where importers can be met etc.

This is a far cry from the closed world of the old Mafia. This is what we might expect in the drugs trade in mainly consumption countries which do not have producer centres. There is no tendency, as Letizia Paoli observes for countries with thriving illegal markets and drug trading to have any tendency to develop mafia type organisations. Rather than organised crime it might be better to talk about network crime: small groups of entrepreneurs who buy from one source but may not do so again, who vaguely know each other but keep at arms length. But know each other's reputations for 'honesty'. Reputation is important in the criminal economy as there is no recourse to law to enforce contracts.

A reflection of this plurality and diversity of organised crime is the increasing problem of working out a blanket definition of organised crime which can include the variety of groups involved. In the UK the National Criminal Intelligence Service (NCIS) since 1998 has published an annual 'threat assessment' based on intelligence gathered by the law enforcement agencies (mainly police and customs). The 1998 assessment attempted a definition of organised crime as follows:

— contains at least three people

— criminal activity is prolonged or indefinite

— criminals are motivated by profit or power

— serious criminal offences are being committed.

This problem of size was repeated in 1998 European Union definition of organised crime as "a lasting structured association of more than two persons acting in concert." This could of course include kids hanging around outside tube stations depriving people of their travel cards to sell on.

Recently NCIS has been more sanguine in trying to capture the complexity of criminal activity rather than trying to devise a catch-all definition. Thus in the 2003 threat assessment we read:

> "While there are certainly some organised crime groups that resemble the traditional British 'firm' or Italian mafia, with permanent members each with a distinct role, and a hierarchy in which there are clear chains of command and communication, there are other 'groups' that are, in practice, loose networks, the members of which coalesce around one or more prominent criminals to undertake particular criminal ventures of varying complexity, structure and length. In the latter instance, the criminals may not think of themselves as being members of any group, and individuals may be involved with a number of sub-groups within the network, and therefore be involved in a number of separate criminal ventures at any one time."

Old mafia and the drugs economy

What has happened to traditional organised crime groups in this context? The paradox is that the traditional types of organised crime such as the Sicilian and US Mafias certainly entered these activities but as peripheral partners to the newer flexible organisations. Yet, paradoxically, as she points out, it is still the mafia that people think of when they hear the term 'organised crime'

We have already seen how the Sicilian Mafia renewed itself by getting involved in public contracts and new political alliances with the Christian Democrat party. The second main area in which the Mafia 'renewed' itself was through involvement in the drugs trade. During the 1970s the trade became a major source of finance and activity.

As far as the Italian Mafia were concerned, Sicily was especially placed to benefit from expansion in the international heroin trade. Its geographical location as a gateway between the Middle East and South Asian producers and the growing consumer markets in bit European and American cities was important as was the nearness of Sicily to local wars and terrorist activities in the Middle East where arms exchanged for drugs in underworld markets. Italian families moreover had connections to both Latin America and the United States where there were sizeable Italian immigrant communities

By the mid 1970's Sicilians had taken over the Middle Eastern supply routes for heroin from South Asia. The learned to co-operate with other organised crime groups in Turkey and Bulgaria. Drugs refineries were re-established in Sicily and also in Northern Italy. The old Mafia had modernised itself, learned to travel and handle banks and international money. The vast profits from the international heroin trade led to increased competition and violence with several internal 'Mafia wars' particularly in the early 1960's and again in the early 1980's.

According to Italian investigators the high point of Mafia involvement in the heroin trade seems to have been the mid 1980's and since then there has been some decline. During the 1980s cocaine consumption was increasing relative to heroin. Meanwhile cocaine prices were falling in the US due to oversupply and the powerful Latin American organised crime groups who specialised in production and global distribution of cocaine were looking to move into the European market.

The Sicilian Mafia, with its unrivalled set of connections and contacts throughout Europe, was able to enter into profitable distribution deals to import and distribute cocaine for the Latin American groups. In the mid 1980s cocaine prices in Europe were three times higher than in the US. Various operations by the law enforcement agencies revealed the growing extent of global international co-operation by organised crime. In January 1994, for example 8 Colombian businessmen, wanted by the US drug enforcement authorities were arrested in Italy and charged with money laundering of $100 million.

But the Mafia remains a traditional organised crime group with modernising tendencies. The old 'family' structure is still important and the aims of the Mafia still include those of traditional organised crime. Thus Letizia Paoli warns the Sicilian Mafia has not become simply an organisation for making money illegally, There has been no abandonment of use of violence in levying massive protection rackets on local business and people and as a means of maintaining domination over an area. The primary goal of thte Mafia, according to Paoli, remains that of power and social domination rather than the accumulation of wealth as an end in itself. The example she gives is that profits from the drugs trade from the mid 1970s onwards could have been more lucratively invested abroad by Mafia and other Italian organised crime groups if they had acted from a purely business or money making standpoint. But in fact much of the profits of the dr ugs trade was diverted to securing dominance over local affairs, and in particular the public building contracts already mentioned.

It is said that the American Mafia families made a decision to go into the heroin trade at a secret meeting in 1957. But they have been largely displaced by newer groups. During the 1980s FBI investigators thought the Mob was running heroin into the US but discovered it was in fact Sicilians (known as 'zips') who had the permission but not the participation of the old Italian-American mobsters. This was one of the discoveries unearthed in the investigations which led to the famous Pizza Connection trial in New York in 1986.

Meanwhile cocaine smuggling and distribution has been dominated by Colombian and Mexican groups. Partly this was about a shift in the drugs market from South East Asian heroin in which, as we have noted, the Mafia had some involvement (together with the Chinese Triads) to cocaine from Latin America which put Mexicans and Colombians at an advantage. The anthropologist Philipe Bourgois, in his brilliant study of New York crack dealers talks about "The Colombian organised crime cartels who... responded vigorously to the new market opportunities in the early 1980s and violently bypassed the traditional networks of the Italian-dominated Mafia that specialised in heroin."

The old Mafia had little power base outside its traditional ghettos but at the same time the latter were being weaked by upward social mobility. Many traditional American organised crime groups had themselves become 'upwardly mobile' and were moving into white collar crime such as financial fraud and insider dealing

Theories of Functions and Dysfunctions

Most scholars other than sociologists generally attribute deviance to a certain biological or psychological abnormality in the individual. But sociologists have long assumed that there is nothing physically or mentally wrong with most deviants. This assumption is a legacy of the French sociologist Emile Durkheim, one of the founders of functionalism in the discipline. For him, deviance is not only normal but also beneficial to society because, ironically, it contributes to social order. Whereas Durkheim emphasised the functions or benefits of deviance, today's functionalists focus on society's dysfunctions or problems as the causes of deviance.

Functionalist Theory

According to Durkheim, deviance can serve a number of functions for society. First, it helps enhance conformity in society as a whole. Norms are basically abstract and ambiguous, subject to conflicting interpretations.

Even criminal laws, which are far more clear-cut than other norms, can be confusing. The criminal act that a deviant commits and is punished for provides other citizens with a concrete example of what constitutes a crime. From deviants we can learn the difference between conformity and deviance, seeing the boundary between right and wrong more clearly. Once aware of this boundary, we are more likely to stay on the side of rightness.

Second, deviance strengthens solidarity among lawabiding members of society. Differing values and interests may divide them, but collective outrage against deviants as a common enemy can unite them, as it did Americans in the aftermath of the terrorist attacks on September 11, 2001. Because deviance promotes social cohesion that decreases crime, Durkheim described it as "a factor in public health, an integral part of all healthy societies."

Third, deviance provides a safety valve for discontented people. Through relatively minor forms of deviance, they can strike out against the social order without doing serious harm to themselves or others. Prostitution, for example, may serve as a safety valve for marriage in a male-dominated society because the customer is unlikely to form an emotional attachment to the prostitute. In contrast, a sexual relationship with a friend is more likely to develop into a love affair that could destroy the marriage. Fourth, deviance can induce social change. Martin Luther King, Jr., and other civil rights leaders were jeered and imprisoned for their opposition to segregation, but they moved the United States toward greater racial equality.

There is a limit, however, to the validity of Durkheim's functionalist theory. If deviance is widespread, it can threaten social order in at least two ways. First, it can wreck interpersonal relations. Alcoholism tears apart many families. If a friend flies into a rage and tries to kill us, it will be difficult to maintain a harmonious relationship. Second, deviance can undermine trust. If there were many killers, robbers, and rapists living in our neighborhoods, we would find it impossible to welcome neighbors into our home as guests or babysitters.

Nevertheless, Durkheim's theory is useful for demolishing the commonsense belief that deviance is always harmful. Deviance can bring benefits if it occurs within limits.

Strain Theory

In the 1930s, U.S. sociologist Robert Merton agreed with Durkheim that deviance is "an integral part of all healthy societies." More significantly, Merton drew on Durkheim's concept of anomie to develop a theory of deviance that later became well known among sociologists for a long time as anomie theory but has also been known since the 1980s as strain theory. Literally meaning "normlessness," anomie is a social condition in which norms are absent, weak, or in conflict. Anomie may arise, said Merton, when there is an inconsistency in society between the cultural goals and the institutionalised (socially approved, legitimate) means of achieving the goals. In the United States, such an inconsistency surrounds the issue of success.

According to Merton, U.S. culture places too much emphasis on success as a valued goal. From kindergarten to college, teachers prod students to achieve the American dream. Parents and coaches pressure even Little League players not just to play well but to win. The media often glorify winning not only in sports but also in business, politics, and other arenas of life. This emphasis on success motivates hard work, thereby contributing to society's prosperity.

But at the same time, people are not equally provided with the legitimate means (such as good jobs and other opportunities) for achieving success. There is, then, an inconsistency between too much emphasis on the success goal and too little emphasis on the availability of legitimate means for achieving that goal. Such inconsistency produces a strain among people in the lower classes, pressuring them to achieve success through what Merton calls innovation —using illegitimate means of achieving success, such as committing a robbery or selling drugs. But most people do not resort to innovation as a response to the goal–means inconsistency. In addition to innovation, four other responses are possible, depending on whether the cultural goal of success and the institutionalised means are accepted or rejected:

1. Conformity, the most popular form of response, involves accepting both the cultural goal of success and the use of legitimate means for achieving that goal.
2. Innovation, the response described earlier, involves accepting the goal of success but rejecting the use of socially accepted means to achieve it, turning instead to unconventional, illegitimate methods.
3. Ritualism occurs when people no longer set high success goals but continue to toil as conscientious, diligent workers.
4. Retreatism is withdrawal from society, caring neither about success nor about working. Retreatists include vagabonds, outcasts, and drug addicts.
5. Rebellion occurs when people reject and attempt to change both the goals and the means approved by society. The rebel tries to overthrow the existing system and establish a new system with different goals and means. An example would be attempting to replace the current U.S. competitive pursuit of fame and riches with a new system that enhances social relations through cooperation.

In short, Merton's theory blames deviance on society's failure to provide all people with legitimate means to achieve success. The theory is useful for explaining the higher rates of robbery, theft, and other property crimes among lower-class people, who are pressured to commit such crimes by their lack of good jobs and other legitimate means for success. But the theory fails to explain embezzlement, tax fraud, and other white-collar crimes because the people who commit such offenses are typically not deprived of the legitimate means for success, as the lower classes are.

As a functionalist, Merton assumes that the same value—belief in material success—is shared throughout society. But this assumption runs counter to the pluralistic and conflicting nature of U.S. society, where many groups differentiated by class, gender, ethnicity, or religion do not share the same values. Some groups, for example, are more interested in pursuing strong relationships than in "big bucks."

Control Theory

A functionalist like Merton, U.S. sociologist Travis Hirschi assumed that the family, school, and other social institutions can greatly contribute to social order by controlling deviant tendencies in all of us. If such control is lacking or weak, in Hirschi's view, people will commit deviant acts. According to Hirschi, the best control mechanism against deviance is our bond to others or, by extension, society. He proposed four types of social bond:

1. *Attachment to conventional people and institutions.* Teenagers, for example, may show this attachment by loving and respecting their parents, making friends with conventional peers, liking school, or working hard to develop intellectual skills.
2. *Commitment to conformity.* This commitment can be seen in the time and energy devoted to conventional activities—getting an education, holding a job, developing an occupational skill, improving professional status, building a business, or acquiring a reputation for virtue.
3. *Involvement in conventional activities.* Following the maxim that "Idleness is the devil's workshop," people keep themselves so busy doing conventional things that they do not have time to take part in deviant activities or even to think about deviance.
4. *Belief in the moral validity of social rules.* This is the conviction that the rules of conventional society should

be obeyed. People show this moral belief by respecting the law.

If society fails to strengthen these four types of social bond, deviance is likely to flourish. Indeed, many studies have found that the lack of social bond causes deviance. But most of these studies, like the theory, have ignored the fact that the lack of bond can also be the effect of delinquency. Just as the loss of bond can cause youths to commit delinquency, delinquency can cause youths to lose their bond to society.

Shaming Theory

While Hirschi sees how society controls us through bonding, Australian sociologist John Braithwaite looks at how society controls us through shaming. Shaming involves an expression of disapproval designed to evoke remorse in the wrongdoer. There are two types of shaming: disintegrative and reintegrative. In disintegrative shaming, the wrongdoer is punished in such a way as to be stigmatised, rejected, or ostracised—in effect, banished from conventional society. It is the same as stigmatisation.

Reintegrative shaming is more positive and involves making wrongdoers feel guilty while showing them understanding, forgiveness, or even respect. It is the kind of shaming that affectionate parents administer to a misbehaving child. It involves "hating the sin but loving the sinner." Thus, reintegrative shaming serves to reintegrate—welcome back—the wrongdoer into conventional society.

Reintegrative shaming is more common in communitarian societies such as Japan, which are marked by strong social relationships or interdependence. Disintegrative shaming is more prevalent in less communitarian societies, such as the United States. Whereas reintegrative shaming usually discourages further deviance, disintegrative shaming tends to encourage more deviance. This is one reason why crime rates are higher in the United States than in Japan.

Braithwaite concludes by arguing that the United States can significantly reduce its crime rates if it emphasises reintegrative shaming in dealing with criminals, as Japanese society does, rather than stigmatisation.

Braithwaite may be correct that the practice of reintegrative shaming can reduce crime, especially if it is applied to first-time offenders who have committed relatively minor crimes. But it can hardly have the same positive impact on hardened criminals with little sense of shame for their crimes. This lack of shame is apparently the result of having been subjected to disintegrative shaming.

Social Conflicts

We have seen how functionalists describe the functions of deviance and attribute deviance to such dysfunctions of society as anomie, weak social bonds, and disintegrative shaming. Now, we will look at how conflict theorists regard social conflict—in the form of inequalities or power differentials—as the cause of deviance.

Conflict Theory

Many people assume that the law is based on the consent of citizens, that it treats citizens equally, and that it serves the best interest of society. If we simply read the U.S. Constitution and statutes, this assumption may indeed be justified. But focusing on the law on the books, as William Chambliss pointed out, may be misleading. The law on the books does indeed say that the authorities ought to be fair and just. But are they? To understand crime, Chambliss argued, we need to look at the law in action, at how legal authorities actually discharge their duties. After studying the law in action, Chambliss concluded that legal authorities are actually unfair and unjust, favoring the rich and powerful over the poor and weak and consequently creating more criminals among the latter.

Richard Quinney blamed unjust law directly on the capitalist system. "Criminal law," said Quinney, "is used by the state and the ruling class to secure the survival of the capitalist system." This involves the dominant class's doing four things. First, the dominant class defines as criminal those behaviors (robbery, murder, and the like) that threaten its interests. Second, it hires law enforcers to apply those definitions and protect its interests. Third, it exploits the subordinate class by paying low wages so that the resulting oppressive life conditions virtually force the powerless to commit what those in power have defined as crimes. Fourth, it uses these criminal actions to spread and reinforce the popular view that the subordinate class is dangerous in order to justify its concerns with making and enforcing the law.

To Marxists, the capitalists' ceaseless drive to increase profits by cutting labour costs has created a large class of unemployed workers. These people become what Marxists call a marginal surplus population population —superfluous or useless to the economy—and they are compelled to commit property crimes to survive. Marxists argue that the exploitive nature of capitalism also causes violent crimes (such as murder and assault) and noncriminal deviance (such as alcoholism and mental illness).

As Sheila Balkan and her colleagues explained, economic "marginality leads to a lack of self-esteem and a sense of powerlessness and alienation, which create intense pressures on individuals. Many people turn to violence in order to vent their frustrations and strike out against symbols of authority, and others turn this frustration inward and experience severe emotional difficulties."

Marxists further contend that the monopolistic and oligopolistic nature of capitalism encourages corporate crime because "when only a few firms dominate a sector of the economy they can more easily collude to fix prices, divide up the market, and eliminate competitors". Smaller firms, unable to compete with giant corporations and earn enough profits, also are motivated to shore up their sagging profits by illegal means. Conflict theory is useful for explaining why most laws favor the wealthy and powerful and why the poor and powerless commit most of the unprofitable crimes in society (such as murder, assault, and robbery). The theory is also useful for explaining why crime rates began to soar after the communist countries of the former Soviet Union and Eastern Europe turned to capitalism. But the theory has been criticized for implying that all laws are unjust and that capitalism is the source of all crimes.

Power Theory

It seems obvious that power inequality affects the quality of people's lives. The rich and powerful live better than the poor and powerless. Similarly, power inequality affects the type of deviant activities likely to be engaged in. Thus, the powerful are more likely to perpetrate profitable crimes, such as corporate crime, while the powerless are more likely to commit unprofitable crimes, such as homicide and assault. In other words, power—or the lack of it—largely determines the type of crime people are likely to commit. Power can also be an important cause of deviance. More precisely, the likelihood of powerful people perpetrating profitable crimes is greater than the likelihood of powerless persons committing unprofitable crimes. It is, for example, more likely for bank executives to cheat customers quietly than for jobless persons to rob banks violently. Analysis of the deviance literature suggests three reasons why deviance is more common among the powerful.

First, the powerful have a stronger deviant motivation. Much of this motivation stems from relative deprivation — feeling unable to achieve relatively high aspirations. Compared with the powerless, whose aspirations are typically low, the powerful are more likely to raise their aspirations so high that they cannot be realised. The more people experience relative deprivation, the more likely they are to commit deviant acts.

Second, the powerful enjoy greater opportunities for deviance. Obviously, a successful banker enjoys more legitimate opportunities than a poor worker to make money. But suppose they both want to acquire a large sum of money illegitimately. The banker will have access to more and better opportunities that make it easy to defraud customers. The banker also has a good chance of getting away with it because the kinds of skills needed to pull off the crime are similar to the skills required for holding the bank position in the first place. In contrast, the poor worker would find his or her illegitimate opportunity limited to crudely robbing the banker, an opportunity further limited by the high risk of arrest.

Third, the powerful are subjected to weaker social control. Generally, the powerful have more influence in the making and enforcement of laws. The laws against higher-status criminals are therefore relatively lenient and seldom enforced, but the laws against lower-status criminals are harsher and more often enforced. Not a single corporate criminal, for example, has ever been sentenced to death for marketing an untested drug that "cleanly" kills many people. Given the lesser control imposed on them, the powerful are likely to feel freer to use some deviant means to amass their fortunes and power.

There is some evidence to support this theory, presented in greater detail elsewhere. It has been estimated, for example, that in the United States, about six industrial deaths are caused by corporate violation of safety regulations for every one homicide committed by a poor person. It is difficult, however, to get direct data on powerful deviants. Compared with their powerless counterparts, powerful deviants are more able to carry out their deviant activities in a sophisticated and consequently undetectable fashion.

Feminist Theory

Many theories about deviance are meant to apply to both sexes. But feminists argue that those theories are actually about men only. Consequently, the theories may be valid for male behavior but not necessarily for that of females.

Consider Merton's strain theory. First, this theory assumes that people are inclined to strive for material success. This may be true for men but not necessarily for women. In a patriarchal society, women and men are socialised differently. Consequently, women are traditionally less interested in achieving material success, which often requires one-upmanship, and are more likely to seek emotional fulfillment through close personal relations with others.

Second, the strain theory assumes that women who have a strong desire for economic success but little access to opportunities are as likely as men in similar circumstances to commit a crime. Nowadays, given the greater availability of high positions for women in the economic world, the number of ambitious women in the so-called men's world is on the rise. But faced with the lack of opportunities for greater economic success, these women have not been as likely as men to engage in deviant activities.

Finally, the strain theory explicitly states that Americans are likely to commit a crime because their society overemphasises the importance of holding high goals while failing to provide the necessary opportunities for all of its citizens to achieve those goals. But this may be more relevant to men than to women. Despite their greater lack of opportunities for success, women still have lower crime rates than men.

The lack of relevance to women in strain and other conventional theories of deviance stems from a male-biased failure to take women into account. In redressing this problem, feminist theory focuses on women. First, the theory deals with women as victims, mostly of rape and sexual harassment. The crimes against women are said to reflect the patriarchal society's attempt to put women in their place so as to perpetuate men's dominance.

Feminist theory also looks at women as offenders. It argues that the recent increase in female crime has not been great enough to be significant. This is said to reflect the fact that gender equality is still far from being a social reality. Like employment opportunities, criminal opportunities are still much less available to women than to men; hence, women are still much less likely to engage in criminal activities.

When women do commit a crime, it tends to be the type that reflects their subordinate position in soci-ety: minor property crimes such as shoplifting, passing bad checks, welfare fraud, and petty credit card fraud. In fact, recent increases in female crime primarily involve these minor crimes, largely reflecting the increasing feminisation of poverty—more women falling below the poverty line. Not surprisingly, most women criminals are unemployed, high school dropouts, and single mothers with small children. They hardly fit the popular image of the newly empowered, liberated woman, who benefits from any increase in gender equality. There has been no significant increase in female involvement in more profitable crimes, such as burglary, robbery, embezzlement, and business fraud. Feminist theory is useful for understanding female deviance. But its focus on female deviance cannot be easily generalised to male deviance.

Symbolic Interactinist Perspectives

Both the functionalist and conflict perspectives portray deviance as a product of society. In contrast, symbolic interactionists see deviance as a process of interaction between the supposed deviant and the rest of society. This process of interaction involves association, societal reaction, and subjective interpretations that shape the world of deviance.

Differential Association Theory

According to Edwin Sutherland, deviance is learned through interactions with other people. Individuals learn not only how to perform deviant acts but also how to define these actions. Various social groups have different norms; acts considered deviant by the dominant culture may be viewed positively by some groups. Each person is likely to be exposed to both positive and negative definitions of these actions. An individual is likely to become deviant if the individual engages in differential association, the process of acquiring, through association with others, "an excess of definitions favorable to violation of law over definitions unfavorable to violation of law".

Suppose a father tells his children that "It's all right to steal when you are poor." He is giving them a prodeviant definition. On the other hand, if the father tells his children that "It's wrong to steal," he is providing an antideviant definition. If the youngsters pick up a greater number of prodeviant definitions, they are likely to become deviant.

While definitions play a crucial role in the process of becoming deviant, Sutherland emphasised more strongly the importance of social interaction because this is the source of definitions. Thus, Sutherland also stressed that deviance will arise if interactions with those who define deviant behavior positively outweigh interactions with those who define it negatively. Which definitions are most influential depends not just on the frequency and duration of the interactions but also on the strength of the relationship between the interactants.

Sutherland developed his theory to explain various forms of deviance, including white-collar crimes such as tax evasion, embezzlement, and price fixing. All these misdeeds were shown to result from some association with groups that viewed the wrongdoings as acceptable. Still, it is difficult to determine precisely what differential association is. Most people cannot identify the persons from whom they have learned a prodeviant or antideviant definition, much less whether they have been exposed to one definition more frequently, longer, or more intensely than the other.

Labeling Theory

Most theories focus on the causes of deviance. In contrast, labeling theory, which emerged in the 1960s, concentrates on the societal reaction to rule violation and the impact of this reaction on the rule violator.

According to labeling theorists, society tends to react to a rule-breaking act by labeling it as deviant. Deviance, then, is not something that a person does but merely a label imposed on that behavior. As Howard Becker explained, "Deviance is not a quality of the act the person commits, but rather a consequence of the application by others of rules and sanctions to an 'offender.' The deviant is one to whom that label has successfully been applied; deviant behavior is behavior that people so label." The label itself has serious and negative consequences for the individual even beyond any immediate punishment.

Once a person has been labeled a thief or a delinquent or a drunk, the individual may be stuck with that label for life and may be rejected and isolated as a result. Finding a job and making friends may be extremely difficult. More important, the person may come to accept the label and commit more deviant acts. Labeling people as deviants, in short, can push them toward further and greater deviance.

Much earlier, Frank Tannenbaum noted this process of becoming deviant. According to him, children may break windows, annoy people, steal apples, and play hooky—and innocently consider these activities just a way of having fun. Edwin Lemert coined the term primary deviance to refer to these violations of norms that a person commits for the first time and without considering them deviant. Now, suppose parents, teachers, and police consider a child's pranks to be a sign of delinquency. They may dramatise the evil by admonishing or scolding the child. They may even go further, hauling the child into juvenile court and labeling the child bad, a delinquent—a deviant. The child may develop a bad self-image and try to live up to this self-image by becoming increasingly involved in deviant behavior. Lemert used the term secondary deviance to refer to such repeated norm violations, which the violators themselves recognise as deviant. Secondary deviants are, in effect, confirmed or career deviants.

Labeling theory helps us understand how secondary deviance might develop, and it sensitises us to the power of labels. But the theory has been criticised for at least two reasons. First, it cannot explain why primary deviance occurs in the first place. Second, it cannot deal with deviance that occurs in secret; unknown to others, it cannot be labeled as deviance. Without the label, logically the theory cannot define it as deviance.

Phenomenological Theory

Phenomenologists delve into people's subjectivity (called phenomenon), including their consciousness, perceptions, feelings, and opinions about deviance. To really understand deviance, phenomenologists say, we must study people's subjective interpretations of their own deviant experiences. Generally, phenomenological studies have revealed that deviants tend to see themselves and their deviance in some positive way and then behave accordingly. This is what Harold Garfinkel found in his classic study of Agnes, a hermaphrodite (a person with both male and female sex organs). Agnes was raised as a boy until high school. At 17, she developed an attractive female figure. She then dropped out of school, left home, moved to another city, and tried to begin a new life as a woman. A year later, she went to the UCLA medical center to request a sex-change operation. Garfinkel interviewed her extensively before she underwent surgery.

Garfinkel found that Agnes saw herself as a normal woman and did her best to convince others that that was what she was. She told Garfinkel that she was merely a normal woman who happened to have a physical defect comparable to any other deformity such as a harelip or clubfoot. Like any other normal person with a deformity, she felt it was only natural for her to want to have hers—the male organ—removed. Her self-concept as a normal woman further led her to claim that, as a sexual organ, her penis was "dead," that she had no sexual pleasure from it and felt no sexual attraction to women. She wanted it to be replaced by a surgically constructed vagina. Her self-concept as a normal woman also caused her to make sure that others would not suspect her of having the male organ, so she always wore a bathing suit with a skirt and never undressed in her female roommate's presence. In his more recent analysis of murderers, robbers, and other criminals, Jack Katz also found a similarly positive self-perception that conflicts with society's negative view of the deviant. Murderers, for example, tend to see themselves as morally superior to their victims. In most cases of homicide, because the victims humiliated them, the killers felt outraged and considered the killing a justifiable way of defending their identity, dignity, or respectability.

Phenomenological theory is useful for understanding the subjective world of deviants. But it is doubtful that all, or even most, deviants have a positive view of themselves and their deviance. Some are bound to develop a negative self-image from having been condemned or ridiculed by society, as suggested by labeling theory.

Social Diversity in Deviance

Race, class, and gender play a significant role in deviance, particularly crime and delinquency. As research has often shown, large differences in deviance rates exist among whites, African Americans, and other ethnic groups; between higher and lower income groups; and between men and women.

Race and Deviance

Self-report studies, in which teenagers are asked whether they have committed any offenses, reveal no significant racial differences in the commission of such minor deviant acts as petty theft, vandalism, and drunkenness. But as the FBI's Uniform Crime Reports suggest, African Americans are more likely than whites to commit and be arrested for relatively serious crimes such as murder and robbery, and Asian Americans have lower crime and arrest rates than whites. Similarly, according to victimisation surveys, crime victims are more likely to identify African Americans than whites as their offenders and are less likely to finger Asian Americans.

These data, however, do not mean that the biological factor of skin color causes deviance. After all, whites in the United States have a much higher crime rate than blacks in African countries. Why, then, do U.S. blacks have a higher crime rate than U.S. whites? Major reasons include a higher incidence of poverty and broken homes, largely the results of racism. But why are Asian Americans, who also experience racism—though to a lesser degree—less likely to commit crimes than whites? A key reason is the close-knit Asian family, with which its members identify so strongly that they are disinclined to commit crime for fear of bringing shame to the entire family.

Class and Deviance

Whether class is related to deviance depends on the type of deviance involved. Lower-income teenagers are just as likely as their higher-income peers to engage in nonpredatory victimless deviant acts, such as drug use, drunkenness, and truancy. But lowerincome youths tend to commit more serious predatory crimes, such as aggravated assault, robbery, and auto theft, popularly referred to as "street crimes."

Lower-income adults are also more likely than those with higher incomes to commit predatory or street crimes. But higher-income adults tend to commit more profitable white-collar or corporate crimes, such as price fixing, tax evasion, and fraudulent advertising. Reasons include greater motivation to be deviant, greater opportunity, and weaker social control among higher-income people, as suggested earlier in reference to power theory.

Gender and Deviance

Deviance is mostly men's activity. With the exception of prostitution, men are more likely than women to engage in virtually all kinds of crime. The types of offenses more likely to be committed by men range from minor economic crimes (forgery, fraud, and petty theft) to serious economic and violent crimes (robbery, homicide, and aggravated assault). But over the last decade, there has been a great increase in female involvement in mostly minor deviances. Men still outnumber women, though, in committing most deviant acts, especially the serious ones.

Several factors may explain the lower rates of deviance among women. One is socialisation: Females are taught to be less aggressive and violent than males. Another is social control: Females are subjected to greater parental supervision and social control than males. A third factor is lack of deviant opportunity: Women are less likely to enjoy deviant opportunities "as a spin-off of legitimate roles or activities." As Darrell Steffensmeier and Emilie Allan explain, "Women are less likely to hold jobs, such as truck driver, dockworker, or carpenter, that would provide opportunities for theft, drug dealing, fencing, and other illegitimate activities."

Analysis of Deviance

Analysis of deviance around the world reveals societal differences in a number of deviant activities.

First, homicide is generally more likely to occur in poor than in wealthy countries, suggesting that poverty is a major contributing factor. Among wealthy countries, the United States has the highest homicide rate, largely because the poverty rate is considerably higher than in Western Europe,

Canada, and Japan. But the ratio of property crimes to violent crimes is generally higher in rich than in poor countries. While poverty serves as a strong motivation for committing a crime, property crimes cannot occur without the necessary opportunities, namely, the availability of properties as targets for robbery or theft. Since such opportunities abound in more prosperous countries, more property crimes can be expected.

Second, prostitution has recently become a fastgrowing global industry. Many unemployed women in formerly communist Russia and Eastern Europe have flocked to more prosperous Western Europe to sell sex. Some of these women, however, have been tricked into prostitution with promises of singing, dancing, modeling, or waitressing jobs from pimps posing as businessmen in their home countries. More women from poor Asian countries have been lured with promises of legitimate jobs to Japan, Western Europe, and North America, only to be sold to brothels. Large numbers of Thai, Indian, and Filipino prostitutes who remain in their home countries cater to local men, as well as to hordes of Japanese and Western men on organised sex tours. Most of these prostitutes come from poor villages. Thus, poverty, along with exploitation by richer countries, contributes to the sex trade.

Third, suicide is generally more common in modern than in traditional societies. But among modern societies, countries such as Finland, Denmark, and Austria have higher rates of suicide than do the United States, Spain, and Italy. The higher suicide rate seems related to greater social equality. In societies with greater equality, people are less subjected to social regulation —and weak regulation is a key contributor to suicide. As Durkheim suggested, less regulated individuals are more encouraged to expect too much from life and thus become more liable to greater frustration when expectations fail to materialise.

Fourth, organised crime differs across societies. Members' loyalty to crime organisations appears stronger in Japan and Hong Kong than in the United States. The syndicates in Hong

Kong, Japan, Italy, and Russia have penetrated legitimate business and politics more deeply than those in the United States. Not surprisingly, antisyndicate measures fail more frequently in those countries than in the United States. There is one important similarity between U.S. organised crime and its counterparts in other countries: They all serve as a "crooked ladder of upward mobility" for the ambitious poor, who can become rich by joining a syndicate

Controlling Deviance

Society transmits its values to individuals through socialisation. If families, schools, and other socialising agents do their jobs well, then individuals internalise the values of their society, accepting society's norms as their own. Even in poor inner-city neighborhoods, many people successfully internalise the norms of the society at large, becoming conformists and lawabiding citizens. Internalisation through socialisation is the most efficient way of controlling deviance. It produces unconscious, spontaneous self-control. As a result, most people find it natural to conform to most social norms most of the time. Violating the norms makes them feel guilty, ashamed, or at least uncomfortable. They act as their own police officers.

Nevertheless, for reasons suggested by the various theories that we have discussed, a few people commit serious crimes, and everyone deviates occasionally, at least from some trivial norms. Thus, control by others is also needed to limit deviance and maintain social order. This control can be either informal or formal. Relatives, neighbors, peer groups, and even strangers enforce informal controls through discipline, criticism, ridicule, or some other treatments. Formal controls are usually imposed by police, judges, prison guards, and other law enforcement agents.

Compared with small traditional societies, large industrialised societies have a more extensive system of formal control. Perhaps formal control has become more important in modern nations because they have become more heterogeneous and more impersonal than traditional societies. This societal change may have increased social conflicts and enhanced the need for formal control, particularly the criminal justice system.

Criminal Justice System

The criminal justice system is a network of police, courts, and prisons. These law enforcers are supposed to protect society, but they are also a potential threat to an individual's freedom. If they wanted to ensure that not a single criminal could slip away, the police would have to deprive innocent citizens of their rights and liberties. They would restrict our freedom of movement and invade our privacy—by tapping phones, reading mail, searching homes, stopping pedestrians for questioning, and blockading roads. No matter how law abiding we might be, we would always be treated like crime suspects—and some of us would almost certainly fall into the dragnet.

To prevent such abuses, the criminal justice system in the United States is restrained by the U.S. Constitution and laws. We have the right to be presumed innocent until proven guilty, the right not to incriminate ourselves, and many other legal protections. The ability of the police to search homes and question suspects is limited. Thus, our freedom, especially from being wrongly convicted and imprisoned, is protected.

In short, the criminal justice system faces a dilemma: If it does not catch enough criminals, the streets will not be safe; if it tries to apprehend too many, people's freedom will be in danger. Striking a balance between effective protection from criminals and respect for individual freedom is far from easy. This may be why the criminal justice system is criticised from both the right and the left, by one group for coddling criminals and by the other for being too harsh.

Most criminals in the United States are never punished. Of the 35 million crimes committed every year, less than half—

about 15 million serious crimes—are reported to the police. Of these serious crimes, only 20 percent (3 million) result in arrest and prosecution. Of the 3 million prosecuted, 2 million are convicted, of whom 25 percent (500,000) are sent to prison. Ultimately, then, less than 2 percent of the original 35 million offenders are put behind bars. Moreover, most of these prisoners do not serve their full terms because they are released on parole. The average prisoners serve only about one-third of their sentences. Does this mean that the U.S. criminal justice system is soft on criminals? Not necessarily. The United States punishes crime more severely than any other democratic nation. It has been for many years the number-one jailer in the world.

Since 1985, the U.S. prison population has more than doubled to about 1.6 million inmates—more than 2 million if local jail inmates are included. Imprisonment is also generally longer than in other democratic countries. The length of imprisonment is generally measured in weeks and months in Sweden but in years in the United States. The United States is also the only industrialised nation in the West that still executes convicted murderers.

Does the comparatively harsh treatment in the United States help reduce crime rates? The increasing rates of incarceration and the lengthening of prison sentences since the early 1980s have indeed reduced crime by removing from the streets many more hardcore criminals, who commit most of the crimes in society. But the decline in crime cannot be attributed to stepped-up imprisonment alone. Other factors are also involved, such as the economic boom in the 1990s, increases in citizen-led policing, and a dwindling population of teenagers—the age group with a very high crime rate. However, "we are sitting on a demographic crime bomb" because in the new millennium, the proportion of teenagers in the U.S. population will be much greater than it was in the 1990s.

The Death Penalty

In 1998, Karla Faye Tucker, age 38, was executed in Texas for murdering two people with a pickax 15 years earlier. She was the first woman put to death by the state since the Civil War and the second woman in the United States officially killed since 1976, the year when the U.S. Supreme Court reinstated the death penalty. Most Americans believe that the death penalty is an effective deterrent to murder. Many sociologists, however, have for a long time found otherwise, given the following forms of evidence.

First, the homicide rates in states that have retained the death penalty law are generally much higher than in states that have abolished it. Southern states, which still practice the death penalty, generally have higher murder rates than the states in other regions, which have mostly abolished capital punishment. This suggests that the death penalty does not appear to deter murder.

Second, within the same states, murder rates generally did not go up after the death penalty was abolished. Moreover, the restoration of capital punishment in states that had abolished it earlier did not lead to a significant decrease in homicides.

A third piece of evidence came from comparing the number of homicides shortly before and shortly after executions of convicted murderers that had been widely publicised. If the death penalty has a deterrent effect, the execution should so scare potential killers that they would refrain from killing, and the number of homicides in the area should decline.

This may sound logical, but reality contradicts it. In Philadelphia during the 1930s, for example, the number of homicides remained about the same in the period from 60 days before to 60 days after a widely publicised execution of five murderers. This finding, among others, suggests that the death penalty apparently does not prevent potential killers from killing even when the state shows people that it means business.

Finally, similar findings have appeared in studies of various societies. As a classic study of 14 nations concludes:

> If capital punishment is a more effective deterrent than the alternative punishment of long imprisonment, its abolition ought to be followed by homicide rate increases. The evidence examined here fails to support and, indeed, repeatedly contradicts this proposition. In this cross-national sample, abolition was followed more often than not by absolute decreases in homicide rates, not by the increases predicted by deterrence theory.

Why doesn't the death penalty seem to deter murder? One reason is that murder is a crime of passion, most often carried out under the overwhelming pressure of a volcanic emotion, namely, uncontrollable rage. People in such a condition cannot stop and think about the death penalty. Another reason is that the causal forces of murder, such as severe poverty and child abuse, are simply too powerful to be neutralised by the threat of capital punishment.

Although it does not seem to deter murder, most Americans support the death penalty, and increasing numbers of people have been put to death in recent years. There is, however, an apparent attempt to appear civilised in doing away with convicted killers. Barbaric methods of execution, such as hangings and firing squads, are for all intents no longer used; they have been replaced by the supposedly more humane methods of lethal injection and electrocution. Concern has also increased that innocent people are sometimes executed.

In 2003, for example, the Illinois governor commuted the sentences of all the death-row prisoners in his state because he believed that "the capital system is haunted by the demon of error." The error of executing innocents usually comes from racial bias, coerced confessions, and unreliable witnesses.

Medicalisation of Deviance

Deviance can be willful or unwillful. Increasingly in modern industrial societies, especially the United States, if deviance is considered willful, it tends to be defined as a crime, and the criminal justice system is called on to control it. But if deviance is considered unwillful, it tends to be defined as an illness, and medicine, as a social institution, is used to control it. This involves the medicalisation of deviance, di-agnosing and treating deviant behavior as a disease. A good example is the common practice of diagnosing hyperactivity in schoolchildren as a medical problem and then treating it with drugs such as Ritalin, Concerta, and Adderall.

Even more commonly, medical psychiatrists, who use drugs to treat mental illness like a physical disease, define many ordinary problems in our lives as mental disorders. Consider, for example, what the psychiatric profession calls the disorder of written expression. This so-called mental disorder consists of the poor use of grammar or punctuation, sloppy paragraph organisation, awful spelling, and terrible handwriting.

It is possible that some students who exhibit these traits may be mentally ill, but it is doubtful that most students with similar problems are mentally ill; they are simply weak or unskilled writers. Also, consider the oppositional defiant disorder, from which children are said to suffer if they often do any four of the following things: lose tempers, argue with adults, disobey adults, annoy people, blame others for their own behavior, or act touchy, angry, or spiteful. It is possible that in the heat of the moment, some parents may say that their disobedient kids are mentally ill. But it is doubtful that most parents believe that these irritating behaviors are signs of mental disorder.

Once diagnosed as mentally ill, the individual is likely to be treated or controlled. Various social and government agencies, for example, often recruit psychiatrists to treat youngsters whose behaviors offend or disturb others, behaviors such as being defiant, using drugs, fighting, hating school, or being disrespectful. Actually, most of these youngsters have experienced poverty, child abuse, or family misery. But instead of dealing with the abnormal environment that causes troublesome behaviors, the psychiatrists label those normal children as mentally ill and then isolate or incarcerate them and give them drugs. In short, kids who stand out as different may be labeled mentally ill and controlled accordingly.

War on Drugs

The war on drugs consists of two basic strategies. One is punitive: using law enforcement to stop the supply of drugs and punish drug sellers and users. The other is supportive: using drug prevention (or education) and treatment to reduce the demand for drugs and help drug addicts. The U.S. war on drugs is mostly punitive, as the government devotes most of its antidrug budget to law enforcement. But the war is targeted mostly at relatively powerless groups, particularly poor African Americans and Hispanics, who are much more likely than affluent whites to be arrested and convicted for drug offenses.

The law enforcement approach has failed to reduce the general level of drug use, and this has led to calls for the legalisation of drugs. Advocates of legalisation contend that, like Prohibition (of alcohol) in the 1920s, current drug laws do more harm than good. They are said to generate many crimes, including homicides, and to encourage police corruption. By legalising drugs, proponents argue, the government can take away obscene profits from drug traffickers, end police corruption, and reduce crime drastically. Finally, legalisers believe that with legalisation, the huge amount of money currently spent on law enforcement can be used for drug treatment and education, which will dramatically reduce abuse. Those who oppose legalisation respond that if drugs are legalised, drug use and addiction will skyrocket. As

William Bennett, a former national drug control policy director, points out, "After the repeal of Prohibition, consumption of alcohol soared by 350%."

Sociologist Elliott Currie has argued that neither drug warriors nor legalisers can solve the problem of widespread drug abuse and crime because they ignore the root causes of the problem—namely, poverty, racism, and inequality. Currie proposes that the government eradicate the causes of the problem by providing employment to all, increasing the minimum wage, expanding the Job Corps, boosting health care for the poor, offering paid family leave, providing affordable housing, and reducing social inequality.

Since 1996, California and eight other states have legalised the use of marijuana by patients with cancer, AIDS, and other serious diseases to ease their pain. More states are expected to follow suit. But the federal government has been challenging those laws and won a victory in 2001 when the U.S. Supreme Court effectively ordered a California group to stop distributing marijuana for medical use. The Court stopped short of invalidating those states' medicalmarijuana laws, however, which meant individual patients still could obtain and use the drug. Even if the Court later finds those states' laws unconstitutional, juries are unlikely to convict sick people for pot possession, as polls have shown that the majority of Americans (nearly 75 percent) favor medicalmarijuana use.

Even so, it is doubtful that marijuana and other illicit drugs will soon be legalised for use by the gen-eral population throughout the United States. Most Americans seem viscerally opposed to the legalisation of drugs. They particularly do not want to have heroin, cocaine, and other hard drugs as easily available as tobacco, alcoholic beverages, and other legal drugs.

What constitutes deviance varies from one historical period to another. Thus, what was not considered deviant in the past could become deviant today if it is labeled as such.

This may explain why a fast-growing number of people are doing something they would not have thought of doing before: going to their doctors for a prescription drug to cure their shyness.

In the past, many people knew that they were shy, but it never crossed their minds that shyness was a pathology, a disease that requires medical treatment. Recently, though, a number of social forces have converged to turn shyness into a mental disorder. First, in 1980, the psychiatric profession labeled extreme shyness as a social phobia or social anxiety disorder. At that time, the condition was regarded as a rare disorder, as it involved experiencing not only a distracting nervousness at parties or before giving a speech but also a powerful desire to avoid these social situations altogether. Next, some movie stars, big-name athletes, and other celebrities appeared on talk shows, in magazines, and on other media to disclose their struggles with shyness. Finally, the pharmaceutical company Smith Kline Beecham entered the picture by advertising and selling its antidepressant Paxil as a medicine for shyness. And thus, Americans were left with the impression that shyness is far more serious and widespread than they had ever realised. As a result, many people today regard shyness as a disease, a medical problem serious enough to require treatment with a drug.

But shyness is a serious problem only for a very few—those who are extremely bashful or truly incapacitated by fears of others' disapproval and need relief through the use of psychoactive drugs. For the majority, however, shyness is only a mild problem. According to a recent survey, nearly half of all Americans consider themselves shy and still manage to carry on a normal social life. Also consider the fact that many of these Americans may actually not be shy at all. In American culture today, it is difficult not to feel shy given the ubiquitous media full of immodest and even brazen talkers, just as it is difficult not to feel fat with the media presentation of extremely thin beauties.

Managing Drinking

Heavy drinking is a serious problem on many college campuses. The traditional approach to this problem has been simply to stop teenagers from drinking. Thus, since 1988, every state has raised the legal drinking age to 21. Doing so seems to have produced some positive results, such as a drop in drinking and in alcohol-related auto deaths among underage youths.

But a growing number of college administrators have argued recently that the higher drinking age has, in some ways, made drinking more dangerous. Before the enactment of the drinking age law, drinking took place in the open, where it could be supervised by police, security guards, and even health-care workers. When the drinking age went up, drinking did not stop, however. It simply moved underground to homes, cars, and frathouse basements, hidden from adults and authorities. In response to this development, campus administrators have tried to find another more effective way to solve the problem of excessive drinking.

A solution was found at Hobart and William Smith Colleges in New York. In 1996, one of the colleges' sociology professors, Wesley Perkins, did a survey at his school and found that students believed their peers were drinking five times a week when in reality they were drinking only twice a week. In another study conducted on 100 other campuses, students also overestimated their peers' drinking. These findings prompted Perkins to ask: If young people believe that most of their fellow students drink a lot, might they be more inclined to join them? But if they believe excessive drinking is relatively rare on their campus, might they drink more moderately? In short, Perkins hypothesised that students would drink in accordance with the social norm of drinking or the dictates of peer pressure at their school.

In 1997, Perkins's school spent about $2,000 to test the hypothesis. Using posters and newspaper ads, college officials publicised the fact that most students drank only twice a week and that just one-third of the students drank three-quarters of the alcohol on campus. Over the following two years, Perkins observed a significant (21 percent) drop in excessive drinking. When the same program was later carried out at other colleges, the reduction in frequent drinking was also significant—from a 20 percent drop at Western Washington Univer-sity to a 44 percent plunge at Northern Illinois University.

Bibliography

Berry, Brian J.L. and John D. Kasarda. *Contemporary Urban Ecology*. New York: Macmillan, 1977.

Castells, Manuel. *The City and Grass Roots: A Cross Cultural Theory of Urban Social Movements*. Berkeley: University of California Press, 1983.

Durkheim, Emile. *The Division of Labor in Society*. New York: Free Press, 1964

Fitzpatrick, Kevin, & Mark LaGory, *Unhealthy Places: The Ecology of Risk in the Urban Landscape*, New York: Routledge, 2000.

Gans, Herbert. *People, Plans and Policies: Essays on Poverty, Racism and Other National Urban Problems*. New York: Columbia University Press, 1991.

Gold, Harry, *Urban Life and Society*, Upper Saddle River, New Jersey: Prentice Hall, 2002.

Logan, J., and H. Molotch, *Urban Fortunes: The Political Economy of Place*. Berkeley: University of California Press, 17-49, 1987.

Macionis, John J., Vincent Parillo, *Urban Sociology*, Boston: Allyn and Bacon, 2001.

Palen, John J., *The Urban World*, 6th ed., Boston: McGraw-Hill Higher Education, 2002.

Shevky, E., and W. Bell. *Social Area Analysis*. Stanford, CA: Stanford University Press, 28-53, 1955.

Simmel, G., *The Metropolis and Mental Life*. In The Sociology of Georg Simmel, edited by K. Wolff. New York: Free Press, 409-424, 1950.

Soja. E. *Postmodern Geographies: The Reassertion of Space in Critical Social Theory*. New York: Verso, 43-75 & 190-248, 1989.

Toennies, F. *Community and Society (Gemeinschaft and Gesellschaft)*. New York: Harper & Row, 12-29 & 33-102, 1963.

Wirth, L. "Urbanism as a Way of Life". *American Journal of Sociology* 44:1-24, 1938.

Index